LOST HOMELANDS

Lost Homelands

Ruin and Reconstruction in the 20th-Century Southwest

Audrey Goodman

The University of Arizona Press   Tucson

The University of Arizona Press
© 2010 The Arizona Board of Regents

www.uapress.arizona.edu

Library of Congress Cataloging-in-Publication Data
Goodman, Audrey, 1966–
    Lost homelands : ruin and reconstruction in the 20th-century Southwest /
Audrey Goodman.
        p. cm.
    Includes bibliographical references and index.
    ISBN 978-0-8165-2881-3 (hard cover : alk. paper)
    1. Southwest, New—Geography. 2. Landscape—Southwest, New—
History—20th century. 3. Southwest, New—Social conditions—20th century.
4. Community life—Southwest, New—History—20th century. 5. City and town
life—Southwest, New—History—20th century. 6. Country life—Southwest,
New—History—20th century. 7. Group identity—Southwest, New—History—
20th century. 8. Social change—Southwest, New—History—20th century.
9. Southwest, New—In literature. 10. Southwest, New—Pictorial works. I. Title.
    F786.G67 2010
    979—dc22   2010006812

Publication of this book is made possible in part by a grant from the
Department of English, Georgia State University.

Manufactured in the United States of America on acid-free, archival-quality
paper containing a minimum of 30 percent post-consumer waste and processed
chlorine free.

15   14   13   12   11   10   6   5   4   3   2   1

Contents

Figures

Acknowledgments

In many ways the ideas I explore in this study developed out of my first book, *Translating Southwestern Landscapes*, and all the people and institutions who directed the writing of it deserve additional thanks for helping me to prepare a strong foundation for this one, too. However, I realized halfway through the research and writing that the origins of this book run deeper. My first serious and exciting introduction to the poetry of American places came from my many wonderful teachers at Princeton, especially A. Walton Litz, William Howarth, and James Richardson. I am still grateful for the knowledge and wisdom they shared with me.

For over ten years, members of the Western Literature Association have provided inspiration, friendship, and a sympathetic audience for this work in progress. Without occasions to share ideas with colleagues like Susan Bernardin, Neil Campbell, Krista Comer, Nancy Cook, Melody Graulich, Bill Handley, Susan Kollin, Nat Lewis, Tom Lynch, Susan Maher, Stephen Tatum, and many others, I would not have written as ambitious a book. My editor at the University of Arizona Press, Patti Hartmann, provided essential encouragement, and the manuscript's readers offered constructive critique and caught errors I might have missed. Thank you.

A Fellowship in American Modernism at the Georgia O'Keeffe Museum Research Center in Santa Fe in 2002–3 allowed me to investigate a wide range of primary sources. Barbara Lynes welcomed me thoroughly, shared her vast knowledge of O'Keeffe's life and territory, and continued to respond to my detailed questions about the "Black Place" long after my fellowship ended. Others at the O'Keeffe Center, including Museum Director George King, Faith Strongheart, and fellow scholars Bette Shumacher, Carolyn Butler Palmer, and Christina Cogdell, made the year I spent there both stimulating and companionable. Dan Pack let me rent his beautiful adobe house in Nambé, down the road from a couple who had lived in the same place for over sixty years; my brief residence on Calle Rivera made me fully aware of how temporary my Southwestern homeland really was.

At the Huntington Library in Pasadena, Jennifer Watts facilitated my study of Charis Wilson's manuscripts, and Susan Coletta showed me Edward Weston's stunning prints. Along with the scholars in residence, they made the library an ideal place for research and intellectual exchange. At the Beinecke Library at Yale, Leah Jehan provided access to Peter Goin's rare book *Tracing the Line* and helped me to procure copies of key photographs. At the Center for Creative Photography in Tucson, Tammy Carter kept working to complete my order for Edward Weston images. I especially appreciate the generosity of Meridel Rubenstein, Joan Myers, Peter Goin, and Geoffrey James, all of whom allowed me to use their work in the book and took time from their current projects to provide images for mine.

My colleagues at Georgia State have supported my work from the start. Bob Sattelmeyer encouraged me to apply for the O'Keeffe Fellowship. Matthew Roudané and Randy Malamud helped me to arrange leave, recognized the value of my efforts even when the book was in its early stages, and provided lucid guidance in many matters. Heather Russel worked with me consistently and with good humor, while Marta Hess and Tammy Mills always made themselves available to solve practical problems. Jan Kroeger and Daniela Fiorentina assisted me with research for the book's final chapters. I am also grateful to Rosella Mamoli Zorzi, Gregory Dowling, Francesca Bissuti De Riz, Shaul Bassi, and Marina Coslovi, who welcomed me to the University of Venice Ca' Foscari and gave me occasion to introduce my work to their fine students.

Closer to home, I have been delighted to discover committed readers, faithful friends, and inspiring dancers in Atlanta, all of whom continue to challenge my mind and my body. Finally, I give thanks, as always, to my family, and above all to Ruth, Charlie, and David, who cheered me every step of the way.

LOST HOMELANDS

Introduction

Out of a ruin a new symbol emerges, and a landscape finds form
and comes alive.
—J. B. Jackson, *A Sense of Place, a Sense of Time*, ix

As photographer Edward Weston and his companion Charis Wilson
drove along the old Butterfield stage route through the Colorado Desert
in the spring of 1937, they discovered two signs. The first was a familiar
warning posted by the Southern California Automobile Club:

DO NOT ATTEMPT

THIS ROUTE

WITHOUT

AMPLE SUPPLIES

OF WATER

GAS ＊ OIL.[1]

Then, near the Carrizo creek some distance ahead, they found a handwrit-
ten sign attached to a wooden cross stuck in the sand: "Carrizo May 17 37 /
Please help sick man at Carrizo Station / Resp Geo T Edwards" (*California
and the West* 43). It was still May 17, 1937, so they returned to the creek and
finally spotted "feet sticking out." The feet belonged to an unknown man
from Tennessee with worthless coupons, sewing implements, a Minnie
Mouse spoon, a bag of rolled oats, and a fishhook in his pocket, dead in
the desert before his time. Wilson recalled,

> We stood a long while looking at him, only the creek running below
> us making a soft sound in the hot silence of the desert afternoon. I had
> never seen a dead person, and had supposed it would somehow shock
> or upset me. And since we had seen buzzards circling up the creek, I
> had been preparing myself for the kind of thing the books describe
> when a man goes crazy of thirst, tears off his clothes, hurls himself on
> the ground gasping for mirages, and finishes, an unspeakable sight.

But this man had died so quietly and easily it was hard to convince myself he was really dead; I kept expecting to see his chest rise and fall in gentle breathing. (*California and the West* 43)

Weston took several pictures of his body and his head while Wilson "copied the name and address of his people" (44), written in pencil on a scrap of paper, and wondered what had lured him west. She speculated that since he had clearly been unprepared for the desert, he may have expected instead the bounty that California commonly advertised: "avocados and oranges and dates growing all over the place" (45). Having seen his last, intimate possessions, she suddenly felt he was "so small and shrunken and lonely I couldn't just stand there looking at him" (44). The corpse's actuality was too intense for a sustained and direct encounter; as Wilson's retreat shows, such scenes of death and ruin require art's mediation.

The visual and written documents produced from this encounter in the Southwestern desert reveal the power of ruins to prompt many kinds of meditation: on the sources of the region's imagined attraction, on the personal history of this unknown migrant, on the significance of the body, and on the capacity of photography to sustain such decisive moments. On this trip, funded by a Guggenheim Foundation fellowship, the duties of producing art and meeting the daily demands of the project were split between Weston and Wilson, his California muse, lover, chauffeur, and keeper of the trip's typewritten journal (fig. 1).[2] They coauthored *California and the West* (1940), a book that calls equal attention to Wilson's narrative commentary and Weston's carefully conceived, meticulously printed images. Wilson explained the difference in their perspectives as: "My viewpoint tended to be literary; his was essentially pictorial" ("The Weston Eye" 117). The first perspective privileged social narrative, the second the aesthetic arrangement that only later came to be incorporated into larger stories about the meaning of the West.

In some ways, Weston's photograph "Dead Man, Colorado Desert" (fig. 2) shows us less than Wilson's account.[3] We could not know from looking at it how they had first discovered the man, or where he was from, or the contents of his pocket. Nor could we know what it was like to stumble upon the body in the desert even if we might begin to imagine it. In other ways, though, the photograph shows us more than the text. It provides intricate details of the man's body and the ground he lay on. His dark, closely cropped hair hugs his skull, while the bristles of his graying beard reflect the light. His hand rests over his breastbone, with his worn,

Figure 1. Edward Weston, "Charis, Lake Ediza," 1937. (Collection Center for Creative Photography, © 1981 Arizona Board of Regents)

Figure 2. Edward Weston, "Dead Man, Colorado Desert," 1937. (Collection Center for Creative Photography, © 1981 Arizona Board of Regents)

parched fingers pointing to his heart. His open shirt and jacket expose the skin and bones of his chest to the air, revealing flesh that looks stiff and slightly mottled. Layers of dirt, trampled eucalyptus leaves, and dry brush create a foreground, middle ground, and background, transforming this found body into a portrait.[4]

Weston tended to resist symbolic interpretations of his photographs, but at the same time he sought to define his work as art rather than document, thus distancing himself from other photographers of the Depression era. His relentless attention to composition invites viewers to read his images as portraits both of his era and of a persistent human effort to find a place in the natural world. Was the dead man a casualty of the West's boom-and-bust mentality? A migrant in search of a better life? A sacrificial figure? This image of a corpse could fit all of these descriptions, or some, or none. Because Weston frames the image in the book with Wilson's text, he both situates it in the context of its production and projects it into the future, when a reader will confront it anew.

Thinking about Twentieth-Century Southwestern Landscapes

Patricia Limerick argues that the West is "the region where we can most profitably study the interplay of ambition and outcome, the collision between simple expectation and complex reality, and the fallout from optimistic efforts to master both nature and human nature" ("Haunted by Rhyolite" 34). As Weston's photograph of the unknown dead man in the desert suggests, the natural landscapes and human ruins of the greater Southwest allow us to conduct such an investigation into the region's private and social histories. Unlike wilderness scenes that might sustain belief in the beauty of uninhabited nature, the automotive, village, desert, and border landscapes that we still inhabit all contain mixed signals of human hope, struggle, persistence, and failure. As landscape historian J. B. Jackson writes in his preface to *Discovering the Vernacular Landscape*, "The beauty we see in the vernacular landscape is the image of our common humanity: hard work, stubborn hope, and mutual forbearance striving to be love. I believe that a landscape that makes these qualities manifest is one that can be called beautiful" (xii).

This book examines how Southwestern landscapes that once represented the dreams of migrants or relatively stable homelands began in the 1930s to articulate the fragmentation and atomization of identity and community. Organized around sites at once real and symbolic—the road, the small town, the bridge, the desert, and the border—this study explores the types of natural, social, and political landscapes that still broadly define the greater Southwest. It shows how each type of shared space has staged conflicts between vernacular use and official designation and how each reveals the persistent and creative processes of reconstructing belief, group identity, and conceptions of environmental stewardship. This book poses questions that concern many of us who continue to settle in the United States in the early twenty-first century, regardless of our place of origin. How do we define and create a sense of home? How does economic hardship effect communal formations? What is sustainable development? How can we live with the legacy and the continued presence of atomic testing and military complexes? What can the violent history of migration from Mexico to the United States teach us about how we should revise our policies regarding border enforcement? Which literary and visual forms best articulate renewed attention to the landscape's historical meaning and spiritual beauty? For each of these questions, the stories and images produced in or about the greater Southwest provide provisional and unsettling answers.

We begin at the start of the Depression, the period when the Southwest suddenly became integrated into much larger economic and cultural systems and later, in the 1940s, was officially designated as a militarized zone dedicated to the war effort and scientific experimentation. I explore the diverse effects of these expanded networks and of military and scientific cultures on local communities, artistic production, and aesthetic form. Following the model of Jackson's study of vernacular landscapes, the beginning of the book describes the literary and visual prominence of Southwestern roads, small towns, and native communities in the 1930s and 1940s. Landscapes and settlements that by the late twentieth century had fallen into ruin or become ghost towns functioned in the Depression era as symbolic sites of imagined communal experience, figurations of the region's mysterious past, or embodiments of aesthetic freedom. Chapter 1, "The Road," introduces the period's narratives of migration, countermigration, and ruin through a selective survey of novels, photographs, and films, including John Steinbeck's *The Grapes of Wrath* (1939); Russell Lee's photographic study of Pie Town, New Mexico; and Weston and Wilson's *California and the West*. By the early 1940s, the collective experience of displacement from rural and village communities began to transform ideas about the city as well. In Nathanael West's novel *The Day of the Locust* (1939) and Preston Sturges's film *Sullivan's Travels* (1941), Los Angeles takes shape as a traumatic present in which the shock of dislocation perpetually repeats itself and the ability to reconstruct a homeland remains elusive. Chapter 2, "The Village," reads Farm Security Administration photographs by Russell Lee and John Collier Jr. beside village stories told by Frank Waters and Cleofas Jaramillo to test the relation between photography's ability to render facts and fiction's capacity to reconstruct communal memory. This chapter also explores how writers alternately used and resisted the conventions of literary regionalism that defined the Anglo Southwest of the early twentieth century to create new positions for themselves as privileged insiders speaking against the reactionary ideology of documentary realism and to lay the foundation for the emerging politicized culture of the Chicano/a movement.

The early chapters of the book prove the critical role writers and photographers played in making visible the effects of displacement and federal programs on the Southwest's diverse communities. The middle chapters then turn to the problem of representing the region's historically significant but neglected ruins. The sites of the nation's major wartime initiatives—Los Alamos, the Trinity Site, the internment camps for Japanese Americans (like that at Manzanar in California), and the Nevada Test Site—were enclosed and concealed in Southwestern deserts, their inner activities exposed only long afterward. Chapter 3, "The Bridge," shows how the lives of two recent migrants, Edith Warner (the proprietress of a teahouse along the Rio Grande) and Robert Oppenheimer (the atomic scientist), crossed at the Rio Grande. This chapter compares the ways that novelist Frank Waters and photographer Meridel Rubenstein represent Otowi Bridge as a site of convergence for native, Anglo, and scientific communities and explores the affinities between different kinds of militarized spaces, from the Los Alamos National Laboratory to Manzanar.

In chapter 4, "The Desert," I consider how images and narratives of Southwestern deserts from the early 1940s on are inevitably and provocatively intertwined with the land's history of contamination. Analyzing how artists and writers from Georgia O'Keeffe to Leslie Marmon Silko and Terry Tempest Williams respond to threats of toxicity with aesthetic rituals that transform profaned landscapes into beautiful objects or stories, I demonstrate how their work variously articulates the trauma of people silenced by the desert's militarization and contamination. I focus here on representations of bodies that test the boundaries between inner and outer landscapes and between past and present. If "[a]n act of representation is an act of embodiment," as Elaine Scarry suggests (*The Body in Pain* 216), then representations of toxic landscapes and irradiated bodies constitute an effort to restore corporeal wholeness and to describe histories that have been officially suppressed. Because they signify within different fields of experience, injuries to the body provide a means of representing the types of trauma that fragmented individual and collective memories in the Atomic and Post-Atomic ages.

The final chapters of the book interrogate the U.S.–Mexico border as a landscape that continues to dramatize the violent conflicts between official and vernacular spaces, first- and third-world consciousnesses, transnational networks and imaginary homelands. Contemporary artists like Peter Goin, Geoffrey James, Cormac McCarthy, Alberto Alvaro Ríos, Arturo Islas, and Luis Alberto Urrea explore the personal, cultural, and social transformations that border crossings make possible and record the longing for home that many migrants carry with them. It is often the body—whether photographed in motion, imagined as being in contact with the dead, or resurrected as a spirit—that articulates the border's ambivalent, hybrid culture and bears the responsibility for sustaining that culture across generations. As they represent what folklorist James Griffith terms a "shared space," the novelists also speak to enduring divisions between the Southwest's contemporary literary cultures and fictional genres. Whereas McCarthy, an Anglo writer, creates heroes who traverse extensive territory on both sides of the border and finally return to a much diminished home, Chicano writers Islas, Ríos, and Urrea tell the histories of extended families and diasporic communities through many distinct perspectives, simultaneously locating these histories in the everyday and sometimes fantastic lives of people in border towns and pursuing their families' long routes of migration. Islas's novels *The Rain God* (1984) and *Migrant Souls* (1990) show how stubbornly the landscapes and realities of exile resist settlement, much less enchantment.

To imagine the borderlands otherwise, as a fully inhabited homeland, would require a fictional form organized around transnational networks rather than individual bodies and families, curious about the practice and power of indigenous belief, and willing to connect the indigenous past with the modernized present. In Latin America such a form, magical realism, already existed; in the Southwestern borderlands, this form emerged only in the late twentieth century. The final chapter of my study examines Urrea's novel *The Hummingbird's Daughter* (2005) as an example of what I call "magical borderlands fiction." Responding to the challenge of restoring and re-storying a region where the histories of migration and knowledge of desert ecologies are so often ignored or erased, Urrea turns to the legends of his family's and his culture's past. By refusing to privilege national identity, political ambition (whether imperial or revolutionary), and rational thinking, his regional version of magical realism rewrites the history of the border as a multivocal and dialogic novel designed to integrate indigenous and rational forms of knowledge and storytelling. Although the complex history of the border is difficult to record, contemporary imaginative works such as Urrea's allow us to see its present condition as not only a political and increasingly militarized boundary but also as a site where new historical understandings, cultural identities, and familial relations continue to be imagined.

This study proves that "landscape" is an elastic term, shaped more by a culture's worldview than by natural formations. Leslie Marmon Silko describes how the Laguna people conceive of human existence as always developing within the earth and the sky; she rejects the notion that a "landscape" can be viewed from a distance, by people who are outside of the scene themselves. She explains,

> Pueblo potters, the creators of petroglyphs and oral narratives, never conceived of removing themselves from the earth and sky. So long as the human consciousness remains *within* the hills, canyons, cliffs, and the plants, clouds, and sky, the term *landscape*, as it has entered the English language, is misleading. 'A portion of territory the eye can comprehend in a single view' does not correctly describe the relationship between the human being and his or her surroundings. This assumes the viewer is somehow *outside* or *separate from* the territory she or he surveys. Viewers are as much a part of the landscape as the boulders they stand on. ("Interior and Exterior Landscapes" 5)

Silko also recognizes the way that landscapes are simultaneously physical and imaginary spaces, real places and dream places. Like dreams, landscapes "have the power to seize terrifying feelings and deep instincts and translate them into images—visual, aural, tactile—and into the concrete where human beings may readily confront and channel the terrifying instincts or powerful emotions into rituals and narratives" (16). The stories inspired by encounters with the landscape thus serve the function of comforting the individual and confirming a group's shared values.

Throughout the book I explore how the meaning and function of landscape in the Southwestern United States have shifted as writers, artists, and scholars have crossed disciplinary boundaries and challenged regional classifications. John Szarkowski explains his understanding of landscape in terms of both artistic technique and the viewer's perspective. For the purposes of an exhibit of photographic landscapes he curated for the Museum of Modern Art in New York, he used the word "to denote a family of pictures concerned with two issues: the formal problems of picture making, and the philosophical meaning of the natural site—those places where man's hegemony seems incomplete" (*American Landscapes* 5). In his assessment of Weston's later work, including the photographs in *California and the West*, Szarkowski observes that landscape posed the greatest challenge, "for in landscape there could be no simple apposition of object and background. . . . Closed, centripetal compositions, in which the subject could be said to exist independently of the picture, are replaced by centrifugal ones, in which the subject is defined by the film's edge" (*American Landscapes* 159). Taking as his example Weston's struggle to manage the relation between subject and space, Szarkowski emphasizes how aesthetic landscapes work to mediate fact, perception, and representation.

Such attention to the formal demands of landscape has guided my thinking about how photographs tell stories through isolating their subjects and suggest meanings beyond mere description, an aesthetic process that extends to documentary texts, memoirs, and fiction. Many photographers and writers work with the tension between "centripetal" and "centrifugal" compositions that Szarkowski identifies in Weston's work. As they explore the greater Southwest's inhabited and abandoned places, they invoke tropes of enclosure and expansion, thus reconfiguring the boundaries that define the region's homelands, communities, and beliefs. Szarkowski concludes his essay on American landscapes by refuting Thoreau's thesis "that the earth is beautiful except where man lives, or has passed through." Since the only real and noble way to maintain a nature preserve is to deny all human entrance to it, Szarkowski proposes instead that we "turn our attention to the rest of the earth, the part in which we live." I share his view that photographers have led us to pay new attention to our inhabited and imperfect environment and continue to explore the implications of Silko's vision of the complex and fragile interrelationships between people and their native places. By making us mindful of the present and encouraging us to excavate the many layers of the past, photographic and literary representations of Southwestern landscapes can engage us in the challenging process of living with ruins and constructing homelands in a culture that overtly values mobility, growth, and change.

Jackson reflected on the word *landscape* in the first essay he published in the journal *Landscape* in 1951, and he continued to do so throughout his unconventional and influential career. A simple word, *landscape* "refers to something which we think we understand," he mused, "and yet to each of us it seems to mean something different." To resolve the lack of consensus, he proposed a new approach. Instead of focusing on the artist's perspective, as art historians traditionally did, he shifted attention to the inhabitants' experience and to the way people use space. His own definition of landscape as "a composition of man-made or man-modified spaces to serve as infrastructure or background for our collective existence" emphasizes its shared human constitution and its contested status

(*Landscape in Sight* 305). "A landscape, like a language, is the field of perpetual conflict between what is established by authority and what the vernacular insists upon preferring," he explained (*Discovering the Vernacular Landscape* 148).

Jackson was always interested in the contemporary social applications of landscape study and continually asked how the history of places "teaches us about the future." Whereas the "nineteenth-century concern for regionalism" led to a productive focus on "local" materials, craftsmanship and agriculture, in Jackson's view the history of these places as told through plans and maps and legal documentation addressed only "an infinitely small fraction of the landscape." While he elegantly analyzed early American and nineteenth-century constructions like the dwelling, the preindustrial town, and the grid, he viewed "the rural or small-town past" as "essentially preparatory" to the study of vernacular landscapes: the road, the parking lot, and the strip. These "unofficial" spaces "often have no documentation at all," and as a result, they provide new opportunities for historians to use their imagination, speculate on the meaning of such ruins, and in the process learn "about ourselves and how we relate to the world" (Preface to *Discovering the Vernacular Landscape* x–xi).

Jackson shows us that the landscapes and regions we inhabit are always in flux. If we look at them carefully, they continue to raise questions about how they have been used and why they change. They are what I call partly articulate ruins—sites where history can be made visible and where possible futures can be imagined. Jackson paid as much attention to the costs of migration as to patterns of settlement, noting the "disturbing mobility of people and spaces, a search for adjustment, for change; an incessant making of structures and spaces and communities, an incessant adaptation and remaking of the landscape, resisted by the political landscape when it could no longer be ignored" (Preface to *Discovering the Vernacular Landscape* xii). His writing thus anticipates more recent spatial theories and regional conceptions, from Arjun Appadurai's analysis of the relation between global migrations and regional imaginaries to photographic surveys of the West's "altered" landscapes and literary reassessments of the greater Southwest.[5]

Throughout this study I argue that landscapes are languages and social texts we can read from multiple and mobile perspectives. Through them we can forge imaginative connections with the histories that haunt abandoned places, understand more fully the lure of mobility, bear witness to the continued transformation of our natural and human environment, and develop broader conceptions of beauty. Photographs of the Southwestern landscape have led me to see the relation between history and place in new ways, and Jackson has provided me with a social, provocative, and often playful framework for describing that relation. At the same time, I am aware that understanding the complexity of any landscape requires a more intimate relation with the people who created it than was possible for this book. As a scholar I rely on documents; as a resident of the South, I necessarily approach my subject as a respectful outsider. Rather than aiming to present a view of Southwestern culture from within, to survey all the region's diverse communities, or to organize the book around figures that might represent such diversity, I analyze selected landscapes for their ability to reveal unseen aspects of the past and to speak to experiences I imagine twenty-first-century readers might share.

Atomic Homelands

Many of the "homelands" I analyze in this book are small New Mexican towns (such as Pie Town, the crossing at Otowi Bridge, and San Ildefonso Pueblo), remembered rural communities (such as those described by Frank Waters, Cleofas Jaramillo, and Rudolfo Anaya), and native lands designated as "reservations." Only in the mid-twentieth century did the many natives and migrants who had settled in these relatively remote desert places or along the exposed borderlands between Mexico and the United States fully articulate and resist their experience of displacement by enacting protests and writing fiction that defined their communities and their conceptions of home. Often working against national and colonial ideologies, through the political lessons of the Chicano/a, Civil Rights, and Red Power movements, and in response to Mexican and Latin American aesthetic models, they created stories and images missing from the twentieth century's dominant narratives of migration, urbanization, and globalization.

Although Native American writers like Scott Momaday, Leslie Marmon Silko, and Simon Ortiz might articulate the importance of finding one's place and communal identity within a land that contains sacred stories most explicitly, the process is not limited to indigenous authors. William Kittredge defines homelands as "simply enough, emotional homes" and the Southwest as a collection of these. He writes, "The Southwest is itself a homeland, the Hopi pueblos are homelands, and middle-class neighborhoods in Phoenix are homelands. They can be as large as our nation or small as the valley where I grew up, large as the Colorado River watershed, small as a village or rural family. . . . Each can be a position from which to enjoy and withstand the gorgeous, evasive, and invasive world, or to despair" (43). Leaving behind the nation as his primary political unit, he imagines a variety of landscapes in which people have come to feel at home. Photographer Peter Goin explains his sense of belonging to a place as "a process of acceptance," which means learning "to live within [the land's] geography, history, character, and, perhaps most importantly, spirit" ("Magical Realism" 254). Creating a homeland requires affirming the value of locality and telling the stories that are connected to specific places, a process that actively links the events of the past with an understanding of the present and mediates individual and communal points of view. Momaday's fiction demonstrates that "one knows one's homeland by recalling some of the countless stories that took place on that land's specific topographical features" and provides a powerful model for how "[i]ndigenous people maintain their social world by pointing to significant places and recalling (often word for word) the legendary and historical events held secure in the tribal imagination" (Teuton 50). In the twentieth-century Southwest, homelands did not necessarily coincide with places of cultural origin. After the displacements of the Depression era, the struggle for survival on reservations, and the destruction of natural lands, people across the region needed to remake their home places through rituals of contact and imaginative acts of storytelling.

The literature I analyze in the early chapters includes narratives of Anglo farmers, Hollywood writers and actors, Hispano villagers, non-professional writers, atomic scientists, and imprisoned Nisei. The book's final chapters turn to narratives of Chicano/a writers and activists, Navajo and Pueblo poets, Mexican migrants, and mestiza curanderas, among others. Their stories cannot be told as part of any unified regional history, and like many scholars I question the value of the regional designation "Southwest," a term that is outdated, "ethnocentric, nationalistic, and misleading" (Lynch, *Xerophilia* 24). Because the region spans the states of the southwestern United States and northwestern Mexico, it should be approached as a series of ever-shifting cultural border zones and a transnational imaginary. Geographer D. W. Meinig writes, "[W]hat is south and west to the Anglo-American was long the north of the Hispano-American, and the overlap of the colonizing thrusts of these two continental invaders—the one approaching west from the Atlantic Seaboard, the other north from central Mexico—suggests a first element in the definition of a distinctive cultural border zone" (3). A significant feature of Meinig's definition of the Southwest as a "border zone" is its geographical isolation: not only are areas of settlement "set apart on the west, north, and east by broad zones of difficult country—the Mohave-Sonoran Desert, the Colorado River Canyonlands, the south Rockies, and the Llano Estacado," but the southern boundary—the U.S.–Mexico border now under increasingly intense surveillance—"cuts directly across the grain of the country and severs some of the Indians and Hispanos from their cultural kin and older connections further south" (4). Even within "this rather detached area" lies substantial division, formalized by the state boundary between New Mexico and Arizona, and between developments along the Rio Grande and the Gila. Throughout the book, I approach the region's landscape elements historically, geographically, and culturally, sketching the features of the Southwest's "cultural border zone" that simultaneously divide the region and define it. Along with other scholars who approach the region from a "postwestern" perspective "as a continually changing and evolving entity in both content and form," I evaluate the cultural processes through which theoretical, geographical, and political boundaries are drawn, contested, and revised.[6]

The stories of the diverse populations who live in and shape the region still commonly referred to as the Southwest, however, can be understood as engaged in a common process of questioning what it means to be part of a community and to claim a meaningful connection to the land. Throughout this study I consider how artists move through the landscape, often shifting their position from outsider to native and back, in order to imagine the collective process that transforms a land into a homeland. I am particularly interested in the roles that women played in the 1930s and 1940s—decades when pursuing an independent career, making art, crossing the border, or merely taking to the road meant accepting risk and declaring independence from conventional expectations. Many women worked in collaboration with male artists or scientists whose work has received substantial public attention, as in the cases of Charis Wilson and Edith Warner. The relation between Georgia O'Keeffe and Alfred Stieglitz has been documented more fully, but the recent publication of letters between O'Keeffe and Maria Chabot, her companion at Ghost Ranch and Abiquiu in the 1940s, shows that the meaning of their relationship, too, is open to revision. The letters women wrote and the journals they kept in the Depression era, not intended for public consumption, provide us with a more intimate understanding of how the connections between people and places are made through sharing everyday life and ordinary encounters with nature, in addition to extraordinary historical events.

I also pursue the question of how the invention, testing, and use of atomic weapons has changed our conceptions of the body and our environment and reconfigured the boundaries of human knowledge. To consider homelands "atomic" means accounting for emptiness as well as acknowledging hidden or invisible histories of contamination. As naturalist Ellen Meloy writes in the epilogue to *The Last Cheater's Waltz*, "Atoms are matter, but they also consist of a great deal of empty space, which anxious seekers of some*thing* might view as a lack of imagination on the part of nature. Electrons lie notably distant from their nuclei, separated by a void. . . . Physicists who study the smallest of particles call the spaces between them a *desert*. On his charts one physicist illustrates this emptiness with drawings of little saguaro cacti" (223). Then she connects this sketch of the "atomic" desert with her own conception of home, which she is still looking for: "Home is both the mass and the space, the red-boned rock and the places where one tries to shape belief around mystery" (223). As this passage suggests, she and other inhabitants of this contaminated landscape may never find a stable and meaningful homeland. As westerners, they share "a keen sense of kinship with the land" and "the certainty that it will never remain the same" (189). Whereas Navajos who live in the Tsé Valley may still connect the valley's sacred origins with its continued beauty, non-native women like Meloy must reinvent their places of origin through a mixture of rituals and devise new conceptions of home and beauty.

For male writers of recent borderlands fiction, it is often the powerful women who migrated to the United States in the early decades of the twentieth century who provide their descendants with the stories that explain what it means to make a home in the United States and to live fully according to one's beliefs. For example, Arturo Islas constructed his saga of a Mexican-American family around three generations of women, while Luis Alberto Urrea took twenty years to complete research about his legendary ancestor, Teresa Urrea, before writing *The Hummingbird's Daughter*. For these novelists, the examples of women from earlier generations both provide access to previously unrecovered histories and prompt serious meditation on which aspects of Mexican culture they want to preserve and cultivate.

I continue to be fascinated with the way landscapes provide access to historical knowledge, cultural practices, and imagined communities.

In his journeys through Southwestern homelands, Kittredge keeps asking how the lives of the region's original inhabitants (the Mogollon, the Hohokam, and the Ancestral Puebloans) and of their descendants (including the Tohono O'Odham, Pueblo, and Hopi peoples) might resemble his own. A westerner but an outsider to the Southwest, Kittredge discovers deep similarities that confirm a shared humanity. When he scrutinizes a Mimbres bowl, for example, he speculates that the patterns refer to native concepts of sacred space. For Pueblo peoples, he explains, "Homelands and community are understood to be at a 'central place,' which was sought for and found by their ancestors, a space both metaphoric and physical." Though cryptic, the images make him "think their lives were ultimately like ours," dedicated to mapping the world and praying for "an orderly, bounded" existence (50–51). At other times he describes his longing for travel and new experience to be at odds with the rituals of the Southwest's "profoundly conservative" native cultures, or considers how his privilege as a white and relatively wealthy American impedes his understanding of life across the U.S.–Mexico border. In Ciudad Juárez, he has trouble fathoming the struggles of people who dedicate their lives to survival and realizes "the degree that I'm insulated from the feelings of people who labor so mightily just to sustain hope. I'm incapable, because of my background, of even seeing much of what's there, or who's there, what they're doing. I don't know how to see it, or them." Still, he knows that "those injustices I have trouble seeing are to a great degree my responsibility" (26). May the knowledge this book conveys come from such joy at discovering that art's common language—and its omissions and blind spots—come from such honest acceptance of any single observer's limitations.

1

The Road

Traveling through the Depression-Era West

> Most foreign visitors to the United States end up liking us. It is
> our landscape that bewilders them and that they find hard to
> understand. They are repelled by its monotony: the long straight
> roads and highways, the immense rectangular fields and the
> lonely white farmhouses, all much alike. . . . We are often asked
> how we who live in the middle of such monotony can have any
> sense of place.
> —J. B. Jackson, *A Sense of Place, A Sense of Time*, 151

Americans in the 1930s were on the road. They took roads well traveled
and back roads, highways and city streets. They left houses that no longer
sheltered them to find better homes elsewhere. If they already lived in the
West, they went farther west, to California. Photographers and writers set
out to see what hard times were, firsthand, and discovered many kinds of
migration: definitive, collective movement that involved "displacement
or social rupture."[1] Migration during the Depression both responded to
and set in motion social and economic transformations within the United
States and it also produced powerful collections of images and stories of
people moving toward unfamiliar places and unknown futures.

J. B. Jackson pioneered the study of the highway as an essential part of
the American landscape, a system for mobility now exported across the
globe. He asserted that the proliferation of roads, grids, webs, and "road-
like spaces—railroad lines, pipelines, power lines, flight lines, assembly
lines" (*A Sense of Place* 190)—in the past century proved the dominance of
the technologies of modernization over traditional attachments to home
and native places, and bewildered people outside the United States. In
contrast to the Navajo conception of the path—the route of a journey
that reconnects individuals with their people's origins, lived experience,
and native landscape—Anglo-European conceptions of the road presume

the primacy, or at least the premise, of a destination. Roads were built to connect houses, towns, states, regions, and nations. With the development of an automobile culture, however, the destination began to matter less. By the 1930s, roads no longer simply led people home or away to a single destination; instead, they became places themselves, landscapes used and shaped by travelers. Though seemingly repetitive and monotonous, these automotive landscapes signaled migrants' common need to find food and shelter, their desire to control social encounters away from the comforts of home, and their anxiety that temporary comforts were all they had. Jackson explained that roads "serve two important roles: as promoters of growth and dispersion, and as magnets around which new kinds of development can cluster" (*A Sense of Place* 190). If, as Jackson argues, roads not only provide routes for migrants but also promote new kinds of group formation, representations of the road provide a means to explore the implications of a society increasingly defined by its "uninterrupted steady flow" and seemingly unlimited potential for development. Our world may now be defined primarily through the dematerialized movement of viewers and images; Depression-era representations of life on the road in many ways anticipated such virtual mobility.

The iconic—and often ironic—photographs produced during the Depression dramatize the highway's potential to erase local histories, often through focusing on the markings and roadside signs that lured travelers ever onward, toward the next site prepared for easy consumption.[2] Other images of the West's open roads perpetuate the idea of available space by inviting viewers to follow the pavement's painted double line all the way to a distant horizon under various conditions of light and storm. A survey of photographs of empty roads by Paul Strand and Ansel Adams would seem to suggest that highways are for driving into the future, not for lingering in the present. Generally lacking any distinguishing natural features, such road pictures allow viewers to project their own experience of driving into the scene, and in this way they can continue to imagine the private transformations that the road traditionally represented for Anglo-Europeans. Jackson observes that the road can represent "an order transcending the political or economic order" and can thus provide a means for examining unofficial experience. He also argues, however, that "we must reformulate the current technological definition of odology so that it recognizes the *private* experience" (*A Sense of Place* 192). The challenge that mobile photographers faced was that of negotiating the public and private meanings of the automotive landscape.

As they explored the roads of the Southwest, many writers as well as photographers began to reveal migration's dark side: the homesteads abandoned and left for ruin; the commercial slogans promising quick fulfillment; the frustration and rage of middle-class whites and working-class African Americans; the forced "repatriation" of Mexican workers; and the imprisonment of Japanese Americans during World War II. During his Guggenheim years from 1937 to 1939, Edward Weston, previously known for his exquisite photographs of everyday objects like egg slicers and bell peppers, his portraits, and his studies of Mexican towns, began to focus on scenes of death and ruin leading to the publication of *California and the West* in 1940. The first part of this chapter looks closely at his work in this period and at his collaboration with companion Charis Wilson to consider how and why the subject preoccupied him on his extensive creative road trip. Other works that define the era tell stories of families alienated from each other and the land they once claimed as their own. These narratives resist the convention of a happy ending in the New West. The second part of this chapter shows how even in stories that seem to commemorate the last wave of westward migration—like John Steinbeck's novel *The Grapes of Wrath* (1939) and photographer Russell Lee's 1940 study of Pie Town, New Mexico—their migrant protagonists fail to find new homes and discover in the end that homelands cannot be easily reconstructed.

Representations of urban disorientation also belie the idea that the trauma of displacement can be healed, as the final part of this chapter illustrates. Instead, we find characters in fiction and film who express resistance or anger at the very notion of purposeful migration: city-dwellers from the Midwest who come to Los Angeles and then refuse to adapt; workers in the movie industry who feel perpetually stuck on the set; ordinary men who leave trails of crime. Stories that revolve around efforts to resist or escape new homes in southern California include Nathanael West's satiric novel *The Day of the Locust* (1939) and Preston Sturges's *Sullivan's Travels* (1941), a film that depicts the machinery of Hollywood.[3] In each of these configurations of migration's end in Los Angeles, we find solitary drifters who cannot attach meaning to their movement, and this lack of coherence often produces deeper alienation and nightmare visions. Rather than the documentary style, the preferred modes for telling such stories of resistance to migration are those late modern or postmodern forms that seek to bring new life to old myths: collage, pastiche, satire, or surrealism.[4] We might think of these stories, often written by artists who for a time shared the experience of displacement, as counter-myths of migration.[5]

Throughout these varied accounts of life on the road we find a struggle between subjective experience and imagined collective formations. Each account shows how perception is shaped by the sensory experience of the body and by collisions between local and commercial cultures. Images and stories of westward movement and regional circulation in this era emphasize the body as a text to be read for its history of labor and experience, for its resilience in the face of hardship, and for its ability to express the frustration and anger widely shared by viewers and readers during the era. If American life in the early twentieth century was already haunted by a modern "sense of the fleeting, the ephemeral, the fragmentary, the contingent" (Harvey 11), the Depression intensified the condition of modernity, and the body became a symbolic site where the period's conflicting feelings could be made visible. Whether through written descriptions of desiring, tired, hungry, injured, pregnant, lethargic, or dying bodies, or through photographs of farmers, workers, and travelers, representations of migration in this era came to express the experience of detachment and deterritorialization shared across racial, class, and regional lines and the rapid atomization of American society. Taken together, they articulate the limits of the nation's nostalgic imagining for an agrarian past, the ambivalence many Americans felt about perpetual movement, and a persistent longing for rituals that could transform places into homelands.

On the Road with Edward Weston

Edward Weston was among the photographers who took full advantage of "the classic age of motoring"—despite his inability to drive. During sixteen trips across California and adjacent states funded by a Guggenheim Foundation fellowship between April 1, 1937, and March 31, 1939, he covered over 20,000 miles in a black Ford V-8 nicknamed "Heimy," chauffeured mostly by his companion (and later wife) Charis Wilson, and occasionally by one of his four sons or his friend Willard Van Dyke. He wrote in his application for the fellowship that he intended "to continue an epic series of photographs about the West, begun about 1929" and to "include a range of satires on advertising to ranch life, from beach kelp to mountains."[6] He chose the region, with the focus on California, partly for aesthetic reasons: "you cannot travel very far in California without being impressed by its startling array of contrasts; without beginning to believe that whatever exists in the rest of the world—from glacier to active volcano—is somewhere represented here" (*California and the West* 125). His concern in limiting the scope of the trip was also practical. Working within a tight budget that required him to economize on all of his expenses, from sleeping bags to canned vegetables, Weston also had to anticipate the costs of photographic supplies and darkroom access. He knew he could use darkrooms in Los Angeles and San Francisco, and he minimized the danger of damaging exposed film by traveling shorter distances. His careful planning paid off: during the two years of the fellowship he produced 1,400 negatives.

Both Weston and Wilson conceived of the trips they took during their Guggenheim years as an escape from the emptiness of commercial American culture, the relentless professional demands of portrait photography, and conventional social and domestic arrangements. When Weston left the United States for Mexico in 1922, he turned his back on the boom times in California—and returned to find himself both less enamored of his native land and distraught that his own personal landscape had turned to ruin: "Too bad for me to have returned to this!—this worn out spot, surrounded by my dead past, the once blossoming fruit trees I cared for so tenderly, sapless, brittle, naked, the plow and garden tools rusty, scattered . . . " (*Daybooks* 115). He applied for the Guggenheim fellowship to support his art, which he was funding through his business as a portrait photographer. When he received the grant, he left behind both his previous interest in human figures and the frustration of serving a culture devoted to the pursuit of easy pleasures.[7] He also distanced himself from the kind of documentary pictures made by his friend Dorothea Lange, choosing to address social issues indirectly if at all. When he made one negative during his travels that actually included people (two fishermen by the Russian River, and four others on the sandbar and the beach), Wilson joked that they referred to it "affectionately as Edward's 'Documentary'" (*California and the West* 76). The very first trip Weston took with fellowship support swept him away from staid Glendale to stark Death Valley, which he called "the most exciting place in the world,—my world."[8]

For Wilson, too, the Guggenheim travels meant liberation. She began her published narrative with a report of the practical tips she had received from well-meaning friends, but both this narrative and her unpublished journal proceed to declare her independence from conventional views. Her texts devote considerable attention to her ability to budget the trip, cook and eat simply, and sleep under any sky—and thus to create the conditions necessary for daily freedom. "Concerning what to take, where to go, and what to go in, we received abundant advice," she wrote. "Our friends argued the advantages of station wagon over trailer, or vice versa; told us about their pet Kollapsible Kamp Kots, and where there were restaurants off the beaten track that served good chicken dinners" (*California and the West* 13). When she went to outfit their sedan for the trip, however, she pared down the necessities of life to sleeping bags from Sears, a stove and basic cooking equipment, a tarp to protect the travelers and Weston's camera equipment from rain and dust, and just enough food to satisfy the healthy appetites they would work up along the way. She cut her hair herself before their departure so that she could care for it more easily, though she later suspected that Weston regretted her practicality. In her journal, Wilson kept track of which brands of canned fruits and vegetables tasted best and thus merited the extra few cents they cost. When she recorded the recipe for her "royal stew," which required one can of tomatoes, one can of corn, some potassium broth (she assured her readers it was tastier than it sounded), crumbled rye crisp, and grated jack cheese, she both flaunted her efficiency and mocked her cooking skills. Many entries recorded her sense that contact with the desert, sea, and freshwater lakes purified her, suggesting that the trips also offered rituals of renewal.[9]

Together Weston and Wilson would disregard common advice and follow less-traveled and often abandoned roads, as they did on one of their last trips through Junction City, California. Wilson noted the recommendation of a local woman to take one road over the other—and their contrary response: "Oh, no one takes the west branch, the east is much faster, and less turns. [We] thank her and take the west, finding the census accurate. No one to bar our way through beautiful farm country" (Journal, April 2, 1939). This episode typifies the way Weston and Wilson worked with a loose itinerary and adapted it according to the weather, suggestions received from people along the way, or the availability of their friends—especially Ansel Adams, who hosted them on several occasions, shared darkroom space, and guided them up Mt. Ediza and through Yosemite.

The two-year project that culminated in *California and the West* was a highly productive partnership that allowed Weston to immerse himself fully in his work. It also gave Wilson the opportunity to develop as a writer, though the practical demands of the trip prevented her from becoming the novelist she aspired to at its start.[10] As "the chauffeur-chronicler of the expedition," Wilson traded her role as muse for the responsibility of mapping the route, managing provisions, and recording the conditions under which Weston made the photographs of each scene (Weston, "Of the West"). During the course of the project, a certain rhythm emerged for each trip, and a structure for the whole became apparent. The trip to Death Valley was their "initiation." The first year provided the foundation for the main narrative. The second year, then, "must come as an epilogue," for although they continued to travel, "we had a home that second year, so everything was changed" (*California and the West* 118). The Guggenheim years also completed a significant stage in Wilson's relationship with Weston: on the second-to-last day of the project, April 24, 1939, she and Weston were married in Elk, California.[11]

The joy Wilson felt upon their initiation into the Guggenheim years is evident in her typed account for Friday, April 9, 1937: "9:45 of a beautiful morning, and we take to the openroad." After Edward jumped out to make "the first Guggenheim negative" of a lone crab apple tree in a green field, they continued on their way, stopping to look at "a mountain laced with fire trails" and, where the desert began, the Joshua trees. Their destination was "Dead Man's Point," twelve miles from Victorville, where Weston had worked before. When they arrived, Wilson walked right "into a Weston-photo," evidently feeling that Weston's image of the site preceded and framed her own seeing.[12] Here and throughout their travels, however, Wilson also recorded her own impressions, which extend, complement, and complicate her partner's images. She wrote of Death Valley,

> [I]t is an exciting place. The flat, conventional, Mojave, dotted with low greasewood bushes, stretches on and away interminably, and here a mass of granite, carved into huge boulders, crazily balanced rocks, tilts wildly to the sky. These black, orange, yellow, grey, top-heavy stones seem to support themselves upright only by clinging to one another. If one important one let go the whole lot would come tumbling down and scatter and bounce away over the desert. This granite mass, rotting, peeling, shrinking, disintegrating,—still is powerful and proud. We drive into a curve sheltered from the road and plan to camp the night.
>
> We've left the planet Glendale's on,—yet its only two: thirty in the afternoon. Edward and his camera start off in a fever of excitement. (Journal, April 9, 1937)

Her perception of the desert's vast scale and precarious rock arrangements, as well as its potential for sudden transformation and destruction, corresponds to some of Weston's many photographs of this landscape, but her language and perspective remain her own. In addition to providing details of colors whose gradations can only be suggested in black and white, she recognizes the ruin before her and conjures a catastrophic future. Elsewhere she scrutinizes the varieties and textures of plants and insects, from small grasses and tiny blue wildflowers to red and brown ants, grasshoppers, and baby hummingbirds, applying her realist eye to scenes that Weston would approach more abstractly. While he photographs subjects like corpses and "tree carcasses" left after wildfires, she inquires into the origins of the dead man, the reasons for the fire, and the natural history of the land's geological formations. Often she, too, opens herself to the depths of space and erasure of time possible in a sublime landscape like Death Valley (fig. 3). "Unbelievably quiet here," she reports on April 11, 1937, "The top of the world on the day of creation. No movement. No life. No time."

This first day established the collaborative pattern and the daily ritual that would hold for the rest of their trips. That night, Wilson reported, "Sleeping bags are warm and comfortable. The wind outside a bit chill. And so many thousand stars to look at, it's hard to stop looking and go to sleep." The next morning, they awoke at dawn and drank the coffee that Edward brewed. Within a few months, Wilson developed an efficient system for recording each day's events: "Except for an occasional note I write nothing that happens on the day, but start typing out the whole in detail at first opportunity the following morning," she explained. "This means that aside from the last day, the record will be typed and complete at the end of the trip" (Journal, September 19, 1937). And so they continued. During this time, Weston abandoned the Daybooks in which he had recorded his ideas about art and his experience. In a final entry in 1944 he wrote, "I laughingly blame Ch. for cramping my style as a writer—and there may be some truth in this charge—." He also judged her narrative in *California and the West* to be "so well-told that I need not recount any of the Guggenheim period" (*Daybooks* 287). He concentrated instead on taking pictures.

Because others did the driving, Weston could "sit in the right-hand front seat with his bright, light, hungry eyes searching the landscape for the meat of his art," as Szarkowski described his working method. Some of the photographs he made "celebrate the pleasure of being driven," while others fulfill his promise to make satires and record his fight against the invasion of commercial culture into the desert, ocean, and forest landscapes that captivated him throughout his career (Szarkowski, *American Landscapes* 11–12). For example, in "'Hot Coffee,' Mojave Desert" (1937;

Figure 3. Edward Weston, "Dante's View, Death Valley," 1937. (Collection Center for Creative Photography, © 1981 Arizona Board of Regents)

fig. 4), the surreal placement of an enormous cup and saucer promising coffee in the scorched desert along Route 66 points out the ubiquity of roadside advertising even in the most remote areas. Without the hand-painted letters, the sign could be a giant sculpture; with them, it becomes a crude invitation to consume. If a car's driver and passenger had not been thinking about buying and drinking coffee, now they were. Weston's photograph shows how commercial interests can easily alter aesthetic or ecological conceptions of the land. "Weston loved nature, and he hated falsity of all kinds"; when he used irony, as in this photograph, it was usually "to contrast materialism or phoniness with nature itself" (Quinn and Stebbins 14–15). At the same time, the image shows how nature can suddenly appear unreal: "the scale of the sign makes the vast distances seem impossible and the desert look like a flat backdrop" (Quinn and

Figure 4. Edward Weston, "'Hot Coffee,' Mohave Desert," 1937. (Collection Center for Creative Photography, © 1981 Arizona Board of Regents)

Stebbins 28). Produced in defiance of the environment surrounding it, the "Hot Coffee" cup changes the relationship between viewer and landscape, interrupting the traveler's free-flowing contemplation with the reminder that more immediate sources of gratification are just around the bend. Weston's photograph, which invites its viewers to look again, beyond the outsized sign, both records this disruption and resists it.

In *California and the West*, Wilson writes of the maddening promise and disappointment of other roadside establishments when she describes their quest for dates in California's Pinto Basin. Informed that she could not buy dates in the general store because "roadside stands do all the business," she, Weston, and Weston's son Brett drove on to find a "trim building" that housed a "date temple" with "spotless showcases" of dates "wrapped in colored cellophane" and "displayed singly on elegant pedestals" (33). The "young goddess" presiding over the establishment clearly disapproved of the party's unkempt appearance and reluctantly sold them a small, overpriced packet of the precious fruit. Later, they started to see a series of signs that seemed to speak just to them (or to any hot, thirsty, and tired driver and her passengers): "28 MILES TO DATE MILK-SHAKES, 25 MILES TO DATE MILKSHAKES, 18 MILES TO DATE MILKSHAKES." Wilson recalled, "Our first mild curiosity was whipped to fever-pitch as the miles grew fewer and the utterly impossible-sounding beverage came closer." This time, though, the product fulfilled the promise. "I have to admit there is no way to describe date milkshakes; they must be tasted to be understood. . . . They are not too rich, not too sweet; and as I say, there is no word for what they are—they are perfectly constructed for desert consumption" (*California and the West* 37). When she, Edward, and Brett returned to Los Angeles, they bought all the dates they could eat for a much more reasonable fifteen cents a pound. Still, the memory of that perfect milkshake sustained her, and her description of it stays with the reader of her narrative.

Wilson's writing implicitly contrasts the way she and Edward looked at the landscape with the hurried efforts of tourists eager to capture the view and move on, the desperate struggles of local people to survive economically and keep their dignity, and the conventions of the popular media. For example, in Death Valley, Wilson and Weston encounter a man eager to take a quick snapshot (though he fears it will turn out looking flat) and a wife even more eager to leave a place she struggles to describe and finally pronounces "just plain weird" (*California and the West* 20). Another trip to Death Valley produces another encounter with a similar couple: "a Florida car drives up and a man and woman emerge to look over the view. The man is well upholstered and clad in a dark blue business suit. He champs on his cigar and after looking the prospect over a while pronounces to his wife and the surrounding landscape—'well it's certainly booful; very booful'" (Journal, March 15, 1938). While many of the people they meet are older tourists who seem anxious to "pop out of their cars, take each others pictures, glance, pop into their cars, and drive off" (Journal, August 11, 1937), Wilson and Weston also come across students on whirlwind jaunts and solitary hitchhikers. One young man who had just graduated from college in Louisiana says that he and his friend have "been to Dallas, up Pike's Peak, through Yellowstone Park, Glacier Park, Crater Lake, and a few more totaling 4500 miles since they left home, then adds that they left home a week ago." Wilson comments wryly, "Sounds like a perfectly delightful way to travel" (Journal,

August 12, 1937).[13] On two successive days on the road in New Mexico, they see couples trying to hitch a ride, suitcase in hand. The first day Wilson notices "the woman looking angry, the man looking hopeful" (Journal, January 1, 1938); the second day she concludes, "I imagine this business of a man, a woman, and a suitcase, is a transcontinental affair" (Journal, January 2, 1938).

Occasionally the written narrative provides an intimate glimpse of how people in California cling to their native places, barely able to make ends meet. In "dismal little" Westport, a town whose only historical artifacts seem to be an old cannery and an abandoned 1914 record book from the Young People's Christian Endeavor Society, Wilson and her friend Gretchen Schoninger see some blackberries on the edge of the road and start picking. Suddenly they find themselves face to face with a woman who appears to be the town's only resident: "[A] weedy old lady with wispy greygreasy hair, half of it knotted on top of her head and half of it swirling around her round face, comes up with fluttering skirts and aprons and says smiling,—say, boys, those berries are ours." Although roadside fruit should be free for the picking, they let "the old gal" and her berries be. Later, Wilson reports, they go to the general store, "a sad sight" with "rows of empty shelves along the walls, broken only by little piles of accumulated junk," where they "apologize for invading her berry patch. She says that was alright, and the only thing is thats all the berries she has for canning" (Journal, August 13, 1937). In the same town, "[a] little old man walks up and speaks sternly to Edward and Willard about dirtying up his spring" when they try to fill their canteen "and shows them just how to do it right and no other way will do. In this country people not only own the roadside berries but the roadside watersupplies" (Journal, August 13, 1937). Later, while staying in a cabin in Barstow, a man named Mr. Ludlow comes in to fix their gas stove. "He says they go wrong every now and then because people try to make them work for pennies or slugs or almost anything." He explains to them, "some people will try to gyp us out of a dimes worth of gas, then go across the street and drink a dollars worth of beer,—not all people, but some people" (Journal, December 7, 1937). Although often unable to defend their positions articulately, these locals reveal to the travelers passing through how custom defines their lives and distinguishes them from thoughtless outsiders. They may not make promising subjects for photographs, but Wilson's narrative of her encounters with them shows how they use and care for the landscape. Even if a town seems abandoned by industry or designed as a campsite for transients, a few inhabitants almost always remain, visible custodians of vanishing rural California.

Meanwhile, Wilson and Weston indulge in the luxury of mobility, the freedom of contemplation, and relatively few documentary demands. In her journal Wilson notes the scenes she finds most exciting, and usually her intensity of feeling comes from the sense that rational time and space have been transformed. As they approach Santa Fe in December of the first year, they see

> an incredibly beautiful evening sea scape,—the mountains down by Albuquerque have become islands rising from a dark blue sea that is marked by whitecaps far out and on near rocks below us the foam breaks around the base of a light house. For fully a minute as we move along slowly in the car the sight persists, then breaks down into its usual parts. Don't know whether this comes in the mirage or optical illusion or revelations and visions, class, but is the most exciting thing I've seen since we arrived in New Mexico. (Journal, December 23, 1937)

With the desert made ocean and all that is solid made fluid, the impression is more powerful for being fleeting and unreal. A photograph Weston made of Albuquerque from the Sante Fe highway surprisingly seems much more solid, leading the eye up toward the horizon but also revealing structured boundaries and evidence of human use in the delicate wire fence and metal debris included in the frame.

Wilson describes a real seascape in a similar manner. One day at Crescent Beach, she and Weston stayed out until the fog rolled out. They notice that "a cockeyed, backsided, newish moon hangs over the water helplessly. The beach is quiet and mysterious, and the voices and laughing shouts of our neighbors are somewhat eerie in the far away." Wilson concludes the entry for August 11, 1937, "Over the flat wet sand we walk with flashlight, then stand where a divided rock rises seven or eight feet from the beach and look between the two halves at the grey soft distance of water and fog and moon. Willard says it has the another-planet feeling and so it has." She, Edward, Willard, and her friend Gret talk into the night around the fire, "scoop out sand beds for our sleeping bags," and go to sleep with "a burned black giant of a log at our heads another just beyond our feet."

Wilson and Weston also discover landscapes that feel mythical rather than inhabited. On a trip a few months later, they camp in a mature redwood forest. "[H]ere I find a woods that is a woods," Wilson declares. "Ever since I read in fairy stories of the woodcutter and his wife who lived on the edge of a dark and gloomy forest, etc. this is what I have thought a real forest would be like." Much of the mythic appeal derives from its pristine appearance and the absence of other tourists. "The place is left as untouched as possible apparently. The ground is deepcovered with redwood needles and enough leaf mold forever and over this is an even carpet of the green clovery stuff (redwood sorrel)." In the heart of such a dense forest, getting lost "is as simple as breathing. Just pay no attention," Wilson advises. For her, it is an otherworldly place (Journal, October 12, 1937). Whereas other people felt compelled to rush and see a great quantity of sites or anxiously staked their claim to a small patch of land, Wilson and Weston took to the road so that they could possess the landscape fully in their imagination, get lost, and allow themselves to be found.

Most of their meditations on the relation between time and place occur either in such untouched regions or at sites of natural and human ruin, which include groves of dead avocado trees and saguaro cacti; old mines and soda works; shacks abandoned to sun, wind, and sand; cemeteries; and ghost towns. Neither found these subjects beautiful in any traditional sense. "Perhaps the old gold towns are picturesque, but the countryside, laid waste by hydraulic mining, is horrible: mountain-sides are scarred and gouged, washed away to the naked earth; ravines are choked with debris piles," Wilson wrote (*California and the West* 87). A broader survey of unpublished prints from the Guggenheim years reveals many variations on the theme of burned remains, especially of automobiles. One image from Bandon, Oregon, frames two scorched and bent cars, one flipped over and the other with the steering column and wheel intact as a backbone. Photographs from Crescent Beach, along the northern California coast, include intricate studies of driftwood—and the remains of a car on the beach, as if washed ashore with the wood. The extensive record Weston compiled of Joshua trees, rocks, and other natural formations in the Mojave Desert also includes the carcass of a car (fig. 5). Another photograph from the Mojave series puts the viewer face to face with the surface of a different abandoned car, once painted deep black like "Heimy" (fig. 6). Looking at the organic, intricate patterns of white cracks in the paint is like apprehending a system of rivers from far above. The decaying exterior reveals what happens to an object when humans yield control over it and let it return to a natural state.

Many observers have noted Weston's apparent preoccupation with "decay and decline" in these years, though he brushed off questions about it.[14] Wilson commented that on their travels across the Mohave "on US 66,

Figure 5. Edward Weston, "Burned car, Mojave Desert," 1937. (Collection Center for Creative Photography, © 1981 Arizona Board of Regents)

Edward specialized in abandoned service stations" and asked herself, "Why are there so many of these desolate ruins dotted along the bleak shore of the desert?" (*California and the West* 101). Later, Minor White commented on Weston's "obsession with death," and Weston replied, "death was not a theme—it was just a part of life—as simple as that" (qtd. in Stebbins 232). Weston claimed elsewhere that when he depicted what others saw as ruins, he had "actually done people" in his own way:

> Wrecked automobiles and abandoned service stations on the desert, deserted cabins in the high Sierras, the ruins of Rhyolite, ghost lumber towns on the bleak north coast, a pair of high-buttoned shoes in an abandoned soda works, the San Francisco embarcadero, the statue of a leering bellhop advertising a Los Angeles hotel—all of these are pictures of people as well as of life. (qtd. in Starr, *Endangered Dreams* 223)

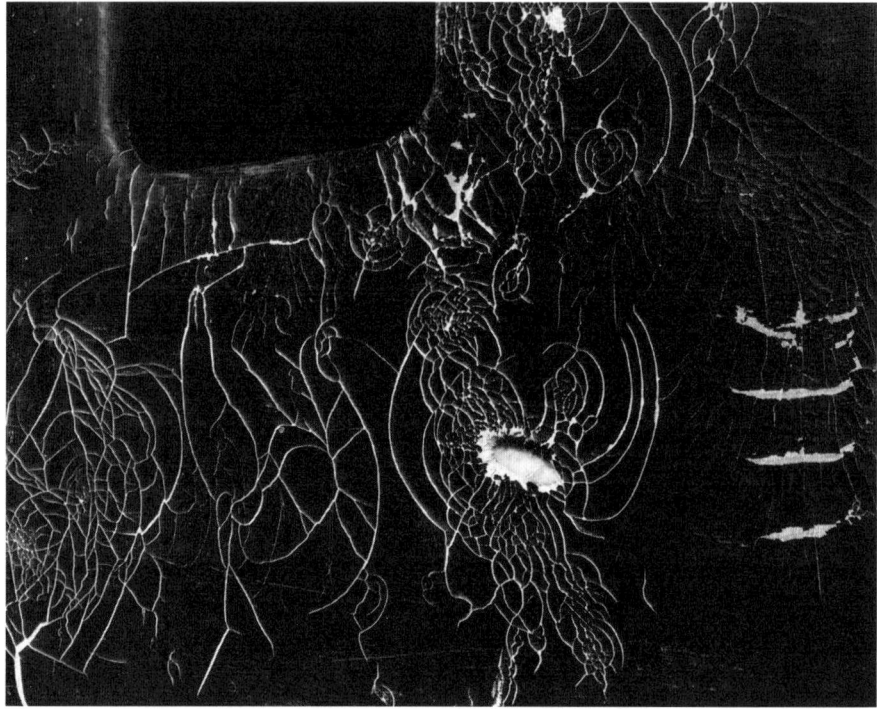

Figure 6. Edward Weston, "Highway 66, Mojave Desert," 1937. (Collection Center for Creative Photography, © 1981 Arizona Board of Regents)

Kevin Starr suggests that Wilson may have written this explanation. In their partnership, she did assume responsibility for expressing Weston's visual ideas in language, not only by keeping the journal but also by drafting any important correspondence.[15] Meanwhile, Weston himself resisted such verbal articulation and "shunned the ascribing of larger cultural or symbolic meaning to his photographs, claiming to choose subjects purely for their form and texture" (Watts 21).

Nonetheless, both photographer and writer resisted the kind of easy interpretation of photographs that newspapers and publications like *Life* encouraged. We have already seen how, after their encounter with the dead man in Death Valley, Wilson and Weston each documented the traumatic experience in their own way. An extensive conversation between them ensued as they kept speculating on how the man could have arrived there and reconstructing the probable sequence of his last hours.[16] The

Los Angeles newspapers, in Wilson's view, "garbled" the story to create a conventional image[17] and at *Life* "the nuts missed the whole point of the contents of bandana—and in the center, carefully wrapped in separate paper, a fish-hook—they just left that part out" (Journal June 18, 1937). When Weston sent *Life* a series of photographs from the first months of their travels, he received instructions to add "a little human interest to wind out the set," like "a man milking a cow, a pioneer on his front porch, ???" (Journal, November 10, 1937). Although Weston did send some additional images, he and Wilson were unhappy with the spread, which placed the photographs in a separate section at the beginning, printed them too dark, and cropped them to bad effect. After these disappointments, they both sought complete control over the presentation of *California and the West*, which required careful editing to produce what Weston called "a cross section of the work, taking the minor notes with the major ones" (126).

The photographs Weston selected for the book balance sweeping views and intimate studies, wild and domesticated spaces, desert and ocean, mountain and plains, life and death—and thus present what Wilson called "Weston's Westerns" (Journal, December 23, 1937), landscapes made beautiful through close attention to their intricate forms. Meanwhile, the narrative Wilson condensed and edited provides a corresponding variety of personal anecdotes, dialogue, and landscape descriptions. Compared with the entire collection of prints the trip produced and the unpublished journal, however, *California and the West* plays down the emphasis on ruins. This difference is especially evident in the treatment of Rhyolite, a town in Nevada that had an extraordinarily short life and, along with the Nevada Test Site, has become a case study on learning how to recover the West's vanished history. In the book, Wilson calls Rhyolite "the western ghost town at its nakedest. Rhyolite's gold boom came in 1906; its death in 1907" (115). She exaggerates only slightly. In the essay "Haunted by Rhyolite," Patricia Limerick concurs that the town was one of the youngest "victims of urban mortality" but expands its life: laid out in 1905, the town ballooned in population to 10,000 people by 1906 before being left for dead in 1911.

Wilson describes in the book how everything portable was carried away, leaving only parts of solid walls intact (fig. 7). These are the structures Weston photographed, two of which he included in the book. Interspersed with images of the lush Columbia River and followed by images of Judge Walker's photography studio in Elk, California; a pristine Aspen Valley in New Mexico; grand Mount Shasta; and Yosemite in heavy snow,

Figure 7. Edward Weston, "Rhyolite, Nevada," 1938. (Collection Center for Creative Photography, © 1981 Arizona Board of Regents)

the first image that was captioned "Rhyolite, Nevada" consists of a grand rectangular doorway with white rocks in the foreground, a two-story building in the background, and a dark hill rising up to the right corner. A second image, also captioned "Rhyolite, Nevada," shows a close-up of the curved archways of what was once a bank building. The third printed photograph of Rhyolite, entitled "Graveyard, Rhyolite, Nevada," (fig. 8), shows four seemingly blank wooden headstones spread out in the desert, one enclosed by square fencing and marked with a wooden cross. In the distance, bare mountains rise from the horizon, but no human settlement is visible. The book situates this image in the center of a group explicitly concerned with destruction's material remains. Preceded by a close-up of a burned tree and a photograph of a dead saguaro and followed by an image that frames the burned remains of a brick fireplace with the

Figure 8. Edward Weston, "Graveyard, Rhyolite, Nevada," 1938. (Collection Center for Creative Photography, © 1981 Arizona Board of Regents)

skeletons of trees that once surrounded a house in Bandon, Oregon, and a cow skull perched on a fence post, it seems to invite inquiry into who made this desolate place into hallowed ground. The published narrative mentions that "Edward was fascinated with the town—Nevada's Athens he called it—and would doubtless have found more to do in better weather" (*California and the West* 115).

Wilson makes no comment on the graveyard in Rhyolite, perhaps because Weston took the negative on their return trip the next year, when conditions favored more leisurely work. In the journal, though, she describes the haphazard effects of neglect:

All graves are heaped gravel, many of the mounds have sunk to be troughs. Some have bars around, some wooden fences, some fallen fences, a childs grave has a broken stick punched into the ground at the head and a little necklace of stones around the outline of the small mound. Date from 1905 to 1930 with 1906 the big year. The mounds are burrowed with gopher holes and the wooden headbouards are often blown clean of letters. Edward thinks he'll come back later to look at lonesome little graves against the mts. Meanwhile rhyolite. (Journal, December 25, 1938)

They spend enough time in Rhyolite for Weston to photograph the Porter Grocery, which he had spotted the previous March, from several directions and for Wilson to talk with a man who "has a mine back in the hill there he bought ten years ago" and lives there "mostly just in the winters, a hard place to make a living." The physical ruins still stand, as seen in the photographs Mark Klett made in 1990 in collaboration with Limerick. Many of Klett's images revolve around the walls of a school (see photographs 23, 27, and 37 in Limerick and Klett) and the bank building's remaining corner and facade, used more recently as a movie set (19–20, 23, 25, and 29). His overview of the "townsite" reveals dirt roads radiating haphazardly from an empty center (leading past the ruins and into the hills, toward a house or trailer, or just out into the desert) and one pickup truck traveling through. As Peter Poole summarizes the contrast between Weston's treatment of "altered landscapes" and the work of Klett and his contemporaries, Weston's "attention was caught, his observations made, but the perspective was different"—more detached and less confrontational (xix).

Weston and Wilson did come back to record the Rhyolite graveyard fully. Weston made at least two photographs of it, and their companion Leon noted writing on the graves that marked the death of Ellery John Olson in 1907, aged six years and four months. If we now return to look at Weston's image of the graveyard, we begin to shift our conception of the landscape's beauty and its history. The contrast between the rough geometry of the handmade fence and the irregular angles of the distant mountains provides an invitation to reflect on the isolation of this short-lived settlement and imagine what it was like to lay one's fortune and hopes for the future at the base of this open sky, only to have them thoroughly swept away as if by the desert wind. Weston's images, I think, encourage aesthetic and historical contemplation by turns; without insisting on documenting the contemporary culture of the Depression, they refract it through the medium of photography. Each carefully planned image preserves the space and time necessary for contemplating the significance of the present. By rearranging the photographs into new groups by place or subject, or by reading them in the full context of Wilson's Journal, we can see how Weston's study of Rhyolite and the West, like the landscape photographs of the "New Topographers" in the 1970s, challenges viewers "to rediscover the relationship between beauty and content" (Poole xvii) and confirms that we have only begun "learning from the landscape of failure."[18]

The Southwestern American Exodus

Photo essays like Dorothea Lange's *An American Exodus* and novels like John Steinbeck's *The Grapes of Wrath*, meanwhile, documented the failures of America's agricultural economy and culture with an immediacy more compelling to contemporary viewers and readers. Published in 1939, these works shaped many Americans' impressions of migration as the struggle of belated pioneers to sustain self-sufficiency and self-respect against corporate interests and a national economy increasingly linked to global markets. The agricultural families that each work depicts seemed to confirm the persistence of an older "Puritan-republican, producer-capitalist culture," a culture that believed in the power of community and the stability of a homeland (Susman, *Culture as History* xx). The "Okie exodus" in particular assumed a mythic power, becoming "the story by which Americans narrated the Depression" (Denning, *The Cultural Front* 262). However, although the images and stories of the Okies and other impoverished groups on the road proved more powerful to viewers and readers eager to reclaim the values of the past than Weston's sublime desert landscapes or material ruins, the survival of farm families and agricultural communities would be only a temporary stay against modernity's uneven spread through the Southwest, a pattern of development that would be epitomized by the installation of atomic laboratories at Los Alamos.

At first, the facts of Depression-era life seemed to speak for themselves, requiring little mediation. Many writers "interrupted their other work to travel around America in search of the thoughts and aspirations of ordinary people—almost as though they might find solace in the discovery that writers shared with the average man a common feeling of bewilderment and despair." From urban slums to midwestern highways to roadside restaurants, "they watched and interviewed and listened to their fellow citizens. . . . [B]efore the simple human drama of the depression experience there was no need to embroider, to speculate, to theorize, to indulge in the conventions of 'art'" (Pells 195–96). As Susman explains the widespread attitude toward gathering such facts: "the whole idea of the documentary—not with words alone but with sight and sound—makes it possible to see, know, and feel the details of life, its styles in different places, to feel oneself part of some other's experience" (159).

Between 1933 and 1935, former journalist Lorena Hickok sent one of the decade's most remarkable documents—a series of reports on ordinary citizens from working-class neighborhoods in New York City to California's Imperial Valley—to Harry Hopkins, President Roosevelt's chief administrator of the Federal Emergency Relief Administration. Meant to assess the effectiveness of existing programs and the need for additional relief across the country, Hickok's assignment aimed to link the "human side" of the Depression with the formation and administration of public policy, giving Hopkins "insight into the thinking of men and women in all walks of life throughout many parts of the United States."[19] She set off in the car she nicknamed "Bluette" and talked "with all sorts of people. There is hardly a type of person I haven't talked with—and at length. Relief officials, WPA officials, state officials, county and city officials, business people, professional people, politicians, both state and local, so-called civic leaders, clergymen, labor leaders, teachers, farmers, relief clients on WPA projects. . . . Certainly if there is any better way to get a cross-section of public opinion in this country, I don't know it."[20] Each night, in her hotel room, she would record her impressions on her portable typewriter. While the introduction to her projected but unfinished book tells the story of the Depression's "unsung heroes" through a sequence of anecdotes, the letters she sent to Hopkins mix portraits of individuals with assessments of regional working conditions. She surveyed coal mines, southern cotton fields, midwestern farms and ranches, California fruit orchards, and struggling cities. She also reported on the effects of regional inequalities, such as different pay scales for Hispanics and Anglos in the West. "She saw with a seasoned reporter's eye and wrote in an earthy, no-foolin' style that managed to be at once unsentimentally cool and warmly sympathetic" (Kennedy 162).

While reporters and historians cited the raw facts of hardship, novelists and photographers explored how people responded to such hardship. Roy Stryker, director of the Farm Security Administration's photography division, distinguished between a newspicture and a photograph taken under his direction in terms of their potential for telling stories: "The newspicture is a single frame; ours, a subject viewed in series. The newspicture is dramatic, all subject and action. Ours shows what's back of the action. It is a broader statement—frequently a mood, an accent, but more frequently a sketch and not infrequently a story" (Stryker and Wood 8). Stryker accordingly defined the purpose of the government-sponsored documentary project in terms of such social narratives: "*We introduced Americans to America.* . . . The full effect of this team's work was that it helped connect one generation's image of itself with the reality of its own time in history" (qtd. in Wood, *Heartland* 20). It was a polite, generous, and naive notion, expressing faith in the ability of images to communicate directly and hope that an imagined community of Americans could be forged. Implicit in this statement is the recognition that by 1935, when the FSA photography projects began, people across the United States felt alienated from their fellow citizens and had lost the ability to see a coherent national culture. Instead of "America," William Stott explains, "there were regions, though again if one looked hard enough, the regions gave way and one had communities—which themselves became, on further scrutiny, classes, factions, groups" (110–11). Patterns of migration during the previous fifty years, along with uneven rates of modernization across the country, certainly contributed to this alienation. Urban life, especially in a major metropolis like New York or Los Angeles, differed substantially from rural life on the Texas plains or in northern New Mexico. Both popular fiction and the FSA projects aimed to bridge such vast divides.

As many critics have shown, *The Grapes of Wrath* achieved iconic status immediately because of its historical resonance, its documentary foundation, and its fictional technique. Interweaving images of the land and masses of displaced people with the heroic story of one farming family, the Joads, Steinbeck came to structure his novel around a series of fundamental conflicts between human and natural forces, migration and disintegration, utopian imagining and material struggle.[21] His narrative begins with a description of the natural disaster that created the Dust Bowl and its far-reaching social consequences: the gathering of dust clouds during the summer of 1934 caused by years of drought and intensive farming, "dusters" that in the words of one historian "swept the full expanse of the Great Plains" but also "darkened the skies over Cleveland, fell on Washington, D.C., reddened the snow of Boston, even created a haze over the ships three hundred miles beyond the Atlantic coast."[22] Steinbeck amplifies the effects of the dust storms by describing the relentless assault on the senses and by endowing the storms themselves with feeling: "In the roads where the teams moved, where the wheels milled the ground and the hooves of the horses beat the ground, the dirt crust broke and the dust formed. Every moving thing lifted the dust into the air: a walking man lifted a thin layer as high as his waist, and a wagon lifted the dust as high as the fence tops, and an automobile boiled a cloud behind it. The dust was long in settling back again" (5). Then he describes a dawn so clogged with dust that the sun cannot show through it. "As that day advanced," he writes, "the dusk slipped back toward darkness, and wind cried and whimpered over the fallen corn" (6). Sounding animalistic but much more powerful than either animals or individual humans, the wind exacerbates the drought, embodies human suffering, and calls for a collective response. The novel goes on to develop the relationship between natural and social catastrophes and makes hardship acutely visible through the paradigmatic experience of a single migrant family.

Steinbeck did not set out to write the epic novel of the Depression. As William Howarth recounts the conception and making of the book, at the beginning of the era Steinbeck was a sympathetic, even guilty observer of other people's hardships. A best-selling author, he capitalized on opportunities to have his work adapted for stage and film, and he knew the limits of his ability to effect social change. However, when he witnessed the floods that devastated migrant camps in California in February 1938, leaving their residents homeless, he was so moved by the natural and social disaster that he began to imagine how he could expand a documentary project on California's migrant workers, which he had agreed to write with photographer Horace Bristol, into a more substantial publication. In the end, though, Steinbeck decided he could not work as Bristol did, gathering extensive material and then editing it into a compressed form. He backed out of the agreement, telling Bristol, "I've decided it's too big a story to be just a photographic book. I'm going to write it as a novel."[23]

In the process of transforming his documentary material into fiction, Steinbeck began to envision how people could form a community capable of resisting commercial economic interests through their shared experience. The novel follows the Joad family and their failure to hold on to the right to work the land with an extensive section that narrates their life on the road. It imagines a series of ideal communities, first among the travelers and then in government relocation camps. Okies like the Joads typically packed their belongings into jalopies and traveled along Route 66, stopping along the way to eat, sleep, refuel, fix flat tires, share stories, and dream about the future. "The highway became their home and movement their medium of expression" (163). Over time, the shared experience of movement produced its own sensibility: "The movement changed them; the highways, the camps along the road, the fear of hunger and the hunger itself, changed them. The children without dinner changed them, the endless moving changed them. They were migrants" (282). Hardship and life on the road, along with continued faith in the opportunities they would find in California, united Steinbeck's travelers and constituted the era's new kind of mobile community.

The Pie Town Settlement

Another kind of improvised community emerged in Russell Lee's photographic portrait of Pie Town, New Mexico, a small farming community Lee discovered by chance in 1940 and quickly identified as a promising subject. Named by a man who sought to broaden his store's reputation for good pies and settled by farmers from Oklahoma and Texas, the town struck Lee as the "last frontier" for homesteaders, a place where everyone seemed "united in an effort to make their community really function."[24] Along with the general store and the post office, institutions typically found in any small town, Pie Town boasted a café on its main street that functioned as a meeting place for all the town's residents. Stryker agreed that Pie Town seemed interesting and urged Lee to emphasize the farmers' productivity and self-sufficiency.

Pie Town seemed to provide ample evidence of a thriving agricultural community and to exemplify a small-town ideal. Lee shot many convivial scenes of church picnics, all-day sings, dances, and family parties, in many ways producing a portrait of an earlier era. As David Kennedy characterizes such social portraits produced under the direction of the WPA, the photographs combine implicit criticism of current conditions with "a persistent subtext of patriotic nationalism," and thus tell two stories simultaneously.

> It was as if the American people, much as they were poised to execute more social and political and economic innovation than ever before in their history, felt the need to take a long and affectionate look at their past before they bade much of it farewell, a need to inventory who they were and how they lived, to benchmark their country and their culture so as to measure the distance traveled into the future that Franklin Roosevelt was promising. (Kennedy 256–57)

Lee's work conformed to this patriotic pattern, but only in part.[25] Lee's wife Joan, who traveled with him and wrote captions for his photographs, correctly identified nostalgia in his enthusiasm for the town. However attractive the town's outdated customs, the homesteading system in Pie Town was "no answer" to the agricultural crisis, she asserted (Myers, *Pie Town Woman* 175–76). Like many women who witnessed the era's hardships, Jean tended to be discerning in her observations and realistic in her judgment.

Upon closer scrutiny, however, the photographs of Pie Town that Lee produced do not merely perpetuate such nostalgia. They also reveal the social costs and economic struggles that threatened rural communities across the West. By the time Stryker sent Lee to New Mexico, the FSA director had already gathered an extensive gallery of images, many of which were published in magazines that circulated nationally, including *Time, Fortune, Look, Life, U.S. Camera*, and *Survey Graphic*. As the agency achieved mainstream status, its photographic subjects and style threatened to become too familiar. The images might be accepted as true, but they were no longer as shocking or as capable of telling effective stories. Stryker trusted his photographers to find stories that linked people from disparate regions, and Lee succeeded especially well in Pie Town and elsewhere in New Mexico. In Taos he followed performers and spectators at the annual San Geronimo Fiesta; in Wagon Mound he attended the Bean Day Rodeo; in Costilla he observed women weaving as part of a WPA project; and in Mogollon he trailed gold miners at work and at quitting time. Each of his studies investigates working conditions, familial relations, and local customs, aiming for portraits both distinctive and typical of the hardship shared by many rural people.

Among his Pie Town photographs are images of the wooden dugouts many families inhabited, lying low in the desert, secure against wind but cramped and dusty inside. From a distance, the houses barely interrupt the expanse of desolate land lacking proper irrigation; indeed, the predominant natural features of Pie Town are dust and dry earth. If the New Mexican landscape had previously enchanted outsiders with visible symbols of its ancient Native American and heroic Spanish past, this landscape of struggling Anglo farmsteads held little recognizable mystery. By photographing land that could not be considered scenic, Lee began to shift his viewers' perception of the region's cultural meaning from Charles Lummis's timeless "wonderland" to an uneven collection of isolated and impoverished rural communities.

Lee repeatedly shot one family, the Caudills, at work and at leisure and thus organized his Pie Town sequence around the daily life of a household, much as Walker Evans organized his study of tenant farmers in Alabama in *Let Us Now Praise Famous Men* (1941) around a few neighboring families. Rather than reproduce the stereotypical small town, both photographers coaxed history and feeling out of vernacular structures and domestic spaces. Lee's photographs show Faro Caudill riding a horse-drawn planter (a piece of machinery seemingly from another century), hauling water five miles, building a new dugout, rolling a cigar, and dancing all night. They show Doris Caudill's constant work, whether milking a cow, placing milk in a cooling box, planting cabbage shoots, patching clothes, ironing, or canning. They show young Josie Caudill still enjoying the rituals and leisure of childhood: chasing goats, combing her hair, sleeping, looking warily over a crooked wooden fence as if into her future.[26] These photographs of domestic life make the process of establishing roots in a place visible, a matter of daily work rather than inheritance. While they connect one family's experience to nineteenth-century homesteading traditions, they also implicitly situate the apparent persistence of earlier modes of settlement within the well-known contemporary struggles of farming families forced to keep starting again, farther west, under worse conditions.

Critics have observed that in Evans's domestic interiors, "the artifacts of a collective culture are also dense with evidence of the living of individual lives" (Galassi 137). Through his calm, precise style, Evans seems to allow things to express their owners and, in the process, to tell the story of how local landscapes are made. In this way he exemplifies his era's use of documentary material as the integration of facts into social fictions. Art critic Clement Greenberg defended photography's status as art precisely for this kind of narrative potential. "The art in photography is literary art before it is anything else," Greenberg claimed in *The New York Review of Books* in 1964. "[I]ts triumphs and monuments are historical, anecdotal, reportorial, observational before they are purely pictorial. . . . The photograph has to tell a story if it is to work as art." According to Greenberg, the photographer's challenge was to "convert" his or her subject from fact to story, since the gap between "the extra-artistic, real-life meaning of things and their artistic meaning is even narrower in photography than it is in prose" (183). Although Greenberg's essay concentrates on the early modernist photographers—Atget, Steichen, Feininger, and Kerstein—he mentions Evans's "super-sophistication" and his creative "demotic eye" toward the end, indicating that Evans's mastery of the medium both fulfilled the pictorial promise of its earlier masters and proved his own general theory.

Evans's work simultaneously recorded local landscapes and incorporated them into stories that connect local and national or commercial cultures. Both Evans and Lee developed the habit "of *picking up* searing little spots of realism and of underlining, quietly, proportionately" through careful framing.[27] In different ways, Evans and Lee dramatized the gap between capitalism's promise of mobility and abundance and the economic limitations that either prevented small-town inhabitants from claiming their share of that abundance or forced them off their land. The photographers represented this gap through their documentary aesthetic, juxtaposing the products manufactured for mass consumption with vernacular architecture and choosing transitional locales as their subjects of study.

Still, there are significant differences in the two photographers' styles. Lee shows greater intimacy with his subjects and pays closer attention to the relationship between people, their houses, and their places of work. He also resists imposing order on the scenes he views. For example, a photograph of a Pie Town farmer's wife washing dishes in her dirt-floor kitchen carries indoors the matter-of-fact approach he brought to the outdoor landscape.[28] By comparison, the uninhabited kitchen of one of Evans's Alabama tenant farmers pictured in *Let Us Now Praise Famous Men* seems a model of cleanliness and simple beauty—and a forced collaboration between absent inhabitant and photographer. Evans worked to create harmonious compositions that integrated commercial and local cultures, whereas Lee tended to photograph his subjects in the middle of their everyday activities, oblivious to the national networks around them. Evans delighted in juxtaposing commercial iconography and vernacular forms. As Jonathan Green has commented, "[n]o commercial item is too mean, too trivial, too out of place for the world of Evans's photographs" (23). For example, in Evans's study "Signs in South Carolina, 1936," a historical plaque and a commercial announcement nailed to the porch railing demand equal attention, as if uniting the remembrance of local history with current practices of consumption into a single frame. Evans organizes the image to create visual contrast between written and illustrated advertisements and real objects, and in this case no people interfere with the arrangement. By contrast, Lee's "Mr. Keele, merchant and president of the Farm Bureau, in front of the general store" (fig. 9) seems to suggest the isolation of people who work in small western towns. The photograph shows a black doorway framed with advertisements for tobacco and horse races and flanked by lists of eastbound and westbound

Figure 9. Russell Lee, "Mr. Keele, merchant and president of the farm bureau, in front of the general store." Pie Town, New Mexico, 1940. (Courtesy of the Library of Congress)

stage stops, complete with mileage. The signs indicate the limits of regularly scheduled travel (in one direction, San Antonio, Texas, 895 miles; in the other Los Angeles, California, 825 miles) and the routes of exchange with the world outside. In the center of the image, we see Mr. Keele carrying a crate of grapefruit, probably a fresh delivery. We notice his straight posture, which conveys a sense of purpose, but with this figure Lee also intimates the future of the agricultural West: life far from the main highway will be economically isolated and psychologically perilous. Despite the roads and the commercial and transportation networks that link the workers in Pie Town with the world outside, human connections seem hard to sustain.

In 1991, scholars and photographers returned to Pie Town, eager to discover whether the Caudill family still lived there and whether the community still existed. A group of students from Southwest Texas

State University organized the project *Retracing Russell Lee's Steps: A New Documentary*, to compare the current appearance of Pie Town and St. Augustine, Texas (another town Lee photographed extensively) with Lee's Depression-era images. They found Pie Town "decrepit," lacking new industries and abandoned by all but a few oldtimers and ranchers. The sprawling desert ranges of Catron County supported 10,000 elk and 2,800 people. They saw "enough to call a community, but not enough to call a town: several abandoned gas stations, a few mobile homes and frame houses, a church, a roadside park where the annual Pie Festival was held, a volunteer fire department, a stucco post-office, a few worn, parked cars, and perhaps, but probably not, a person" (Smyth n.p.). This characterization implies that a settlement could barely be sustained by people who remained isolated, out of public view, and who lacked official or commercial support. Fifty years after Lee organized his study around the vital idea of a frontier community, the notion and the possibility of its realization had lost all force. The families who had come to Pie Town during the Depression had been hoping for a second chance. If they could not survive in Texas by farming cotton, they would come to Catron County to claim a homestead. Yet, by the early 1940s, they had begun to leave, joining the army, working in defense plants, or looking for jobs in the city. Several elderly farmers who had held on, like Bob Magee who "got my Ph.D. in 'Post-Hole Digging,'" admitted that their children had done better by leaving the town and getting a university education. In 1991 their own land was being threatened by environmental groups who proposed a substantial increase in grazing fees. Each family the researchers spoke to described their struggle to survive in Pie Town and the difficulty of imagining its next generation: "A young couple, if they get married and expect to raise a family and live decently out here, they can't do it," stated Colita Schalbar, a resident of Albuquerque who taught elementary school in Pie Town until 1957 and had been photographed by Lee at a dance. Pie Town's apparent cohesion in the early 1940s was short-lived, a brief pause in the region's relentless pattern of migration, social rupture, and reconstruction.

Unsettling Los Angeles

Los Angeles, always the city of America's future, exposed and reinvented this pattern so often during the Depression era that displacement became as much a state of mind as a social condition. "[I]f we understand the history of the last two centuries as dominated by migration," as Henry Yu and other scholars propose, then Los Angeles becomes a model for imagining modern locality and post-regional identity. Taking the metropolis as his rule for community formation in the Americas, Yu proposes that we reconceive settlers as "migrants who fantasize about stopping and making an organic tie between themselves and the land they occupy" and a region as "an act of imagination, an organizing and categorizing of a smaller subset of the ideas generated at these nodes of intersection" (Yu 540). Pie Town and Los Angeles may seem worlds apart, but the challenge that both posed to any essential notion of rootedness confirms the dissolution of any absolute division between rural and urban categories of experience.

"The history of Los Angeles is the history of its booms," Carey McWilliams wrote in his seminal study *Southern California Country* (1946). Each boom had its boosters. The speculative boom of 1887–89 brought real estate wizards, boosters who put "Joshua trees in a desert tract advertised as the only region in Southern California in which the orange was indigenous!" (120). In the 1890s the Los Angeles Chamber of Commerce and the magazine *Land of Sunshine* publicized southern California to midwesterners who could travel in comfortable Pullman cars. During the tourism boom of 1902 to 1920, street life lured curious but cautious moderate-income observers to the city—and sensible subdivisions kept them there. In the 1920s, oil and motion picture production brought about the nation's largest internal migration in history (and the first accomplished by car), swelling the population of Los Angeles by nearly 115 percent. This boom of the twenties brought lower-middle-class migrants; it also brought, in McWilliams's words, the "dwarfs, pygmies, one-eyed sailors, showpeople, misfits, and 50,000 wonder-struck girls" (159) attracted to the movies, the "odd and freakish types" that populate Nathanael West's *The Day of the Locust* and inspired Preston Sturges to pay homage to the "motley mountebanks, the clowns, the buffoons" who inspire laughter.

Only after a final boom during the Depression, which brought new groups of working-class migrants, did a regional literature and local consciousness begin to develop from within southern California. Carey McWilliams, Kevin Starr, and Mike Davis all suggest that the 1930s mark a transitional period in the region's economy, patterns of migration, and master narrative of development. The hopes for the future that sustained so many white migrants through disappointed dreams had produced an *anticipatory*—rather than an actual—regional identity. In the 1930s this utopian orientation began to change. According to Starr, the hopes raised

in anticipation of the West's riches became enmeshed in the urban landscapes of southern California in the 1920s, and they "did not evaporate
with the anxieties and social conflicts of the Depression."[29] Instead, these
wishes became more intense, and the urban landscape became saturated
with dreams and disappointments. Starr further explains, "By the mid-
1920s myth and reality, dream gesture and landscape had so interpen-
etrated each other in an actual place . . . that each aspect of architecture,
of lifestyle, social psychology and infrastructure bespoke an integrated
condition based upon the Hollywood myth" (Starr, *Inventing* 334). Davis
also chronicles a shift in the city's dominant stance in this decade from
boosterism to debunking—that is, from sunshine to *noir*, with the latter
sensibility articulated most fully by European intellectuals (Adamic,
Horkheimer, Adorno), by writers of the new "Los Angeles Novel" (Cain,
McCoy, West), and by producers of *film noir*. David Fine has observed
that the California novel that took shape in this period is "obsessively
concerned with puncturing the bloated image of Southern California as
the golden land of opportunity and the fresh start" (*Los Angeles* 44). By the
time West wrote *The Day of the Locust*, Los Angeles was simultaneously
a place of material riches and cultural impoverishment: a "dream dump"
where people came to fulfill their last hopes or to die.

West's novel and Sturges's film *Sullivan's Travels* articulate these shifts
in the experience of migration, the loss of the boom mentality, and the
trauma of urban life through tropes of spatial immobility. In these works,
survival in Los Angeles produces a passive but urgent desire for escape—a
desire that can be satisfied only by detaching dreams from places. The
previous decades had brought millions to Los Angeles; these narratives
suggest that suddenly the problem might be the difficulty of leaving.
Kaja Silverman describes historical trauma as an unraveling of a culture's
dominant fiction and as a social formation without a mechanism of
achieving consensus. While she analyzes such unraveling in films of the
mid-1940s that document the "ruins of masculinity" after World War II,
I think that the fiction and film of the wartime years locate trauma in the
ruins of migration: the destruction of middle-class hope for new opportunities in a region whose commercial development relied on migrant
labor but demanded migrants' social marginalization. Both West's satire
and Sturges's comedy depict writers and producers locked in positions
and places they have chosen, repeatedly forced to recognize the losses
of both a sense of place and the possibility of progress toward a better
future. It is an active paralysis—and in *Sullivan's Travels* the paralysis is the

comedy's conceit—but one that questions whether migration's trauma can be worked through. In both works, Los Angeles takes shape as a traumatic present in which the forces of shock and recovery, of location and dislocation, remain in perpetual struggle.

According to Rita Bernard, "Nathanael West's distinctive contribution to the literature and social criticism of the thirties lies in his recognition of the importance of collective dreams and desires." West understood that people required not just the necessities of life but also the everyday practices that could produce transformation: "to add inches to the biceps and to develop the bust . . . to write and live the life of an artist . . . to be an engineer and wear leather puttees . . . to develop a grip that would impress the boss" ("'When You Wish Upon a Star'" 325). In *The Day of the Locust*, such efforts at self-improvement are repeatedly frustrated. The poetics of shock keep estranging the past from the present while withholding the means for self-transformation. Refracted through an eastern intellectual protagonist, much of the narrative dismantles the fake fronts of Los Angeles architecture and, by extension, its claim to generate culture. Tod Hackett's critical gaze exposes any seeming vestige of natural beauty as artifice from the start. His trip home from the studio in chapter 1 immediately disenchants a twilight scene in Pinyon Canyon into ugly artifice: the "pale violet light" that outlines the edges of the trees suddenly becomes a "violet piping, like a Neon tube" that traces "the tops of the ugly, hump-backed hills" (West 61). Along the path to Earle and Miguel's camp, Tod encounters orange poppies; "Their petals were wrinkled like crepe and their leaves were heavy with talcumlike dust." Tod notes that "the air itself was vibrant pink" (113). Instead of a natural paradise or a collective realization of dreams, here Los Angeles is a city filled with sickly light and inscrutable objects—indecipherable not because they have a mysterious aura but because they lack stylistic consistency and historical meaning. The houses do not fit the landscape, just as Tod's "large sprawling body" does not connect with his apparent talent. His personalities snap "one inside the other like a Chinese box" (60).

West makes urban fragmentation visible in the landscape, in architectural styles, in patterns of dreams, and in art. Pastiche penetrates even the most unremarkable private spaces, like his protagonist Homer Simpson's ersatz "Irish" cottage—with roof thatching made of "heavy fireproof paper," hinges "stamped to appear hand forged," a "Spanish" living room, a fireplace filled with cacti (some real, some rubber and cork), and two identical New England–style bedrooms. Just as this mixture of styles has been drained of the possibility of producing sensation or meaning, so has the person who apprehends it. The novel "thematizes the problem of feeling," Jonathan Greenberg argues, making "the mere experience of particular feelings . . . the source of conflict" (590), both for its characters and its readers. Often it is the very absence of feeling that perplexes the reader of West's fiction and, at times, his characters as well. For example, West's narrator tells us that, along with the afternoon sun and the exertions of a lizard in the back yard, the house "fairly well occupie[s]" Homer. Homer's only real sensations—inchoate surges of desire—derive from the memory of his own sexual trauma; they remain buried in "the refuse of feeling" (87) or in the uncontrollable movement of his hands.[30] It is critical that Homer, as a typical modern migrant, *not* feel acutely, so as to protect himself from despair. As Edmund Wilson wrote of the novel,

> Mr. West has caught the emptiness of Hollywood; and he is, as far as I know, the first writer to make this emptiness horrible. The most impressive thing in the book is his picture of the people from the Middle West who have passed on from their meager working lives to the sunlit leisure of the Coast, wanting something more than they have had but not knowing what they want, with no capacity for the enjoyment of anything except gaping at movie stars and listening to Aimee McPherson's sermons. ("Hollywood's Dance of Death" 73)

The narrator describes Tod as a typical victim of the Hollywood dream, someone "whose anguish is basic and permanent," someone "without hope." His body registers that anguish by disconnecting the sensations of its parts, his mind by disconnecting the memory of rejection from the present experience of it. Homer's pain will be perpetual: his crying, Tod notes, "has no progress in it" (167).

Because it is preoccupied with the city's spatial and imaginative fragmentation, *The Day of the Locust* resists aesthetic transcendence, progress, or what we now think of as a postmodern acceptance of the absence of solid history. West's Los Angeles keeps producing the experience of shock, and such repetition demands either the numbing of the imagination or its routinization. T. J. Clark has written of the "emptying and sanitizing of the imagination" that accompanies modernity's "horrible, intolerable" disenchantment, and he characterizes modern art as "caught interminably between horror and elation at the forces driving" modernization (7–8). West's novel reveals an awareness that it, too, is "caught between horror and elation" through two figures of dreams:

Faye Greener's nonchalant deck of cards and Tod's painting. Through Faye, West reveals the routinization of the imagination to be an everyday response to the trauma of modernity; in the painting Tod creates, "The Burning of Los Angeles," West reproduces modern art's perpetual vacillation between despair and hope.

At the center of the painting rushes the mob, the dark counterpart of Baudelaire's Parisian crowd. In front, a small group flees; behind, the burning city rises in "a great bonfire of architectural styles" (184). Here we have both the dialectical structure of modernism (high art versus mass culture) and the elements of an exemplary postmodernism that "swims, even wallows, in the fragmentary and the chaotic currents of change" (Harvey 44). But the painting and West's novel do not yet accept spatial and stylistic fragmentation as inevitable, much less pleasurable. Instead, they document the painful loss of transcendence that modernism traditionally gestured toward while lacking the detachment from the past that would bring delight to pastiche. Because the painting cannot decide between a vision of the future as a "terrible holocaust" and the happy chaos of a "holiday crowd," it functions merely to neutralize the pain of the present, to detach Tod's imagination from the reality of his pain.

In the novel's culminating riot, however, collective boredom is finally pushed over the edge into an orgy of violence. Like the ersatz mourners at Mr. Greener's funeral, the audience for the premiere at Kahn's Pleasure Dome is "tired of oranges, even of avocado pears and passion fruit," full of anger at the incompatibility of an engineered Los Angeles and their own experience of it. The riot releases repressed class rage, which is also the rage of disappointed migrants, and repressed sexual desire: an old man hugs a young girl, his hand in her dress and his mouth biting her neck. A woman pays no attention to a man with his arm around her and simply continues her conversation. The crowd as a whole moves in monstrous mimicry of the city, like an unruly body, through jerks and spasms and screams. The "wailing moan" and screams of the ambulance speak more humanly than the crowd does—so much so that Tod finally thinks the noise must be coming from him. The shock keeps repeating itself in this last scene, which extends into the reader's present through Tod's unending laughter. Cathy Caruth develops her theory of traumatic suffering through an analysis of Freud's *Beyond the Pleasure Principle*. She observes that in Tasso's story of Tancred, so fundamental to Freud, the voice of suffering is released *through* the wound. So, too, does Tod utter the trauma of urban emptiness through his wounded body. In the end, no one leaves

Los Angeles. Mr. Greener dies, Faye has not yet achieved her big success but cannot admit failure, Homer's exit is literally blocked by the mob, and Tod succumbs to delirium.

Analogous to the novel's spatial, psychological, and class paralysis is its paralysis of genre. A composite of scenes, plots, and characters from films of the 1930s, the novel surveys the many forms available to the literary imagination. However, the restless montage confirms the thematics of entrapment.[31] *Sullivan's Travels* also aligns the motivations of plot (the desire to leave Los Angeles) with an investigation into how generic mobility might provide a means of escape. In the film, a successful director of lighthearted comedies, John L. Sullivan, resolves to get serious and find out what "trouble" is, firsthand, so that he can make a "meaningful" film from the book *O Brother, Where Art Thou?* Conceived partly as "a satire of the making of the movie *The Grapes of Wrath*," it begins with Sullivan (Joel McCrea) presenting his plan to research the experience of the struggling poor to a group of highly skeptical studio executives.[32] First he must leave Los Angeles; then he must live among the poor and share their hardship. He does not get far: after being pursued by a "land yacht" full of Hollywood insiders eager to take down his "story of vagabonding," his first solo ride lands him back in a Hollywood coffee shop, where he meets a tough and disillusioned actress (Veronica Lake) who intends to be on her way out of town for good. Sully's generous nature, not to mention his attraction to the girl, kicks in. He cannot help trying to help her, and after reluctantly revealing his identity, he takes her to his mansion. Instead of making the girl happy, however, the experience of real contact with a Hollywood director makes her "sore." "You've taken all the joy out of life," she accuses. She expresses rage at his swimming pool, his limousine, and his barbecue. At breakfast she reveals all the things she did not have (pearls, a yacht, a new girdle), and now those lacks are writ large. Unlike Sullivan's fellow movie executives who lie about the hardships of their youth, the girl and the real vagabonds do not need to invent pain. They live it, and occasionally they escape into the manufactured fictions of romantic comedies, musicals, and cartoons. It is the old model—art as compensation or catharsis, predicated on the gap between everyday struggle and entertainment's pleasures—that Sturges's comedy calls into question.

Sullivan and the girl eventually set off to look for trouble together. As they sit at a lunch counter in Vegas with the land yacht down the road, Sullivan voices doubt at the possibility of escaping the city through embracing pain himself. Something keeps pushing him back, he complains, "as if some force was saying, 'Get back where you belong. Don't try sticking your nose out here. You don't belong to real life, you phony,' . . . Maybe there's a universal law that says, 'Stay put! As you are, so shall you remain.'" Here Sullivan tries to explain the problem of immobility by naturalizing it: the force that prevents him from leaving his professional role, his class, and Hollywood is "like gravity," a "universal law." Sturges generally plays the naive director's frustrated encounters with reality for laughs, and Sullivan's observation here confirms that any effort at class and gender reversal will not succeed in the end. A disavowal of probability provides the film's license for humor and its "tonic against sentimentality" (Lane 86).

While the plot uses the "real" geographic boundary between the city and the periphery to oppose rich and poor, private and public life, capital and labor, the film reinserts such oppositions into the city itself. At the railroad station, hobos gather just down the tracks from the orderly depot. When Sullivan tries to show his generosity to the poor by dispensing five-dollar bills, he plunges deeper into the city's underclass than he ever intended to go, getting involved in a fight that lands him in a prison camp. The railroad is also a symbol of historical trauma in the old style, like the "Octopus" that destroyed the common farmer in the name of progress. By contrast, the cars that have replaced the train for middle- and upper-class Angelinos announce the arrival of mobility for its own sake, without regard for destination or geographical boundaries. The freeway will soon spread development farther and farther away from the already fragmented city center. With both its name and its luxurious interior, the land yacht further mocks the predetermined routes of the railroads and their meager allotment of personal space.

The happy ending of *Sullivan's Travels* insists on sustaining the structure of comedy without giving up the film's many examples of suffering. The film thus uses generic convention to lift the hero out of his endless, painful labor and his repeated physical punishments. Sturges makes a knowing display of film technique, from the first page-turn, imitating the opening of a novel, to the melodramatic tragedy-within-the-film that begins the story, the montage of silent workers shown to the film's viewers, and the Disney cartoons shown at the prison camp. After such an extensive survey of form and genre, the return to stock comedy is ironic, and as in West's novel, a cacophony of demonic laughs fills the concluding frame.

The modern metropolis—which Los Angeles epitomized, exaggerated, and superceded—was created and reconfigured by diverse and ever-changing groups of migrants. Histories and archaeologies of Los

Angeles—such as the exemplary studies of Davis, William Deverell, and William Fox—must negotiate layers of the past that have been buried, eroded, or shaken into fragments and find ways to integrate them into understandings of an urban landscape where change only accelerates. Many other sites significant to the experience of migration in the twentieth-century Southwest, however, are substantially abandoned, not fully visible without the supplement of aesthetic, imaginative, or historical perspectives. By foregrounding the problem of visuality, landscape studies like Weston's *California and the West* and FSA photographs like Lee's Pie Town series ask us to think about how our understanding of and feelings about a place and a period derive initially from what we see and only later from how we supplement this initial impression with other sources of knowledge.

Our understanding of the Southwest's twentieth-century histories of migration and resettlement is still emerging, as I show in the chapters that follow. Jackson wrote in *The Necessity for Ruins* that "there has to be that interval of neglect, there has to be discontinuity; it is religiously and artistically essential" (102). Small towns and rural landscapes were not all ruins in the late 1930s, even if the migrants who left them for the city or the promise of California made no provisions to sustain the places left behind. In the decades that followed, viewers and readers began to look back to these rural places and see the origins of a trajectory of modern disintegration. "[R]uins provide the incentive for restoration, and for a return to origins," Jackson explains. Rephotography projects like Klett's studies of Rhyolite and Joan Myers's return to Pie Town, documented in *Pie Town Woman*, provide one kind of restoration. As we will see in the chapters that follow, revivals of older fictional genres, from the village story to the magical realist novel, provide other literary forms for documenting atomization and reconstructing Southwestern homelands.

The Village

Romance and New Mexican Rural History

A landscape should establish bonds between people, the bond
of language, of manners, of the same kind of work and leisure,
and above all a landscape should contain the kind of spatial
organization which fosters such experiences and relationships;
spaces for coming together, to celebrate, spaces for solitude,
spaces that never change and are always as memory depicted
them. These are some of the characteristics that give a landscape
its uniqueness, that give it style. These are what make us recall it
with emotion.
—J. B. Jackson, *The Necessity for Ruins*, 16-17

The last chapter showed how representations of the road revealed the
difficulties Depression-era migrants faced in trying to reconstitute new
communities and senses of home, especially in Los Angeles. In the years
leading up to and following World War II, stories and novels of urban and
suburban life seemed especially well suited to expressing and interrogating
the emergence of a coherent national culture. Although a traditional unit
of spatial and social organization in many parts of the country, the village
or small town seemed to be, at the latest, a nineteenth-century idea. As
Jackson discusses in the conclusion to *The Necessity for Ruins*, the small
town corresponds to "the most picturesque and appealing aspect of our
past." Because it belongs to an earlier era, writing about it always poses the
danger "of lapsing into sentimental antiquarianism, a glorification of the
simpler days of the early Republic" (117). For writers, a focus on village life
in the 1940s seemed to mean either aligning themselves with the literary
ambitions and conservative politics of the Southern Agrarians or admit-
ting to "sentimental antiquarianism." In the case of New Mexico, however,
writers of the village also manipulated such sentiment and deployed it for
political purposes. Acutely aware that the rural communities of the Rio
Arriba valley were becoming invisible in the face of national and global

networks, native Anglo and Nuevomexicano writers turned to the histories of their own villages as a means of resisting the pressures of modernization. I begin my analysis of New Mexican village stories with a brief survey of photographs taken by Russell Lee and John Collier Jr. of small towns in northern New Mexico. Both Farm Security Administration employees studied villages that still preserved traditional ways of life well into the twentieth century and were ill-equipped for the changes that would be wrought by federal improvement projects, war, and uneven postwar prosperity. Yet, like the work of New Mexican folklorists Lorin Brown, Fabiola Cabeza de Baca, Annette Hesch Thorp, Lou Batchen, and Cleofas Jaramillo, their photographs do not merely capture vanishing customs, like so many snapshots of the Old West. Particularly when read with contemporary novels and memoirs, these photographs announce a new orientation toward local objects and rural spaces, both as part of a social record and as material that could later be put to aesthetic use. As Peter Galassi has written of Walker Evans, they prove that "if an artist looks outward rather than inward, beauty and emotion"—qualities previously claimed by literature and high art—"will take care of themselves" (qtd. in Slusher 223).

Whereas *The WPA Guide to 1930s New Mexico* provided suggestions for road tours; descriptions of major cities; and essays on agriculture, Indians, folklore, religion, and art, all with the intent of luring readers to visit many remote places, the stories of rural life produced by the *Guide* and FSA photographers located the reader in a single village, mapped the village's vernacular landscape, and described the secular and religious rituals that in Arjun Appadurai's terms both "embody locality" and "locate bodies in socially and spatially defined communities" (*Modernity at Large* 179). Most of this chapter concentrates on Frank Waters's novel *People of the Valley* (1941) and Cleofas Jaramillo's memoir *The Romance of a Little Village Girl* (1955), which I approach as twentieth-century American variants on a much older British genre, the village story. Instead of encouraging tourist mobility, they articulate the traditions that keep villagers attached to their home territory. By organizing their representations of local customs and village life through circular patterns and the perspective of native figures, each of these works both reenacts local knowledge and mediates it. Thus they create a complex and gendered dynamic of identification and detachment that reveals the difficulty of seeing and coming to know a rural community in an era of migration and urbanization.

I view both of these texts as fully engaged with ongoing debates concerning the status of Spanish-speaking people both within the region and the United States as a whole, the role of women's work in a society that values production primarily in economic terms, and the importance of food in sustaining cultural identity. As John Nieto-Phillips discusses in *The Language of Blood*, the "Spanish American identity" claimed by New Mexico's Spanish-speaking people, Nuevomexicanos, "had its origins in diverse struggles against political and social marginalization, and was nurtured by a burgeoning tourist industry, a Hispanophilic cultural movement, and locally authored histories and scholarship" (2). To resist such denigration and political marginalization on the basis of race and class, some elite Nuevomexicanos promoted their blood ties to Spanish ancestors, claiming a racial purity that could pass as whiteness, distinguish them from recent Mexican migrants, and ally them with the Anglo Americans who seized power in the territory and then the state.[1] "By the 1940s," Nieto-Phillips explains, "both 'American' and 'Mexican American' observers regarded it as little more than a Spanish façade masking widespread poverty and profound tensions among Anglos and Nuevomexicanos, and among Mexican-origin people in the Southwest more broadly" (8). I argue here that Jaramillo both constructed and reworked that façade to control her public identity and protect her private family history.

Furthermore, Louis Mendoza has observed that the political work of Mexican American women during the first decades of the twentieth century has been obscured because of the Migrant Generation's patriarchal constructions of gender. "It is only in the specialized histories of labor, journalism, and 'women' that these women's work is acknowledged," he argues (105). I conclude this chapter by considering whether folkloric figures, like the heroine of *The People of the Valley* and the aristocratic "Spanish American" women constructed by Jaramillo in her memoir, perform political work that has been overlooked by critics and writers, including Denise Chávez, who define cultural resistance as explicit political engagement. "The literature and history of other sites of containment have yet to be written," Mendoza claims, and this chapter performs such writing as it explores the emerging significance of Nuevomexicanas, whose literature reimagines past patterns of settlement against received histories and anticipates more profound reconfigurations of rural space.

Seeing Northern New Mexico

By the time FSA photographers were assigned to work in New Mexico in 1940, the focus of the national project had shifted toward representations of village life, though it continued to document vernacular objects and architecture. Director Roy Stryker worked in response to particular images produced by Ben Shahn, Dorothea Lange, Walker Evans, and Edward Rothstein, his earliest and most skilled photographers; he discussed the images with each photographer and used the discussion to guide later assignments (Hurley 50–54). The early studies had recorded forced migration or "relocation" and urban and rural poverty: in 1936, Stryker asked Dorothea Lange to "take for us some good slum pictures" in San Francisco and Los Angeles because "[w]e need to vary the diet in some of our exhibits here by showing some western poverty instead of all south and east" (Hurley 70). Later studies like Lee's Pie Town series concentrated on small towns, agricultural labor, and the ethics of cooperation. The typical "shooting scripts" modeled on literary examples still held: "record a variety of commonplace activities such as 'Home in the evening,' 'Listening to the radio,' 'Visiting and talking,' and 'Men loafing and talking,'" and seek opportunities in private houses and public recreation sites, like pool halls, lodges, saloons, and street corners (Bustard 35). But now Stryker supplemented such scripts with instructions to include typical rural landscapes. He advised Lee,

> We are certainly looking forward to seeing the pictures which you are getting in the upper Rio Grande valley and in and around Taos. Don't forget a good ranch to go along with some of the more impoverished and small subsistence ranches. A few pictorial shots, please, such as: a row of Lombardy poplar trees with clouds in the background; shots of juniper and other trees, flowers in the background. Don't forget the picture of sagebrush you were going to get for me; a sheepherder and sheep on a hill, silhouetted against the sky; don't forget that the burro is an important part of that agriculture—we could stand quite a few shots of the little animal, taken in various poses and in various types of work in which he helps; a few pictures of the adobe churches. . . . (qtd. in Wood, *Heartland* 8)

In another letter to Lee, he took the matter further: "try to take 'a few Westons,'" he wrote, referring to Weston's formalist work prior to *California and the West*.

> You have no idea how important these highly syrupy pictures are going to be, especially when someone comes in here who isn't particularly

sold on our other photography, and is in a position to go out and do a lot of talking. NM, Ariz., and Utah and the rest of the country do have skies filled with white clouds, so you had better get that red filter out. However, you'd damn well better not go too far, and spoil the picture. (qtd. in Myers, *Pie Town* 108)

Stryker knew his political purpose, his audience, and his photographers—even if his impressions of New Mexico seemed to come from popular Westerns and from pictorial and high-modernist photographic landscapes. When images became overly idealized and detached from the social world, they became "syrupy"; what he had in mind was some new and irregular combination of beauty and grittiness, utopian fantasy and social truth.

In fact, photographers in New Mexico could not avoid signs of hardship. In 1930, 40 percent of the state's population lived in poverty. In 1933, 28 percent of New Mexicans received federal relief, the highest state percentage in the country. Half the banks had folded. Major New Deal programs like the Rural Electrification Administration, the Soil Conservation Service, and the Bureau of Reclamation's monumental dam construction provided some relief.[2] Yet, even with these programs under way, by 1940 electricity reached just a third of rural women (Myers, *Pie Town* 124). Five years after the New Deal began supplying steady help to impoverished families, conditions remained virtually unchanged, largely due to government corruption in the state. Lorena Hickok's report from New Mexico emphasized the scarcity of available, fertile land: the state "has an area of 78,000,000 acres, of which only 2,000,000 will produce crops!" she exclaimed.[3] About a third of the state's land was in the public domain, generating no income from taxes; new migrants from Oklahoma, Arkansas, and Texas quickly discovered that their land was good only for grazing; and the state's Hispano majority persisted in traditional methods of farming and irrigation. For all these reasons, to an outside observer the prospects for quick improvement seemed slim.[4] Nancy Wood recently catalogued the facts that limited the state's economic recovery: "The illiteracy rate remained at 15 percent; malnutrition and infant mortality were 30 percent higher than the rest of the country. Per capita income remained two-thirds of the national average. . . . [T]he average value for New Mexico farmland was about $4 an acre, one-eighth of the national average" (Wood 245). Photographers like Lee and John Collier Jr. recorded such hardship, which was often rooted in cultural resistance to change as well as natural conditions and the national economy.

Lee's 1940 study of Chamisal and Peñasco, in Taos County, includes impoverished as well as prosperous ranches, typical shots of rural families working the land, and, as in Pie Town, depictions of communal and village life. Lee shows us Chamisal's Main Street and a typical farmstead. In these images, the distant Sangre de Cristo Mountains and the sky dominate the human settlements, which have clearly been constructed by the hands of those who live in them.[5] The adobe buildings and the fences that surround buildings and enclose grazing areas require local materials and constant maintenance, as Lee notices. Many of his photographs show women working to replaster adobe houses. Other images show farmers working together, whether helping each other to push a mower onto a truck or slaughter a pig, women baking bread in an outdoor *horno*, or couples and children sharing the domestic labor of canning, roasting corn and chiles, and cooking beans. He wrote to Stryker that even though he did not know how to speak Spanish, the people he met were "really grand"—able to convey pride in their work and way of life (Wroth 133). All members of the community cultivated land and engaged in physical labor together, and they gathered to observe saints' and holy days through processions and masses. In her analysis of the region's acequia culture, Sylvia Rodrí- guez argues that such shared secular and religious practices constitute "practices of place" that connect identity to location through feelings of communal belonging ("Honor, Aridity, and Place" 33). Lee documents these place-making practices from a respectful distance, providing only close-ups of the religious structures (the church and the entrance to the cemetery)that he chose not to disturb with his presence.[6]

In Collier's photographs of Trampas, the village also expresses its dis- tinctive culture through work, religious observance, and daily routines. He predicted, "[T]he pictures that we find to be the most important are going to be the ones that people think of as dull. . . . The dramatic pictures will never finally be the thing that will tell us what was going on" (qtd. in O'Neal 288). Instead, it is the images that show the materials of daily life, the ordi- nary labor, and the local religious rituals that will signify the coherence and determined resistance of Nuevomexicano culture. His study of the local store reveals a place where local people meet and exchange informa- tion (fig. 10). Many images show residents working with materials gained from the land, as in one photograph of the town's mayordomo (manager of the acequia irrigation system), Juan Lopez, sorting beans with his son,

Figure 10. John Collier Jr., "Trampas, New Mexico. A Store." (Courtesy of the Library of Congress)

and others of his wife, Maclovia Lopez, cooking tortillas, washing, sewing, and spinning wool (fig. 11). Collier notes that "the family has ten sheep and they spin the wool for blankets, which are woven for them in Cordoba." Collier paid especially close attention to the interior of the Lopezes' house, framing each of his images to mediate the viewer's access to the family's intimate space. We might be looking through a thick doorway at an old man rocking in his chair, not really welcome to enter the next room; or we might see just a single wall of the room, with the man (identified as Grandfather Romero, ninety-nine years old) sitting still enough to seem like one of five objects arranged against a blank adobe wall (fig. 12). Collier seems to play with the idea that Romero, too, is becoming an image, just like the relatives and religious figures framed nearby. Elsewhere he shows that saints and Hollywood movie stars share space on the same wall. In this family's imagination, they seem to belong to the same mythic world.

Figure 11. John Collier Jr., "Maclovia Lopez spinning wool," 1943. (Courtesy of the Library of Congress)

In this last project for the FSA, Collier deliberately narrows his focus. These close-up views capture the vernacular art that families created in their houses and implicitly invite comparison to assemblages by artists like André Breton or Joseph Cornell. While Collier conveys the visual perception he cultivated through a mixture of formal art education at California Institute of the Arts, friendship with Dorothea Lange, and previous work for Stryker, his photographs of the Lopez family collaborate with his subjects to an unusual extent—and at times shield them from unwelcome

Figure 12. John Collier Jr., "Grandfather Romero, a member of the family of Juan Lopez, the majordomo, is ninety-nine years old." Trampas, New Mexico, 1943. (Courtesy of the Library of Congress)

scrutiny. Because it is clear that Grandfather Romero or another member of Lopez's household has assembled the objects on the wall, Collier's studies of them begin to transfer authorship from observing photographer to observed subject.

Writing about Soviet documentary film in the 1920s, Victor Shklovsky defined the genre's task as "broader than the problem of fiction and nonfiction. . . . Our problem is the priority of raw material" (qtd. in Tyrus Miller

"Documentary" 228). We have seen through representations of the Dust Bowl, California and Nevada ruins, and Los Angeles in the 1930s that America's raw materials were all the people and places left behind during the heady rush of the Jazz Age. To keep making these materials new and visible, photographers had to keep testing and alternating formal techniques. Their vision of reality also had to encompass an ever-wider range of raw materials: public symbols and private life, commercial products and handmade artifacts, industrial production and manual labor, city crowds and small-town isolation. Photographs of rural life in New Mexico in this period extend such a shift away from romanticized landscapes and idealized experiences, although they still present the subject from a respectful but curious distance, thus upholding the norms established by Stryker. Fiction and personal narratives, by contrast, can alternate points of view, imagine varying degrees of attachment to rural landscapes, and project new home places, as the literary renditions of village life by Waters and Jaramillo reveal.

New Mexican Village Stories

In an effort to promote the Southwest's regional identity, workers for the Federal Writers' Project and the Farm Security Administration collected several village stories. These accounts of rural New Mexican life did not reach many readers and generally failed to articulate a coherent cultural identity, either because they alternately resisted and "accommodat[ed] Anglos' ascendancy and touristic fantasies" (Nieto-Phillips 8) or because the fieldworkers did not fully understand the culture they documented. Although some stories appeared in *New Mexico: Guide to the Colorful State* (1940) and a substantial number were collected in *Women's Tales from the New Mexico WPA* (2000), most written documents from this project remain in the New Mexico State History Archives and the Library of Congress. The invisibility of rural experience was sensed acutely by those who lived it. "There was a time when standardization was rampant and all efforts, social and economic, converged on the idea of making the country uniform to the point where Southwestern villages would be identical with Middletown," explained native New Mexicans Nina Otero-Warren and J. F. Zimmerman in order to justify their recovery project for the FWP. To remedy the problem of Anglo ignorance and the cultural divide between Nuevomexicanos and Anglo Americans, they proposed to focus on the "person who is a product of the soil" and thus find "the true America that lies hidden in the Southwest."[7]

Henry Alsberg, director of the Federal Writers' Project, agreed. In the manual he sent to Ina Cassidy, New Mexico's state director until 1939, he advised that "[e]mphasis should be placed on groups that are indigenous or rooted in the local life," and "[w]orkers should be assigned to their own communities and groups on the strength of full familiarity with the materials, the people, and the problems involved."[8] All published material needed to have sufficient atmospheric detail to appeal to general readers. When Alsberg wrote to Aileen Nusbaum, FWP director in 1939, he explained that he wanted "to make the readers see the white mid-summer haze, the dust that rises in unpaved New Mexico streets . . . [as well as] the social cleavages and jealousies." In short, "We want the type of visual description John Steinbeck would give."[9] Documentary photography had already provided a model for how rural landscapes could be made symbolic. Now writers had to follow the same method of selecting representative details. This official agenda shaped all the state guides, often producing homogenous documents and superficial introductions to regional culture.[10]

Novelists and writers familiar with New Mexico's native cultures, however, represented rural experience in literary forms not so easily assimilated. Several writers revived a literary genre that languished until the late 1930s: the village story. Focusing primarily on the Nuevomexicano and Pueblo communities of the Upper Rio Grande Valley, Frank Waters's novel *People of the Valley* and Cleofas Jaramillo's memoir *The Romance of a Little Village Girl* record the persistence of local tradition and the reinvention of Spanish American identity. In both narrative form and stylized characterization, they testify to the continued importance of an inherited homeland as the foundation for cultural identity, the effects of a class hierarchy among Nuevomexicanos, and the power of religious rituals and folk remedies. Although evidence of the traditions that urban viewers and readers might have found alluring occasionally appears to signify an idealized rural past, more often it refutes Anglo paradigms of Southwestern romance. Both works present a regional perspective at odds with the national ideals often imposed on materials collected by writers for the Federal Writers' Project. Village stories thus constitute narratives of resistance to the era's dominant stories of migration, accommodation, and harmonious diversity. Further, the voices of resistance that speak through these texts have often been discounted by critics because they belong to women marginalized by their own culture and passed over during critical reassessments of regional or Chicano/a literature and historiography. By reading these texts again in the multiple contexts of local New Mexican history, the gendered politics of regional literature and its reception, and our contemporary deterritorialized culture, we can begin to see how their formal features negotiate a complex set of literary and cultural expectations both within and beyond the greater Southwest.

Franco Moretti has revealed enclosed narrative space to be the "fundamental chronotope" of British village stories of the early nineteenth century. Examples from New Mexico also use this chronotope to make "urban readers . . . look at the world according to the older, 'centered' viewpoint of an unenclosed village" (*Graphs* 37, 39) and refract historical pressures on rural land. In early-nineteenth-century England, parliamentary enclosure transformed the countryside; in early-twentieth-century New Mexico, Anglo-American settlement, land appropriation, and public works projects threatened communities in the Upper Rio Grande Valley. The stories of these villages begin at moments of sudden and irreversible transformation and then return to memories of rural experience, written with the awareness that urban and non-native readers longed for what Moretti calls an "alternate homeland" (*Graphs* 52). By articulating the details of lives traditionally defined by place of birth, agricultural labor, and seasonal rituals through the bodies and perspectives of native inhabitants, New Mexican village stories allow readers to escape from the contingencies of modernity and imagine themselves as participants in rural communities. At the same time, the stories exert control over readers' access to local knowledge, thus flaunting—and to some extent protecting—its value.

The stories I examine here end either with an abrupt departure from the village or with the re-creation of an earlier cultural era and a more-enclosed space. These conclusions test the limits of the form's implied collaboration between Nuevomexicanos who claim "deep primordial attachments, particularly in terms of their history, blood, soil, and language" (Nieto-Phillips 8) and Anglo and urban readers' desire to imagine rural communities. In both cases, aspects of rural experience remain unnarrated. Village stories, like the documentary photographs of the period, test the ideology that rural life constitutes authentic American culture. If detailed portraits of Nuevomexicano families and adobe buildings risk seeming too particular to the region, the stories of village life in the Upper Rio Grande are certainly too isolated to be integrated into a coherent national script. The genre also tests the vitality of local traditions and the role that women play in sustaining them. Which traditions, and which type of woman, will be sacrificed to modernization? Which will persist as a foundation for resistance to Anglo colonization and the dominant national culture? Village stories in New Mexico provide a new perspective on the processes of reconstructing the rural and articulating imagined homelands that would become essential to Aztlán, the Chicano/a idea that the American Southwest was originally the home of the Aztecs, and to Chicano/a political consciousness and literature in the 1960s.

People of the Valley

Frank Waters claimed that he wrote most truthfully about New Mexican life "from an outside viewpoint, an honest and direct attempt at translation, rather than the fictional method of working out from within."[11] While never claiming to be native to the Hispano, Pueblo, and Hopi communities he wrote about, he did develop intimate knowledge of them during his long career. In 1911, at age nine, he lived on the Navajo Reservation in New Mexico while his father worked as a trader. After studying for a few years at Colorado College, he moved to California's Imperial Valley—where he wrote his first two novels—then back to Colorado and finally, in 1935, to the Rio Arriba region in northern New Mexico, his primary residence for the rest of his life. The setting for his first New Mexico novel is a "beautiful blue valley" modeled on the Spanish-American village of Mora, located between Taos and Las Vegas in the Sangre de Cristo Mountains, where he lived cheaply with two Anglo friends between 1935 and 1938. He also became close friends with Mabel and, especially, Tony Luhan. He lived in a guesthouse on Mabel's property in Taos in 1938 and traveled to New York with Tony and her in 1940 to deliver the manuscript for *People of the Valley* to Farrar & Rhinehart for publication. The Anglo-European artistic community of Taos greatly influenced Waters's development, according to biographer Thomas Lyon, but Waters still managed to keep his distance and cultivate a strong relationship with Tony and the people of Taos Pueblo. When he aimed to publish his major novel about the pueblo, *The Man Who Killed the Deer* (1942), he made sure to clear it first with the tribal council. He did not want to repeat the mistake of anthropologist Elsie Clews Parsons, whose monograph based on her studies of tribal life in Taos in 1923 and 1924 caused outrage because it violated tribal secrets. According to former Taos Pueblo governor Tony Reyna, "Frank was more respectful than most people who want to write about us. He came as a friend" (Holley 46).

The novels Waters wrote about the villages of New Mexico best display his power to develop symbolic and political ideas from everyday rural experience. Joe Holley identifies Waters's literary strength to be his physical understanding of place, explaining that "Waters is a better writer the further away he gets from airy, esoteric, psychological concepts . . . at his best when he allows the symbolic and the mythic to evolve naturally out of vivid, tangible experience" ("A New Mexican Writer's Long Life" 49–50). According to Tom Lynch, "Waters demonstrates a bioregionally informed sense of the value of preserving the traditional Hispano agropastoral community" (*Xerophilia* 60). Although Waters's relation to the people of Mora has not been fully documented, his novel about this village tests the extent to which he could penetrate the mentality of the community and the region as he articulated its transformation.

While some historians claim that residents of villages like Mora and Taos did not feel the effects of the Depression so acutely because they could provide for themselves through agriculture, the 1930s nonetheless marked a critical stage in their development.[12] Resisting the cumulative pressure of decades of U.S. appropriation of common lands, the construction of irrigation systems, and the appropriation of sacred sites, the villages began in this decade to organize collective protests. Waters accordingly constructed *People of the Valley* from a variety of native perspectives, relocating the voices of authority from government officials and outsiders to symbolic characters with intimate knowledge of the history of the land and the people who settled it. The novel describes critical events in this history: Spanish settlement in the area in the early nineteenth century, the shift of official control to the U.S. government following its conquest in 1846, the construction of Fort Union in 1851, the influence of French trader Ceran St. Vrain after he opened a store and mill in Mora in 1855, and the effect of the railroad's arrival in Las Vegas in 1879. These developments shaped the economy of the Mora Valley in the early twentieth century and, in *People of the Valley*, set the stage for a series of confrontations that would determine the relation between the traditional culture of the village and the national bureaucratic culture of rational improvement and capitalist growth.

People of the Valley begins as an unnamed narrator tells us that the people here have always used the acequia system to control the streams flowing into their steep-walled canyons. They have endured floods small and large and always survived, rebuilt their huts, restored their herds, and replanted their crops.[13] Now the government, a distant abstraction to the "forgotten" people of the village, intends to bring progress: to build a dam at the canyon's mouth, create a lake, and lay a road for automobiles. All the people ask why the dam should be built: "There has never been one before; it is not the custom. The floods come, like sunshine and the drought. They are all God's will. Else why should there be floods? No doubt it is wrong to stop them. No; I do not see why there should be a dam. Why should there be a dam, Señor?" asks one anonymous voice (5). With this objection Waters introduces the beliefs and customs that define this community and set it apart from the nation to which it legally belongs.

Although they have witnessed changes, from the arrival of French Hudson Bay trappers from the north to the influx of Mexican settlers up the Chihuahua Trail to the invasion of Anglos "from the strange, unknown and barbaric east" (20), the people in the novel have sustained the practices that connect them to this place. They understand the imme-diate physical world: their land in the upper Valle de San Antonio and in the lower Valle de Santa Gertrudes, the single street of their village, and the ringing of the church bells. Plans for the dam drawn by engineers merely exist on paper, or in a "thunderbolt sentence, a flowery phrase" (6). Neither this written language nor political rhetoric describes their lived reality. The officials in charge remain vague, too: "El Estado. The gover-nor. The políticos for whom we made crosses on our votes, as instructed. Perhaps the Presidente himself. . . . Who knows these things exactly when he is busy in the fields?" (4). What they do know is the land, "mother to us all. An enduring truth that only her sons can know" (20), and the power of such rooted tradition becomes knowledge that Waters imparts to the reader. Constructed around the events that force the people to sell their land and make way for the dam, the novel dramatizes the conflict between modernization (articulated through bureaucratic language) and local cus-tom (articulated through the collective voice of the people)—or, in Lynch's terms, between "modern faithlessness" and "primal faith" (*Xerophilia* 62). The narrator and, later, the central character, Maria, will work to mediate these positions and articulate the ecological and historical arguments for and against modernization.

The conflict over the dam that drives the novel most likely did not occur so dramatically. According to Gary Rogers, who performed a care-ful comparison of the history of the Mora valley and Waters's representa-tion of it, the state engaged in "a small amount of flood control" in the late 1930s in order "to lessen dangers of flood at Mora" (140). While it is possible that the county's report minimized the extent of the project or the displacement of the villagers, it seems more likely that Waters chose to intensify the effects of government intervention on village life, just as he later dramatized the fear that the government would claim permanent ownership of the lake sacred to the people of Taos Pueblo in *The Man Who Killed the Deer*. The novel stages "a reenactment, in microcosm, of the history of colonialism" (Lyon, *Waters* 101).

The opening chapter also establishes the circular pattern that defines the novel's form: The people leave their land to gather in the village, first for the speeches about the dam and then for the annual feast for their village Saint's Day, and at the end of the day set off toward home. The path confirms the boundaries of their earthly experience and the power of their customary motion. Although outsiders occasionally migrate to the valley, none of the natives emigrate until the very end, when the families who lost their land start a new settlement in a fertile, unsettled, "hidden little valley behind these mountain walls" (Waters, *People* 192). Waters identifies few individuals in this opening scene, indicating merely where they have come from: "weary, flint-eyed men who have ridden out of the dark mountain fastness of Las Colonias and El Quemado," families "who have bumped since sunrise over the rocky roads from Vallecito and Lucero," and people traveling "from El Alto with brown faces tinged red from Indian Picuris" (5). Like Steinbeck's migrants in *The Grapes of Wrath*, they meet on the road because they share a destination, and they speak in an anonymous, collective voice. The rituals of gathering, including the barbecue of steers, sheep, and pigs "basted with a mess of brown sugar, vinegar, black and cayenne pepper, tomato paste, salt and chile" (6), and the common sentiment of confusion and uncertainty about the dam matter more than the identities of individual characters. Waters narrates the valley's origin, the people's behavior, and their speech in a single, fluid voice before narrowing his focus to a few characters as he describes the crowd's dispersal. At this transitional time of day, "the crespusculo vespertino" or "the blue hour between yellow sunset and black night," the people finally seek to resolve the critical issue at hand and appeal for advice to an old woman sitting "stiffly upright in imperious silence" (8). Pausing on the ridge above the valley, they have yet to complete their ritual circle, and this interruption suggests that return to their customary ways may not be so easy.

The old woman introduced anonymously continues into the upper canyon, through a village consisting of "a scatter of six or seven steep-roofed adobes, aspen corrals and anthill ovens" (9), and farther up the road toward the forest. In this remote place Waters presents his central character, Maria del Valle, illuminating her face with the flare of a match:

Its powerful and primitive features, timeless with sorrow and fecundity, are savage and enduring as if cut out of rock: a rock beaten, smashed and worn by waves but still jutting the promontory beak of nose, high cheekbones and solid jaw into the surge of life. The eyes are small and black and bright, the eyes of a hawk. Only the dark, red-brown flesh of her seamed and sagging cheeks appears touched and worn by time— but still timeless and enduring as the red-brown earth forever furrowed by the plow. (10)

The melodramatic illumination of Maria's face here recalls the exaggerated chiaroscuro of late Renaissance painters like Georges de la Tour, whose solitary subjects emerge from shadows holding a single candle. Yet, rather than framing her as a painted figure, Waters connects her body to the physical elements: rock, sea, and earth. Seemingly made from the materials of nature rather than human flesh and blood, more bird than woman, Maria symbolizes the difference between people who derive their entire being from the land and those who merely use and trade it. Waters shows her as both archaic and vital, alternately an icon and a living presence. We could read her as a symbol of nature, a synecdoche for the valley, an embodiment of traditional knowledge, or a prototype for the mestizaje figures in later Chicano/a fiction, for Waters represents her as all of these.[14]

Throughout the novel, however, Waters insists that Maria is also a philosophical being, fully engaged in debates about the nature of god and man. Lyon identifies the combination of Maria's "poetic-philosophical life and vision" and "the cultural conflict within which her destiny works itself out" as responsible for the novel's "consummate form" (Lyon, *Frank Waters* 96). "The book is at once a private, poetic song of an individual and a historical documentation" (97), he concludes, and so Maria "must be seen as both real and symbolic" (102). This accurate description confirms the novel's affinity with contemporary fiction. Waters's treatment of Maria recalls Steinbeck's depiction of Ma Joad in *The Grapes of Wrath*, for example, since both characters function simultaneously as individuals and ideal women able to anchor and guide their communities at times of crisis. What requires further attention, I think, is the way that the figure of Maria controls the reader's perception of the village community. If a "knowable community" is "a selected society in a selected point of view," as Raymond Williams defines it, then this novel tests the extent to which representing the village's communal identity requires limiting the narrative point of view.

Because Maria's life coincides with the past century of the valley's development, she functions as a device for revealing, decade by decade, critical aspects of local history and the effects of the region's development on rural communities, but the distance we keep from her shows that this history might easily become irrelevant to the modern era. The novel's second chapter takes us back to the time of Maria's birth and subsequent chapters narrate her rise to self-sufficiency and then to authority. Made an orphan when her Indian mother from Picuris Pueblo died in childbirth, Maria was raised in the mountains by two goatherds, *viejos* who divined the future by reading goat skulls. When they die in a flood, she fends for herself and becomes self-reliant, tending her goats, trading her cheese, and teaching herself how to apply herbs and other remedies. Thus she comes to embody "the beauty of the wild" (33). Neither her passionate sexual encounter with a gringo soldier, which leads to the birth of her son Teodosio, nor her stable relationship with the devout muleteer Onesimo, father of her daughter Gertrudes, challenges her original deep connection with the land, which becomes the source of her independence and her power: "The beautiful blue valley grew and prospered. So did Maria" (75). Out of this congruence comes the name by which she is known, Maria del Valle.

In the novel's early chapters, Waters uses Maria to reflect on the village's Catholic foundations, elaborated earlier by Willa Cather in *Death Comes for the Archbishop*, and on the secret rituals of the Penitente brotherhood, described sensationally by Charles Lummis and more evenly in *The WPA Guide to 1930s New Mexico*, which characterizes the Penitente ceremonies as "a genuine and deeply sincere folk-survival" (124). Although always an outsider, Maria initially sympathizes with Onesimo's faith. Catholicism interests her because it seems to be based on triumph over human frailty, and she easily transposes Jesus to her own land: "She imagined him riding down the dusty valley road astraddle a burro, 'the short and simple animal of the poor'" (50). Still, she feels that the elaborate ornamentation of the church in Santa Gertrudes is meaningless and inhuman, and the arrogance, greed, and hypocrisy of the Catholic priests repulse her. The brutal faith of the Penitente Brothers, which Onesimo embraces with greater zeal after the Catholic priest rejects his request to marry him and Maria, seems cruel and inhuman, too. As Onesimo endures the lashes from the yucca whip that allow him to share Christ's suffering during Lent, Maria's "heart bled like his back" (60). She finds Catholicism less powerful than the lessons of the two men who nurtured her and "taught her that even the skulls of goats reflect the pattern of the stars and the power of the earth below" (50), knowledge that Georgia O'Keeffe would similarly explore in her paintings of cow skulls in the desert nearby.

Following Onesimo's death, Maria turns back to the earth, bringing vegetables and fruit to sell in the valley, gathering weeds and herbs to cure sickness, making dyes from leaves and roots, preparing food "in the old way, the way of the poor who know neither sugar nor salt, the way of the hungry who watch each apple fall, chicos, posole, nixtamal, panocha; ribs dried in the sun, jerked beef, dried corn and squash and apples, green chile roasted, peeled and hung up to dry" (76). This catalog of native foods and their methods of preservation resembles those found in WPA reports and local cookbooks, but here it is integrated into a narrative of loss and resistance, made to overcome the emptiness of Catholicism, the anguish of death, and the poverty of the city. Lynch notes the pleasure that Waters seems to take in writing the name of each native food, "the biological treasures of the landscape." In the process, Waters conveys "the abundance of the natural world and its more-than-sufficiency for the people who reside in the valley" (Lynch, *Xerophilia* 64). We learn later that one exemplary family took the money received from selling their land and moved to the city. They discovered that the excitement of watching the railroad, walking on a street lit at night, and going to the movies did not compensate for the father's hard work on the railroads, the money stolen after their house burned, and the illness the children developed from eating too many peaches and tomatoes spooned from "those shiny cans with the beautiful pictures on them which can be pasted on the windows" (Waters, *People* 173). They returned to the valley "penniless, homeless, starved and shamed," while Maria stayed in her hut, bathed in the stream nearby, touched the silver pesos she received for her land, and sustained her aging body with posole, tortillas, and weak tea.

The novel refuses to romanticize Maria's physical existence or to extend her embrace of the past to the entire rural community, however, emphasizing instead her rigidity and isolation as well as the lack of consensus among the rural folk. Maria enforces with a vengeance traditions that others have forgotten, as she does with the custom of borrowing from neighbors on the *Día de los Inocentes*. She penalizes her neighbors by forcing them to pay for their goods if they did not speak the requisite phrase, "pero no por inocente," at the time of the loan. She administers remedies and utters *dichos*, the sayings of the common people, in a way that makes other people fear her power. Her adherence to ancient custom surely constitutes "an act of cultural resistance," as Lynch describes the revival of San Isidro Day later in the novel, but the community does not share Maria's faith in the land as a means of fighting modernization. She seems backward and stubborn to them, and her authority extends only to those people who continue to have faith in the old ways. For all who come to her door for advice, more go to the Murphys, or "Los Mofres" as they are called, an Irish peddler and his brother who settled in the valley during Maria's childhood and built a prosperous business by managing a store, running a mill, buying land, and eventually engaging in the politics of dam building that secured their economic dominance.[15]

Maria comes to occupy a powerful position at the margins of the village, simultaneously distorting and enlarging the reader's perspective on the role of traditional beliefs in sustaining this rural community. Feared and admired, "tolerated with fustian phrases, hated in whispers, and respected silently" (93), she remains isolated in her "small mountainside hut." From the perspective of "unseeing eyes"—presumably those of the thoughtless villagers and the reader—the hut is located "just below the tall weathered cliffs which jut out to separate the crescent halves of the beautiful blue valley." From Maria's perspective, it is "the point of a completed circle" (116). On one level, this statement presents a truth perhaps most visible in rural spaces: one's home always seems the center of the world. Yet, Maria's marginality with respect to the people who threaten to dominate her, from the villagers to the local judges, the Anglo officials, and agents of the federal government, makes her assertion of centrality an act of will. Waters chooses her to organize competing perspectives on the village's contemporary significance, just as he later chooses to organize his novel about Otowi Crossing around the fictionalized Edith Warner, precisely because she alone can exercise her will.

As Raymond Williams observes in *The Country and the City*, "under the pressure of urban and metropolitan experience" many readers think that "a country community, most typically a village, is an epitome of direct relationships." But this transparency is often a function of idealization or a stable but imaginary point of view. What we need to see, he suggests, "is not only the reality of the rural community" but also "the observer's position in and towards it; a position which is part of community's being known" (165). In *People of the Valley*, the narrative allows us to observe Maria and to understand the land and the village; we watch the arrival of outsiders through her and through the sympathetic but more philosophical narrator. As Waters keeps shifting the perspective and mocking the language and values that define the culture of his readers, he makes Maria's humble home a stable if not entirely desirable position for observation and a place of refuge. From her "little hut" she can see the laws of nature and "all the passions that warp the mind, flesh and spirit of man" (123). From there alone it seems possible to know not only the practices of the community but the meaning of its existence.

Subsequent chapters introduce Maria anew, from multiple perspectives, and then gradually draw the reader into her consciousness, allowing us to understand her way of thinking without forcing identification. In the process, readers grasp Maria's power and its limits. For example, when her wealthy neighbor Don Fulgencio proposes marriage, we see both the villagers' interpretation of Maria's hesitation (she must be shrewd and deliberate) and her own confusion. Don Fulgencio never showed any romantic interest in her before, and now, at age seventy, he must have a reason for proposing to "a simple, old and nameless woman" (96). As she keeps questioning him, she lays out their stark differences. "You have been rich and I have been poor. You are of the Garcías, and I am of the people. Your power is of the Government of politics, of important things understood only by the intelligent. And they are good, doubtless. But my power is that of the wisdom of the people who do not think, but feel. And that is good too" (96). She doesn't see how these two powers can unite, so she delays until her resistance ebbs. Assured that she will maintain title to her land and her independence, she finally accepts Don Fulgencio's plea to "grow together in our gentle age, and so be wise at last" (97) and agrees to be married for the first time at age fifty. The depiction of the wedding itself alternately reveals the grotesque appearance of the bride and groom to the villagers, the crude splendor of the celebration, and Maria's discomfort and perplexity. When she returns to her hut rather than staying in her husband's house, the people dismiss her: "She is not only too old to learn, but too simple to forget" (102).

The truth turns out to be more complicated, as Maria learns after her husband's death. She consults Don Fulgencio's friend Sanchez and discovers that her husband devised a scheme for appropriating the land outside the valley included in the titles granted to the original seventy-six settlers under both Spanish and American rule. Because the people could not read the terms of the grant, they did not know that for every piece of land inside the valley they also held title to pieces ten times larger outside.

Don Fulgencio took advantage of their ignorance, buying the entire property from farmers when they needed money and then returning just the smaller portion when they came to buy the land back. He knew the land would be valuable for the timber it provided for the new railroad and for its position on the watershed, and finally Maria held the only outstanding piece, "[t]he perfect site for a dam that must be built" (132). By marrying Maria, Don Fulgencio thought he would guarantee his controlling interest in the company that sold water rights to the government, and he planned to spend the last years of his life idly guarding his money—until a historic flood violently washed both life and fortune away.

Throughout *People of the Valley*, natural catastrophes like floods and modernization projects like the dam seem to be cyclical events that occur and pass, leaving the heroine and the structure of the community intact. Maria's longevity, combined with her habitual return home, suggests that the village's rural mentality will survive even the most violent challenges. Waters renders her as a folk figure to make her "too simple to forget." Yet, as development accelerates, the road (or "Máquina of progress") bisects the circle that encloses and defines the community of Santa Gertrudes. The narrator compresses and dramatizes the people's response to it with vivid personification:

> From strange cities it came. Up from the plains of tall grass and short grass where the buffalo had rolled, and the long horns had tossed their square bow. Over arroyos and mesas into scrub oak and piñon, into pine and spruce. Through the forest it cut a swath; through the little mountain meadows where the deer had come down at night from the picachos to bound lazily over log fences and stand, ears up and unafraid, listening to the sound of squeaking wagon hubs. With iron girders it straddled the lower river. On white concrete and black asphalt it lumbered through the blood-red adobe of Buena Vista, the yellow clay of El Questo, the chocolate brown hillsides of La Cueva and the whitish talc near Romeros Corner. Into the beautiful blue valley it came. (178–79)

The villagers watch it coming with wonder, feeling it to be "unreal." At this point Waters confirms the difference in perspective between the people of the valley and his readers that has been implied throughout the novel. His readers know the machines of progress to be real and, probably, no longer wondrous—knowledge that Maria, the most traditional of the villagers, also intuits or anticipates. In Waters's portrayal here, the rural mentality admires innovation and detaches it from everyday life, simultaneously re-enchanting progress and containing it within a mythic narrative. The personification of progress attempts to convey a clear picture of the feeling that first greeted modernization and will fade again into history. Waters's Máquina exaggerates the excitement and the destruction brought by the dam in order to render it a historical spectacle—and thus to dramatize the difference between modern technology (with its elaborate discourse of progress) and tradition (with its repetition of folk beliefs and direct speech).

On a practical level, the people continue to ignore the "Máquina of progress." Even when the law specifies that a family must leave its land by a certain date, no one begins packing until the sheriff arrives with notice of eviction. In fact, because Waters resolves the people's crisis by discovering a new, "untouched" valley nearby with land for them to buy with their silver pesos, wood to build their new houses, and game to hunt, it seems that the people will continue their rural existence as before, this time with their cultural isolation reinforced geographically. In the words of Maria's grandson, "Rock walls enclosed it; it was dark and triste; it was high and cold. But a little stream ran through it" (192). Wagons reach it with difficulty, and there will be no road. The conclusion makes a new virtue of hardship, which "whet their appetite to enjoy frugality. So they began to build their dreams" (193). By displacing the community into a new valley, Waters renders it forever unknowable and preserves the idea of the village as "a place in itself, the source of its own terms of meaning and identity."[16]

Maria continues to be the figure who mediates the relation between progress and tradition and who elicits what seems to be Waters's philosophy of time. As she reverts again to the anonymous role of "old woman," she approaches death in the "lofty little valley" that "was her cradle" (199). Earlier she had opposed the dam with her "feeling for the land," a position that the narrator elaborates in his own language, paraphrasing Maria: "It is impossible to fight the new with its own weapons. But to go back, back to the dimly understood truths that lie dormant in dead faiths and living bloodstreams—that is the secret of seers and dictators, of power and success. For mechanical progress, being change, is evanescent. What endures is only the enduring" (141). Maria soon expresses the same idea in her own words: "I do not oppose the dam, new customs, a new vision of life; I oppose nothing. But I uphold the old ways for they are good too. I awaken in men their love for their land for they are a people of the land.

It is their faith" (166). Between these two expressions lies the motivation behind the narrative itself, which combines the narrator's ability to integrate intellectual reasoning, local knowledge, and sympathy for a coherent community with Maria's deep historical knowledge. The dialogue between these worldviews continues as the narrator interprets Maria's life and Maria is pressed to articulate her position regarding the dam.

Williams writes that George Eliot's fiction marks "a new kind of break in the texture of the novel, an evident failure of continuity between the necessary language of the novelist and the recorded language of many of its characters" (*Country* 169). As Eliot combines "an analytically conscious observer of conduct" with "people represented as living and speaking in mainly customary ways" in a single form, she tries to solve the discontinuity between the educated position of her readers and herself and the socially inferior position of country folk by distributing aspects of her own consciousness to her rural characters. So, too, does Waters give his own consciousness to Maria in *People of the Valley*—and in the process suggests that his thoughts and his novelistic technique have been substantially shaped by his understanding of the faith and language of the region's indigenous people. His concluding meditation, presented at Maria's death, seems to derive from her consciousness and restates her wisdom in language his readers would understand: "There is nothing ever lost but unreal, evanescent images; nothing ever gained but a perception of the enduring reality behind them. This is difficult to learn. We must first learn that there is only one time, and that it contains all, eternally. Maria, having learned it, was content" (201).

Waters's own philosophy derived from Eastern metaphysics, the works of Carl Jung, and the teachings of Pueblo and other Native American leaders.[17] He "habitually insisted upon overcoming the dualism of rational thought versus intuition," according to Lyon's introduction to the *Frank Waters Reader* (xiv), and valued equally nature's "particular" and "abstract-philosophical" dimensions (xiii). In a speech entitled "The Regional Imperative" delivered at Colorado College in 1985, he argued that "regional writing is the common denominator of all literature," for "a writer must know who he is, what he comes from, how he stands in relation to his own region." At the same time, the writer's local position also "should provide him a glimpse of the horizons beyond" (Sturdevant, "Sundays in Tutt Library" 128). The regional novel, in other words, must aspire to universality. Waters advocates a unified effort to save the earth from the ravages of atmospheric pollution, water contamination, and nuclear testing, calling it a "planetary imperative." In *People of the Valley*, however, that imperative is still rural and regional, defined by Waters as "allegiance to one small portion of Earth" (123).

Reversing the documentary method of coming to know a rural community through its outer appearance, its rituals, and its domestic spaces, Waters writes from individual and collective positions within the village and keeps estranging the appearance and language of Anglo outsiders. Whereas FSA photographers like Lee and Collier were charged with finding fundamental similarities among diverse rural communities as they sought to isolate distinctive local elements, Waters begins with the conviction that some people in the communities he represents know more about the unity of the natural and spirit worlds than he does, and he develops individual characters from rural types to articulate that difference. Rather than maintain a sympathetic narrative detachment, he devises plots that intervene in the villagers' fate and protect them from misinformed scrutiny. Lynch accurately classifies the novel within a genre he calls "the Southwestern," one which takes the perspective of the invaded culture and seeks "to preserve cultural integrity and protect already settled land from appropriation and degradation at the hands of Anglo newcomers and their descendants" (*Xerophilia* 42).

As Waters makes a strenuous effort to imagine a new village that could sustain the community's cultural integrity at the end of *People of the Valley*, he also shows the boundaries of any home as permeable and subject to revision. We might think of the difference between the "beautiful blue valley" at the beginning of the novel and the untouched valley at the end as that between a home and a projected homeland. As Paul Giles explains, a home is "a zone in which domestic comforts could be taken for granted," whereas a homeland, reconstructed after trauma, is "one in which they had to be anxiously and self-consciously guarded" (51). Waters suggests that villages like Mora can survive only through passionate reattachment to the land, traditional beliefs, and local rituals. This is a lesson that other New Mexico writers, like Cleofas Jaramillo, had to learn firsthand, and that subsequent Chicano/a writers rewrote into new forms of rural and regional romance.

Village Girls and Working Girls

Cleofas Jaramillo was the great-granddaughter of José Manuel Martínez, who owned three thousand acres of land in northern New Mexico as part of a Tierra Amarilla land grant; the granddaughter of Vicente Martínez, who managed sheep on a land grant in Arroyo Hondo, and Jesús María Lucero, a trader on the Chihuahua Trail; the daughter of established rancher and merchant Julián Antonio Martínez of Taos; and the wife of a rich businessman and state senator, Venceslao Jaramillo (Rebolledo, Introduction to Jaramillo, *Romance* xv-xvi). Although her childhood and the early years of her marriage were defined by her family's land and prominent regional position, she later suffered the deaths of three children and her husband and the substantial sacrifice of both land and wealth. When Jaramillo began to reconstruct her past in collections of "Spanish" folk tales, recipes, and personal narratives, she wrote with an acute awareness of personal, cultural, and material loss. Thus she follows the "retrospective narrative habit" that Genaro Padilla identifies in *My History, Not Yours: The Formation of Mexican American Autobiography*: "an individual life is measured within a communitarian configuration and against the disruption of identity as identity is situated within an imagined cultural community of the past" (232). Along with the powerful contrast between an imagined past and an impoverished present, Jaramillo's writing articulates the division between native Nuevomexicano traditions and their nonnative, Anglo-American appropriation. Her collections of folklore and her narratives unevenly respond to, duplicate, and resist the dominant Anglo discourse that defined the region's villages from the turn of the twentieth century through the 1940s.

Jaramillo provides ample evidence of nonnative cultural appropriation of New Mexican village life and local traditions in her memoir, *The Romance of a Little Village Girl*, published in 1955 at the end of her life. As a resident of the area around Taos and Santa Fe, she could not avoid Anglo artists. As she explains in *Romance*, "writing and art are contagious in this old town. We have caught the fever from our famous '*cinco pintores*' and author Mary Austin, and some of us have the courage to try" (167). Familiar with the writings of Lummis, Austin, Cather, and Ruth Laughlin Barker, among others, Jaramillo often borrows their language and their romantic perspective. However, as she does so she records the pressures of Americanization on her own culture and her social position, and she responds strategically to the power of their discursive network in her representations of New Mexican villages. She describes her homeland, the valley of Arroyo Hondo, as "a fertile, green refuge" and an "isolated nook" that preserved old customs. Yet, she claims that because they were so familiar to her, she did not think about recording them in writing until

Anglo writers showed her their value and, implicitly, her own value as their chronicler.

The critical status of New Mexican writers of the 1930s and 1940s like Jaramillo has been largely determined by their overt dependence on non-native forms of cultural representation and by their class position. Among the elite landholders of northern New Mexico, Jaramillo, Fabiola Cabeza de Baca Gilbert, and Nina Otero-Warren found literary material in their own family histories, often paying little attention to the struggles of more recent migrants or to contemporary expressions of Mexican American culture. Like Charles Lummis, one of their Anglo predecessors, they glorified their Spanish past—in their case, because they recognized its power to generate myths that would heighten their cultural and political status in an increasingly Anglo-dominated state. Raymund Paredes uttered the first and lasting critical assessment when he attacked their "hacienda mentality" and wrote that Jaramillo's writing "seems a literature created out of fear and intimidation, a defensive response to racial prejudice." To him, Jaramillo was too invested in a culture "locked in time and barricaded against outside forces" (56). Padilla continues this line of critical reasoning in his study of Mexican American autobiography, which devotes one chapter to a close analysis of *Romance*. In his view, "the literary activity of an entire generation of Nuevomexicanos was at once selected, organized and controlled by a powerful nonnative discursive network that divided their ability to see straight to the heart of their own historical and material condition, or, to the extent that they did, muted their capacity to speak without fear of nullification or erasure" (*My History, Not Yours* 207). He argues that by writing folklore from a master script provided by Anglo newcomers, they reified "a heroic Spanish colonial past that would salve a colonized people's psychological wounds, even while they continued to surrender their land and social status" (202). Padilla pays close attention to the ideological and social forces that shaped Jaramillo's defensive posture, identifies moments when she articulates resistance through the master discourse, and even suggests that her "innocuous" collection of *The Genuine New Mexico Tasty Recipes* "opens an interstice for counterhegemonic expression at a level that is all but overlooked" (224), but he returns repeatedly to the problem of Jaramillo's "narrative nostalgia." Neither Jaramillo nor her early Chicano critics, in other words, have been able to get past the distorting power of romance.

Héctor Calderón has recently provided an even blunter critique, claiming that in their writings, Otero-Warren and Jaramillo recall only "a familiar gloss of history: we are descendants of heroic conquistadors who in this isolated region of the world fought the Indians, shed their blood, tamed the wilderness, and built a civilization that was a model of conduct" (13–14). Both writers share "nostalgia for the past" and "both recall a harmonious world of aristocratic pretense," Calderón continues, professing himself to be "amazed at this conservative strain of Mexican American thought" (14). However, Rebolledo, leading other Chicana critics, has argued that the "auto-ethnographies" of colonized Nuevomexicana writers narrate ongoing social struggles to maintain a culture threatened by modernization and testify to experiences that would otherwise be silenced and forgotten.[18] While their knowledge of folklore and ritual, combined with their education in both English and Spanish literary forms, gave them the authority to define themselves for both Anglo and Spanish-speaking audiences, their limited access to publishers prevented them from realizing it. Manuel Martín-Rodríguez characterizes Jaramillo's story of having a professor want to publish her work as his own as "representative of the usurpation of authority that until recently has threatened the survival of many texts and documents from the early stages of Chicano/a literature" (68). As a writer who insisted on credit for her authorship, Jaramillo is a key figure in the formation of a Chicana literary tradition.

Historians have explained the complex motivations for emphasizing "Spanish" heritage, and in relation to Chicana writers we can add the motivation to speak authoritatively to a national audience about regional traditions. In an essay on Otero-Warren, author of *Old Spain in Our Southwest*, Elizabeth Salas notes that many native New Mexicans continue to distinguish their pioneer past from that of later Mexican immigrants. "During the 1930s, the term 'Spanish' was the polite term, the respectful term, a marker of class distinction, in contrast to the term 'Mexican'" (144). The distinction became more significant and more wishful as immigration from Mexico increased: between 1900 and 1930, the number of Mexicans in the Southwest grew from 100,000 to over a million. As Vicki Ruiz and Virginia Sánchez Korrol point out, beginning in 1848, when Mexicans on the U.S. side of the new border suddenly "became second-class citizens, divested of their property, political power, and cultural entitlements" (*Latina Legacies* 12), racial stereotypes intensified for all classes of Spanish-speaking people in the United States. In the 1930s, Anglo-American migration and Mexican immigration continued to threaten the culture, social status, and economic security of native New Mexicans like Jaramillo, Cabeza de Baca, and Otero-Warren—"these writers not only were describing the loss of their lands and culture, but they also were actively resisting culturally defined roles for themselves and for all Hispana women" (Rebolledo, *Women* 33).

During the Depression many Hispano families suffered the loss of income from wage labor as well as the loss of their land. After establishing patterns of seasonal migration to Colorado to harvest beet fields, herd sheep, work the mines, or work on the railroad to supplement income from family farms, they suddenly found themselves forced to retreat to their home villages. Whereas seven to ten thousand workers in northern New Mexico's Upper Rio Grande Valley migrated north to work in the 1920s, in the 1930s that number shrank to two thousand. In her study of this region, Sarah Deutsch clearly explains the challenges of the Depression era, beginning with the decision of most employers in Colorado and New Mexico to cut wages and hire fewer workers. Nuevomexicanos also found themselves subject to two new laws that controlled their mobility: first, the enforced "repatriation" of Mexicans to Mexico between 1930 and 1935 following federal legislation to restrict the number of immigrants; and second, the closing of Colorado's border in 1936, an illegal initiative proposed by Governor Johnson to limit the number of Hispanic workers on relief rolls by deporting them over the state line (Deutsch 164–66). Although both efforts to control migration and immigration were short lived, they irreparably split the Spanish American communities in northern New Mexico. According to Deutsch, after the blockade few workers ventured back to Colorado and "Hispanics were powerless to repair the migrant webs" (166).

Meanwhile, their villages provided little refuge. Unpredictable weather, including heavy snow, hail, and drought, made farming and sheepherding very difficult. Farm women continued to sell and trade chile and handcrafts like weaving, woodwork, and tinwork either to tourists who visited their villages or at the "Native Market" established in Santa Fe in 1934 (Jensen, "'I've Worked'" 237–38). However, craft work paid poorly, and its cultivation by Anglo patrons and upper-class Nuevomexicanas—like Cabeza de Baca, who gave cooking and canning demonstrations at women's homes as a government extension agent, and Otero-Warren, who fostered traditional Spanish crafts while superintendent of Santa Fe county schools—reinforced the cultural and class divisions between rural families and their urban or more cosmopolitan counterparts. Unable to support themselves—the majority of families relied on government relief—some chose to move to cities like Denver or Albuquerque.

Although Jaramillo's wealth and status protected her somewhat from the economic hardships faced by other rural families, evidence of material loss is undeniable in her writing. *Romance* recounts an effort to show her friend Ruth Laughlin Barker "an old Spanish-style house" of the type Jaramillo frequented as a child. The author of a popular novel, *Caballeros*, Barker may have wanted material for her next book. While the beauty of the Taos valley remained intact, instead of gracious houses, she and Jaramillo encountered only absence and decay. "We rode to Ranchito, but where was Aunt Piedad's attractive old home, or the new one grandpa had built for her? It was hard to believe my eyes that what I was seeing were the melting remains of these once big, fine lively homes," Jaramillo writes. She looks for the house of the Valdez family in Placita and cannot find it. Then she approaches the Gonzales's house in Arroyo Seco and finds that "the whitewashed porch with the blue railing posts was gone, and the whole house was in ruins" (119). Her formerly rich friend Juanita appears at the door, shabbily dressed, and sells a few remaining pieces of family silver to Barker for a low price so that she can repair the house. Much later, Jaramillo returns to her home village of Arroyo Hondo and similarly discovers her "once lively, happy home, now in melting ruins" beside the "new, modern-looking schoolhouse" (187). The store her father owned and managed, renovated by her brother, also seems entirely new, and "buses on their way to Colorado, roar by twice a day" (188). Ruins or the bland façade of modernization—Jaramillo dramatizes the opposition and provides no hope for compromise.

Other chapters reveal outrage rather than grief at Anglo appropriation of Nuevomexicano culture, and this anger led Jaramillo toward her own career as a writer. The example often cited by critics is her indignation at the bad recipe for tortillas she read in *Holland Magazine* in 1935.[19] In response, she immediately established La Sociedad Folklórica, a group to consist of "thirty members of Spanish descent," to converse solely in the Spanish language, and to raise public awareness of Spanish traditions, especially during Santa Fe's yearly Fiesta; wrote a cookbook, *The Genuine New Mexico Tasty Recipes/Potajes sabrosos* (1939); transcribed stories her family had passed down to her, published as *Cuentos del hogar/Spanish Fairy Tales* (1939); and explained the customs of her village in *Shadows of the Past/Sombras del Pasado* (1941), a book she illustrated herself. To find a publisher for *Shadows*, she submitted the manuscript to "some of our Western universities" and received many rejections, but when one professor asked to use some of her stories in his book she realized, "All they wanted was to read my manuscript and get ideas from it, so I decided to have it published by a small private press here in my city" (168).

Her brother, Reyes Martinez, worked as a field writer on Hispanic Folk Life for the New Mexico WPA. Jaramillo's writing may have also been an unofficial response to this official endeavor. The reports that Martinez produced for the Federal Writers' Project record popular songs about changing customs among local youth, comic verses about sheepherders who migrated to Wyoming for work, and recollections of new entertainments like the phonograph (which arrived in Taos in 1893), the George Bailey circus (which performed in Arroyo Hondo in 1914), and "Las Panoramas," or movies.[20] One report explains the history of his own family, "The Martinez Family of Arroyo Hondo," emphasizing their "pure Spanish stock" and resistance to intermarriage. Another reproduces common "Spanish Proverbs," like "Lo que es de todos, no es de nadie," or "That which belongs to everybody, belongs to no one"—a saying that apparently referred to past attitudes toward public property.[21] Martinez also discusses the ethic of cooperation that prevailed in Taos County before 1900; people used to help each other harvest, card and spin wool, plaster houses, wash clothes, and make syrup from corn husks. With changes in modes of travel and farming, such cooperation waned. Elsewhere he describes places in Taos Country suitable for picking pine nuts and explains the nutritional value of food commonly grown and prepared in the region, like chile, tamales, and panocha ("a cereal food prepared from malted wheat" that he deems "one of the best all-around foods . . . which should be used regularly by every American family").[22] Many of these accounts give "personal knowledge," his family, or his neighbors in Arroyo Hondo as the source of information, effectively presenting materials for his own auto-ethnography. However, Martinez did not pursue publication of his material outside of his contribution to the WPA guide. In fact, while his district supervisor, Taos artist Muriel Haskell, commended his access to local knowledge, she complained about the quality of his writing. Martinez "is particularly able to gather material on the northern villages, folklore and customs—and additional oldtimers' stories," she reported in February 1936, but "his wordage is not entirely satisfactory."[23]

Jaramillo's writing assimilates the observations about Nuevomexicano life contained in WPA reports like her brother's into open narratives of cultural loss and invented renewal. Critics tend to emphasize the idealization of her childhood and marriage, which coincided with her life in the villages of Arroyo Hondo and El Rito, and see the accounts of her struggle after the deaths of her husband and daughter, which brought her to Denver and Santa Fe, as elements of a separate and contradictory narrative. Because the traumas of losing her land and witnessing her daughter's murder are linked in her memory and remain the intense motivation for her writing, however, they prevent her from imagining any home as a place of refuge. These traumas structure a circular narrative pattern that revises and critiques the popular histories of her village and her adopted city. Before recounting her husband's illness and premature death, Jaramillo includes a description of village life in each chapter; afterward, she never fully returns to the villages of her childhood. As memoir, *Romance* remains faithful to Jaramillo's own migration from rural to urban space, and its conclusion can be seen to imitate larger patterns of Hispano displacement.

Jaramillo indicates her awareness of her role as a Nuevomexicana writer through the form of her narrative, rather than through explicit ethnic identification. With its almost obsessive pattern of return to her past houses, *Romance* is in many ways a traditional village story—with the difference that Jaramillo's viewpoint becomes more and more modern as the narrative progresses, making her the representative of both old and new orders. The first chapter, devoted to the "romance and adventure" of New Mexico's first explorers, describes how Jaramillo's ancestors, the Martinez and Lucero families, settled land and, more importantly, established villages: first Ojo Caliente, then Los Luceros, then Arroyo Hondo, where Jaramillo spent her childhood. By the time New Mexico became a territory of the United States, commercial networks extended throughout the region and into Mexico, and everyone from trappers to "towering gold seekers" somehow discovered "the little hidden valley of the Arroyo Hondo." Jaramillo extols the isolation and natural beauty of her home:

> This verdant little basin lies low between two high ridges of hills, closed up on the east and west by the river canyons. It is isolated from the rest of the world. Through the center of the basin splashes the noisy, rocky river. Its crystaline waters create green-carpeted meadows and fields. On the west the river surges through the stupendous gate of the Rio Grande and mingles its crystal waters with the musky green ones of the Rio Grande. Three picturesque villages add charm to this small section of the beautiful Taos Valley. (7)

In this first description, the valley's waters lose their pristine clarity only when they flow through the western gate. Its fertility sustains three villages and its canyons protect the inhabitants from invasion from "the rest of the world." Thus the valley is made the center of the world and the origin of village culture. The sudden invasion of prospectors and miners, saloons and gambling places, however, immediately disrupts "the quiet that had surrounded the village before" (8), leading to the decline of the family and its wealth. "Our families now remained more secluded in our enclosed *placitas* courtyards," she writes. The constructed and socially enforced enclosure shrinks and exaggerates the natural boundaries of the valley, establishing a centripetal pattern that will leave native families no easy routes of escape.

Subsequent chapters resist dwelling on the changes wrought by the strangers to the valley, focusing instead on the harmonious mixture of work and leisure that seemed to make Arroyo Hondo self-sufficient. Jaramillo makes a virtue of the villages' isolation as she recounts the freedoms of her childhood: gathering berries and butterflies, fishing and hunting, cooking and preserving. She remembers her parents' "energetic labor": "They had time for everything—work, hospitality, religion and even politics" (11). They created a sense of leisure by shifting from one kind of work to another, such as from managing the dry good and grocery store to supervising the vegetable garden. According to Jaramillo, "The compensation for an everyday full day's work was not material, but rather the kind that is felt in the soul" (12). As Jaramillo describes the feasts of San Geronimo and Santiago and the Penitente ceremonies in the next chapters, however, she begins to distinguish between the realms of domestic harmony and traditional religious rituals, confined within her rural valley, and of entertainment and education, largely occurring or imported from cities without. When Mexican performers arrived to give puppet and circus shows, they "broke up the quiet, and enlivened everyone" (23).

Her own departure for boarding school, first at a convent school in Taos and then at the Loretto Academy in Santa Fe, intensified the romance of home as it introduced her to more exotic worlds. When she describes her return from her first fall at school in Taos, for example, she lingers over the description of how her Indian cook Lupe, her nurse Tiodoro, and her mother made dough for sopaipias, empanaditas, tamales, and chapitos. This description both accentuates the newly felt abundance of her home and confirms the authority she claimed later for herself when she published "the right recipe" for "white, light and fluffy" tamales, "so different from those served at restaurants" (32). The food culture of the village, documented more fully in *The Genuine New Mexico Tasty Recipes*, also attests to the richness and complex origins of her native culture. For example, Gary Nabhan notes the Persian and Arabian origin of one of her recipes for lamb and garbanzo stew (*Arab/American* 33). Other recipes reflect local adaptations of indigenous Mexican and Pueblo traditions. When read as part of her extensive effort to chronicle her homeland, the descriptions of village life provide evidence of how Arab and Spanish culture migrated to and changed in the context of the New World.

Against the comforts and tastes of home, Jaramillo then articulates the already commodified enticements of the world beyond her village. The language she uses to convey her first impressions of Santa Fe, a two-days' ride from Arroyo Hondo, echoes that of tourist guides, emphasizing the city's "glamorous early history," its "old Spanish customs," its "attractive, old-style homes," and its charming antiques (*Romance* 49–50). Like many Anglo tourists, she attended a Corn Dance at Santo Domingo Pueblo and the feast of San Lorenzo at Picuris Pueblo, and she found the ride toward Peñasco "scenic," the small church "picturesque" (56). As she describes more distant travels, such as her "enchanting trip" to Mexico, Jaramillo continues to act as a tourist, marveling at fine crafts in each city, the "antique picturesqueness" of Cuernavaca, and the formal and elegant hospitality of her friends in Mexico City. Though she claims "a natural sympathy and understanding of the people in this our neighbor country," she still concludes with an assessment of Mexico as condescending as one that Anglo tourists of an earlier generation might have used to describe her own homeland: it seemed a "languid, exotic land of leisure that lies drowsing under scorching suns, in this paradise of souls, where the sole ambition of most is to obtain just enough for their daily needs" (106).

As Jaramillo relates her worldly encounters, she expresses greater attachment to her native valleys. Each time she narrates her return, she intensifies the valley's isolation, natural beauty, and shared rituals. En route to a family wedding in Abiquiu, she passes "the green valley of El Vallecito" where "little adobe houses slept peacefully between the green farms strewn along the rich trout stream." After crossing the divide, she glimpses "the El Rito valley lying green at our feet, drenched and sparkling with raindrops" (57). At Abiquiu, she finds refuge in her cousin's enclosed garden, attends the wedding mass, and dances with the guests (including her future husband) until dawn. Her own wedding took place in Taos in 1898, when "the town and its surrounding villages . . . were still but little changed from the time Don Juan de Oñate established the first capital of New Spain there" (77). Although she found her husband's village of El Rito lonely at first, she returns to her own with joy:

> A hymn of gladness sang in my heart as we came in sight of the villages nestling in their natural setting at the foot of the high ridges of hills that shelter the green bowl of the valley. It appeared like an oasis in a desert after the ride across the plain. To the quietness of the evening, shedding its peace and serenity on the inhabitants, the meadowlarks, *charas* and *tildios* added their sweet vesper songs from the meadows along the river. (87)

Here she conjures the idyllic valley with full knowledge of what lies beyond it and laments again the necessity of leaving: "Oh, time, turn back and let me live again, just for a minute, those happy days!" (88).

With her husband Venceslao's death, "the happiest epoch of my life had ended," she writes (130). Beneath the "exterior reserve" that she had been taught was proper to display to her husband "there had always burned the most ardent love" (128). When he died, Venceslao left a bereft widow and substantial debt. After a lifetime of privilege, even extravagance, Jaramillo suddenly faced the responsibility of sorting through her husband's business affairs, including managing his property in Denver and his sheep ranch in Chama, New Mexico. Many of his properties carried substantial mortgages. Jaramillo immediately went to work managing the Denver apartments and planned to pay off the mortgage and take control of the building, but the structure required extensive repairs that she could not afford. So she found a buyer and sold the property at a low price, realizing that "[t]he depression after World War I had started to hit the country" (133). Later she returned to her house in Santa Fe, rented one bedroom for income and company, and turned her attention to renting the farms at El Rito and selling the Chama ranch. Although she succeeded in selling her husband's additional nine lots in Denver, she priced them "below cost" and still owed back taxes. She offered "the sheep ranch at half price, but buyers could not pay even this, as most of the cattle and sheep men had lost considerably during the last few years" (136). In the meantime, her bank and several others went into bankruptcy, wiping out her estate money, a savings account for her daughter, Angelina, and nearly all of her life savings. Just as she made contact with a possible buyer for the sheep ranch in Texas, a banker (who had depended on Venceslao's investment to get started in local business) foreclosed the mortgage. At that point, Jaramillo writes, "My last thread of hope in saving a home for my daughter broke, after nine years of hard work trying to save something" (137).

Jaramillo's failure to maintain her husband's property reveals a much wider breakdown of the local networks of power and a new restructuring of the regional economy. This failure also led her to hold tighter to the cultural traditions she hoped to pass on. Although she could not afford boarding school for more than one year, Jaramillo still imposed strict standards on her daughter. She forbade any correspondence with potential suitors, evening dates, short stockings, and improper friendships, and she continued to exercise the emotional restraint taught by her own mother. She recalls, "I had tried to bring up my daughter in the old Spanish rule, sheltered in her home" (146). After Angelina was brutally murdered in her bedroom in Santa Fe by an escaped convict, Jaramillo grieved and deeply regretted the limits she had imposed on her daughter. "My mistake was, I see, that in trying to keep her free from gossip and innocent of worldly knowledge, I had failed to see that she was living in a different age" (146). The process of sorting through her daughter's affairs took much longer than sorting out her husband's estate; at the time of writing *Romance*, Jaramillo admitted that even though fifteen years had gone by, she still kept Angelina's books and clippings about her father and her family. One clipping announced the inaugural ride of '*El Jaramillo*,' "one of the Santa Fe's newest all-steel Pullman observation cars." According to the newspaper report, "'*El Jaramillo*' is a beauty, finished in the most exquisite of polished woods and with about every device for safety and comfort. It is the first of a series of cars which will be named for famous families in the Southwest" (165). Whereas Cleofas identified herself as a woman descended from the first families of Spanish pioneers, Angelina chose to celebrate the popular and commercial value of her father's family name. Significantly, it was Angelina who first encouraged her mother to write of the customs of her childhood, and the memoir is partially refracted through Angelina's imagined point of view. While there is certainly nostalgia at work in her reconstruction of family and village life, Jaramillo alternately celebrates and reveals deep ambivalence about the isolation she experienced and imposed upon her daughter.[24]

Whereas the early chapters of *Romance* keep returning to the happy isolation of village life in northern New Mexico, the chapters following the deaths of Venceslao and Angelina newly associate return with grief and shift the author's sense of home permanently to Santa Fe, which she no longer sees through a tourist's eyes. Her final visit to the village notes the popularity of Taos among artists and tourists, who tend to see "only its customs rather than its soul" (186), and the absence of her old house. In its place is "a new, modern-looking schoolhouse—with nothing left but memories of a once lively, happy home" (187). Reflecting one last time on the positive value of rural labor for providing stimulation, happiness, and longevity, she leaves "the sunny, sheltered little valley which imparts a sense of security" (189), resolved to save what she can of the old ways through architectural preservation and the seasonal performances of the folkloric society she founded.

It was the re-creation of village and Native American culture through performance, rather than its textual representation, that captured public attention in the 1930s and 1940s—and continues to lure spectators. According to Calderón, "La Sociedad Folklórica still participates in the Anglo-inspired Santa Fe Fiesta by staging La Merienda—An Old Fashioned Style show, an afternoon fashion show of Spanish heirloom dresses, shawls, mantillas, and jewelry and serving bizcochos and hot 'Spanish' chocolate as refreshments" (32). Santa Fe also holds an annual Indian Market that displays Native American art and food, including mutton stew, roasted corn, blue-corn pancakes, fry bread, and salted piñons.[25] At the end of *Romance*, Jaramillo correctly identifies the problem with her lifelong project to recover her heritage as her own culture's lack of interest. "The glamour and beauty which appeals to the senses of the artists and the writers who have come into our country, should appeal more forcefully to us, the heirs of the artistic culture and of the poetry and the religious traditions which our Spanish ancestors left to crystallize on the crests of our New Mexico mountains" (183). The attractions of "their" rural past to the current generation, however, were not immediate, largely because of their association with upper-class Nuevomexicanos and their appeal to Anglo tourists. As much as Jaramillo tried to negotiate her readers' desires for an "alternate homeland" and her own longing to return to places whose traumatic destruction she had witnessed, she found herself caught between a generation struggling to manage material and social losses and an emerging Chicano/a sensibility that sought to remake communal history in different terms. Instead of merely sustaining a restorative, if nostalgic, older viewpoint or anticipating how Chicana writers might recover domestic stories for political purposes, Jaramillo articulates the trauma of losing her home through the circular narrative of the village story, inviting her readers to experience it without providing a clear way out.

Women's Work in Chávez's Las Cruces

As we have seen, the reception of Jaramillo's writing by Chicano critics provides one perspective on its limitations. Denise Chávez's recent writing provides another, as it deliberately rejects Jaramillo's privileged "Spanish" culture as archaic and leisured, and her "little village" as hopelessly rural—while preserving into the late twentieth century the values of women's work and family tradition to which Jaramillo devoted her life and her career. Both critiques, institutional and literary, reify the marginal status of rural women in the mid-twentieth century in a globalizing United States and, more specifically, in the formation of the Chicano/a literary canon. Because Jaramillo belongs to neither the "Migrant Generation," as historians describe the Mexicans who came to the United States between 1900 and 1920 to escape the turmoil of the Revolution, nor to the "Mexican American Generation," a group that spans the Depression and Civil Rights eras and often struggled to assimilate into mainstream culture, she challenges the dominant models of Chicano/a historiography, which tends to privilege explicit challenges to the master narratives of regional difference or national assimilation. The result can be the failure to recognize histories of resistance, like Jaramillo's, that neither overtly resist these narratives nor conform to a typical postcolonial paradigm.

Along with the differences in cultural affiliation and status as established residents rather than recent migrants, New Mexican women writers of the 1930s occupied different class positions than the Chicana writers who succeeded them. In "between [their two generations], value systems changed," explains Rebolledo:

> [W]orking and middle-class women began to write where before mostly educated upper-class women were writing; in the first generation the emphasis was only on Spanish culture, but in the second a pride in the combined Indian and Spanish heritage becomes much more dominant. The first generation of writers still generally perceived themselves as Spanish; the second generation saw themselves as Chicana. ("Tradition" 97)

In a collection of stories, *The Last of the Menu Girls* (1986); two novels, *Face of An Angel* (1994) and *Loving Pedro Infante* (2001); and a memoir, *A Taco Testimony* (2006), Chávez explores the ways that female characters express their ethnic affiliation and responsibility to their community through work. She defines her own purpose similarly: "My mission as a writer is to write the stories women and men never tell, are afraid to tell. And in that writing, to bring mercy" (Brown-Guillory Interview 36). Claiming to "get [her] material from Safeway and in [her] own four walls," Chávez connects her immersion in the demands and material sensations of ordinary life in the modern, southern New Mexico town of Las Cruces with her own family history and imagination. From these sources, she produces fiction that serves a diverse community of readers. She brings a defiant, working-class sensibility to her writing, one that has been informed by the cultural politics of the Chicano Renaissance and Rudolfo Anaya's example. She has said in an interview that Anaya first made her aware that it was possible to write about her native state. Before reading *Bless Me, Ultima* (1969), she thought that all New Mexican writers published cookbooks poorly illustrated by their nephews.

When she made this comment, Chávez undoubtedly had Jaramillo in mind. She did not appreciate Jaramillo's defensive, aristocratic position with respect to "Spanish" tradition and clearly objected to the appearance of Jaramillo's publication of *The Genuine New Mexico Tasty Recipes*. In *A Taco Testimony* she explains, "There are always those who want nothing to do with the country of most of our ancestors. There exists an invisible membrane of denial for so many. The Spanish look down on the Mexicans, who sometimes look down on the Native American *nativos*," and even her own father distinguished between his own identity as a "Spanish white man" and her mother's as a Mexican from Texas (78). Still, Chávez, too, learned to negotiate her relation to cultural and literary traditions through characters who prepare and serve food, as well as consume it. For example, in *Face of An Angel*, her heroine, Sovieda, is a waitress in an anglicized Mexican restaurant struggling to complete her university education. She decides to take the course Chicano Culture 210 at the local college and immediately finds herself caught between real and academic identities. The course begins with a quiz: "*Define and distinguish between the following*: Hispanic, Chicano, Mexicano, Mexican American; *Relate the Stories of the Following*: Our Lady of Guadalupe/La Morenita, La Sebastiana, La Llorona, El Coco." Then her professor demands, "Write a brief essay on why you are taking this class" that addresses whether Chicano/a culture "is part of the American tapestry" (286–87). Just off from her shift, Sovieda scans the quiz and feels dizzy. As she writes, she silently taunts the professor who comes to represent the disjunction between lived knowledge and intellectual training. "Dr. Velasquez, you want to know about Chicano culture? Well, here I am, smelling of hard work" (287). Chávez takes the idea of food preparation as metaphor for political and social struggle in interesting directions—certainly away from village and rural domesticity and into commercial and institutional spaces. Her widely anthologized story "The Last of the Menu Girls" and her novel *Face of an Angel* test food's metaphorical values while using it to ground her characters' experiences in the materiality of daily life and work. Her memoir continues to explore the significance of food to family tradition, giving her "a better understanding of the unique culture that is southern New Mexico, Far West Texas and northern México—alternate sides of the tortilla to you, life and sustenance to me" (*Taco Testimony* 11).

The title story of Chávez's first collection introduces Rocío Esquibel, a young woman just about to finish high school and beginning to think about her future. She takes a summer job as a nurse's aide and learns that her specific duty will be to take food orders from patients—that is, to be a "menu girl." An aging, repulsive man named Mr. Smith, who reminds Rocío of a gnome made of green Jell-O, offers her some iced tea, his specialty. Then he hands her "a pile of green forms. They were menus," the narrator explains. "In the center of the menu was listed the day of the week, and to the left and coming down in a neat order were the three meals, breakfast, lunch and dinner. Each menu had various choices for each meal" (*Taco Testimony* 19). The choices include Salisbury Steak, Fish Sticks, Enchiladas, and Rice Almondine—a mixture of debased Continental entrees packaged for institutional consumption and one native dish, the enchiladas. Mr. Smith boasts, "[T]hey're really good. Trini makes them, she's been working for me for twenty years" (20).

Though the job may not seem difficult to master, Rocío discovers that she cannot predict how she will respond to patients, or how they will treat her. For example, one young woman entrances Rocío with her "translucent beauty," even though she yells at her to go away. Another man, an illegal immigrant from Mexico, had his nose bit off in a barroom brawl. Rocío stares at him as he sleeps off his "hard drunken wanderings" (33). From time to time she returns to Mr. Smith's office in the basement for refuge, always aware of the suffering above her: "The bodies of patients twisted and moaned and cried out, and cursed, but for the two of us in that basement world, all was quiet save for the occasional clinking of an iced tea glass and the sporadic sound of Mr. Smith clearing his throat" (22). In the scenes in Mr. Smith's office, Chávez plays with a set of striking oppositions: aging Anglo man and young Chicana woman, sickness and health, social conventions of hospitality and the economic demands of running a hospital.

Over time, Rocío comes to have some sympathy for Mr. Smith, who takes over her job himself when she leaves. In no small measure it is the ritual of drinking tea together that promotes this cross-cultural and inter-generational understanding. Likewise, the ritual of eating together in the hospital cafeteria with her friend and coworker Arlene allows Rocío to declare her commitment to serving others: "It was there, in the coolness of the cafeteria, in that respite from the green forms, at our special table, drinking tea, laughing with Arlene, that I, still shy, still judgmental, still wondering and still afraid, under the influence of caffeine, decided to stick it out. I would not quit the job" (25). We seem to be a long way from the gracious dining room of Jaramillo's family home in Arroyo Hondo, and surely Chávez means to challenge our notions of cultural tradition and women's work. I would argue, however, that the cafeteria, too, is a hos-pitable and privileged space into which the narrator invites the reader to share food and ideas through the bodily experience of a Chicana protago-nist. Although Chávez here chooses a public place rather than a domestic sphere, Jaramillo made her hacienda and her city house public by writing about them, just as other Chicana writers, notably Sandra Cisneros in *The House on Mango Street*, deliberately remapped the social meanings of private kitchens and houses.[26] For these writers and their heroines (whether autobiographical or fictional), shared work is more important than consumption, companionship more valuable than private interest. Rocío eventually declares her vocation to be that of writer, and the history of her work and friendships as presented in this story establishes a model for the kind of working artist she will become.

In an interview granted while writing *Face of an Angel*, Chávez explained that she was "questioning what it means to serve. Women have traditionally been in service, so I think it is about time that we question it." Annie Eysturoy asked, "So you explore what it means to serve, both for the recipient and the giver, and what kind of relationship that creates?" Chávez responded, "You can take that into the metaphysical or the spiritual, what-ever. What is a life of service? Then what is work? Is it not in a way service, too? . . . Whatever your life's work is, if you are a plumber, if you design flower baskets, there is always that search for order and clarity in whatever you do. . . . It is the sense of love and devotion and commitment that you put into your work that I celebrate" (Chavez, Interview 166). In *Face of an Angel*, Sovieda approaches her life's work with just such devotion and commitment. She not only works as a waitress; throughout the novel, she also compiles her own manual for the waitresses who will follow her, *The Book of Service*. Sovieda may mock academic formulations of Chicano/a culture, the commodification of Native American culture, and the Santa Fe style (as she certainly does with her descriptions of the Turquoise and Kachina "theme rooms" at the restaurant where she works, El Farol). Nonetheless, she completes the course and serves the restaurant for fifteen years, both recording these cultural stereotypes and resisting them.

Chávez also reveals the importance of women's work in sustaining communal traditions through the characters of "Chata," a cleaning woman who originally worked for Sovieda's grandmother, and Oralia, her housekeeper whose father was a Pueblo Indian and whose mother worked for Sovieda's great-grandfather. Perhaps because Chata "lives in a tiny two-room shack," she can teach "what home really means, what comfort really is, . . . what work is and how every woman should continue to work, even in the worst of times, day after day, week after week, year after year" (*Face of an Angel* 216–17). When Chata praises her for being a good worker, Sovieda cherishes the words as "the highest honor." She loves the Mondays that she works and eats with Chata, "talking in Spanish and laughing in no particular language" (215). At those times, the rituals of work and shared meals bridge differences in age, class, and ethnic identity. Oralia, too, creates an ideal community through the work that she shares—her herbs cure all ills, her little yellow kitchen beats at the heart of her mother's house. When asked of her dreams, Oralia replies that she wants "everyone to know what it is to belong, to be committed to something, to know they are brother and sister and mother to everyone" (311). Memories of Oralia at work—"making empanadas, sealing the edges with fork grooves, or boiling oil to just the right heat so that the sopaipillas puffed up high once they touched the hot grease" (140) or weeding her garden or telling stories—are the real materials of native New Mexican cultural history, as Sovieda herself recognizes when she chooses Oralia as the subject of her "Oral History" assignment for the Chicano Studies class. From her own work and her relations with Chata and Oralia come the lessons for aspiring waitresses that she writes in her *Book of Service* and that Chávez herself articulates in her testimony: "Never forget who you are, and where you come from" (451).

Such lessons about the connection between identity and place of origin were also taught by Maria in Waters' *People of the Valley* and by Jaramillo in *Romance of a Little Village Girl*, but these older works admitted the possibility that other members of their community and their readers might not accept their wisdom. To return to Rebolledo's point, "value systems" changed between the two generations. The value of the village did not seem apparent in the 1940s and 1950s, either within New Mexico or to readers from elsewhere, except as a place where vanishing traditions could be imagined or appropriated. Writers like Waters and Jaramillo realized the fragility of the culture they valued and the limitations of their authorial power. Many readers and writers in later generations did not want to associate with the village's backwardness or its implicit class and ethnic hierarchies; they repudiated such self-sufficient representations of village life in order to imagine places more fully integrated with contemporary economic and political struggles. After an interval of neglect, however, I think that we can return to these texts and find new value in their representations of tradition, work, and ritual. They reconnect us to the past while making it clear that histories of private lives are not equally accessible, nor are such lives immediately meaningful. Like material ruins, the ruins of social landscapes provide incentives for restoration—and leave open the question of the best aesthetic form for this cultural work.

The Bridge
Cultivating Community in the Atomic Age

> A monument can be nothing more than a rough stone, a fragment
> of ruined wall as at Jerusalem, a tree, or a cross. Its sanctity is
> not a matter of beauty or of use or of age; it is venerated not as a
> work of art or as an antique, but as an echo from the remote past
> suddenly become present and actual.
> —J. B. Jackson, *The Necessity for Ruins*, 91

On most maps of northern New Mexico, Otowi Bridge is not marked.
One can follow the Rio Grande north from Albuquerque and find the
pueblos of San Felipe, Santo Domingo, San Ildefonso, Santa Clara, San
Juan, and Taos, continuing all the way to the Colorado border without
noticing one of the river's crossings. For the driver who speeds along the
main road north from Santa Fe, turns left at Pojoaque and follows Route
502, a new bridge will rush beneath the tires, carrying her far beyond
Black Mesa and the juniper-covered hills of the high desert, up the hill to
Los Alamos. Anyone who glances along the road, however, might notice a
small, unused railroad suspension bridge running parallel to the highway,
as well as two unimposing adobe buildings. This is Otowi Bridge, located
near what remains of a railroad station, a teahouse, and a private dwelling.

Otowi Crossing is now an abandoned site, a place unmarked on the
maps that chart scenic routes, urban growth, or native lands, although
the site of Otowi Ruins nearby officially became a section of Bandelier
National Monument in 1932 (Rothman 251–53). Around Otowi Bridge and
Los Alamos, there were a variety of native settlements, including those of
Pueblos living by the Rio Grande at Po-Woh-Ge-Oweenge, "Where the
water cuts through," now San Ildefonso. Hispano families also farmed and
ranched on territory originally included in a 1746 Spanish land grant on
the Jemez Mountain's eastern slope. Now, however, little intimates these
native patterns of use—that tourists once chose it as their destination for

a rest along their way, or that atomic scientists once found refuge there. The very absence of a commemorative plaque suggests that Otowi Bridge fits neatly into neither the Anglo regionalist myths that transformed the Southwest into a diversion for tourists, nor the recreational model of the National Parks System, nor the national narrative of scientific and military triumph originating in Los Alamos. Instead, it could be another site on a map of "GhostWests," as Ann Ronald conceives in her book about the West's often invisible history. Like the headquarters at California's Donner Memorial State Park, or Tucson, or Ghost Ranch, all stars on Ronald's map of haunted places, "its artifacts and its ambience feed a hunger for a personal connection between history and sense of place" (6). Otowi Bridge poses the challenge of finding ghosts who left few traces. There, in a landscape "everywhere spotted with ruins," one must listen hard to hear echoes of the people and communities who could bring the site back to life and render it as the prehistory of the present rather than let it remain a relic of a vanished age (Jackson, *A Sense of Place* 15).

Many studies have been conducted about Los Alamos and its director, J. Robert Oppenheimer; a memoir and a novel have been written about Otowi Crossing and its longtime resident, Edith Warner; and anthropologists and historians have explored the cultures of northern New Mexico's pueblos and villages. In this chapter, I am interested in how representations of Otowi Bridge produced after its decline show how Warner's private, domestic world has come to haunt the public triumphs of the Manhattan Project. I focus in particular on how Frank Waters organizes his novel *The Woman at Otowi Crossing* (1966) around the figure of Warner, using her historical experience to imagine a new kind of nonrational space and to create a counter-mythic heroine. Waters juxtaposes one woman's practice of hospitality against the accelerating pressures of scientific achievement and world war, seeking to understand the relation between these two incompatible worlds. I explore the ways that Warner's figured body has become a bridge between physical and metaphysical realms and a trope for a conception of space that integrates lived experience and utopian theory.

I then consider *Critical Mass*, a multimedia exhibit about the converging histories of Otowi Bridge that photographer Meridel Rubenstein, performance artist Ellen Zweig, and videographers Steina and Woody Vasulka created in 1993. The exhibit locates Warner's house and identity both within and beyond the discourses of war and modernity. It aims to reconnect physical experience and the historic space of Otowi Bridge with our contemporary knowledge of the bomb's toxic legacy and the global scientific world it helped to produce. This mixed-media installation introduced new methods for coding and decoding the ruins of an everyday life made virtually mythic by an unprecedented convergence of historical forces. Rubenstein and Zweig found a formal solution to the problem of bridging humanist and poststructuralist discourses, thus realizing through art the desire of social geographers like Henri Lefebvre to reach "beyond theory." The combination of personal narrative, oral history, poetry, philosophy, artifacts, and photographs in their project articulates the diverse human and environmental traumas of the Atomic Age without integrating them into a new master narrative. Gary Okihiro and Joan Myers's collaboration *Whispered Silences: Japanese Americans and World War II* similarly assembles a range of written and visual documents to articulate the private and largely marginalized experiences of Japanese Americans imprisoned in internment camps across the desert West between 1942 and 1945. The second half of this chapter explores how each of these works pursues contingent and collaborative narratives to make private and public memories of the war "present and actual."

Crossing Otowi Bridge

The now-ruined building at Otowi Bridge might have displayed the mixture of technology, native and imported labor, and leisure that produced distinctive western places like the trading post, the railway station, or the Harvey House. It first provided a repository for supplies left in boxcars for the Los Alamos Ranch School founded in 1917. Adam Martinez of San Ildefonso Pueblo, son of the potters Maria and Julian, supervised the deliveries. Then, in 1923, it functioned as a post office and general store. In 1928, Edith Warner began to remake the house into a place where railroad crews, passengers, tourists, and eventually scientists could stop to have a snack, a dinner made from homegrown vegetables, or a slice of chocolate cake. Warner had first explored this part of New Mexico in 1922, when she moved from Pennsylvania to a ranch in Frijoles Canyon to recover from a breakdown, and she settled there for good in 1928, when she accepted the job of station agent at Otowi Bridge. Warner's Pueblo companion, Tilano Montoya, had also traveled widely before returning to northern New Mexico, having performed traditional dances with a group from San Ildefonso in London, Paris, Berlin, Rome, and Coney Island (Church, *House* 55). Santa Fe and Taos were already established regional centers, destinations for Anglo writers, artists, and tourists who sought to experience Southwestern culture. Warner worked hard to make Otowi Crossing a local destination as well, and she and Montoya completed an additional house for overnight guests in 1934.

Soon after Warner and Montoya's development of Otowi Crossing, however, Los Alamos was conceived, built, and put to use in developing the atomic bomb. Los Alamos appeared suddenly in this remote and rural landscape; it was an instant community, but one meant to be invisible to outsiders. A few decades earlier, Edgar Lee Hewett had made a strenuous attempt to preserve the area from development altogether. He argued for the archaeological value of the entire Pajarito Plateau and proposed a national park that would include the prehistoric sites of Frijoles, Puye, Tscherige, and Navawi'i. By 1906, however, his idea was a lost hope: the new Forest Homestead Act instead made more of the plateau's land available for settlement.[1] When Ashley Pond designated ranch land for use as a sportsman's club on the top of the plateau and later built the Los Alamos Ranch School, a new phase of development began, one that would force cooperation between the plateau's native groups. As the government appropriated the Ranch School and began to build laboratories and houses for the Manhattan Project, it hastened local cultural, economic, and ecological changes by replacing farm work with jobs on "the Hill,"[2] as the Los Alamos National Laboratory came to be known. In the process, the federal government restricted local access to wood, water, hunting grounds, and sacred territory and failed to protect the sovereignty of tribal lands.

The government, guided by Oppenheimer, chose and imposed its will on Los Alamos, creating what Peter Bacon Hales has called the "origin myth" of the Atomic Age. "Nature and technology, science and faith, fear and arrogance: these dualities, central to our uneasy sense of ourselves, come together on the three sites of the Manhattan Engineer District, and in the enterprises of war and inventions for which they were made" (5). Even though the Manhattan Project itself lasted only twenty-seven months, from the spring of 1943 to the fall of 1945, the war "creat[ed] a network of scientists and scientific laboratories in New Mexico, where there had been very few before," permanently transforming the region's landscape and linking local and global interests (Nash, "New Mexico" 8–9). In the words of Waters's fictional scientist Mitch Gaylord, Los Alamos developed so quickly and systematically that it seemed "fantastic and unreal." While even the newer buildings at Otowi Bridge appear premodern in Waters's novel, either as a "small adobe squatting on the bank" or like an "old print of a woodcutter's hut in the Black Forest" in an edition of Grimm's fairy tales, the buildings at Los Alamos seemed to be models of compartmentalization and scientific rationalism, surrounded by fences and accessible only through carefully monitored gates (*Woman* 36, 74).

The reality of Los Alamos was less glamorous. According to Charlotte Serber, a scientific librarian, when the first group of workers arrived in 1943, "Everything was makeshift. . . . The fence around the Post was half-finished. The Tech Area was an empty shell without power, gas, telephone, furniture, or equipment, and it was separated from the Post proper only by fence posts" (Serber and Wilson 58). Construction proceeded quickly and did not always seem to realize a master plan. Serber recalls, "The first buildings were drab and badly planned with soft, unvarnished floors, small windows, and poor incandescent lighting. Later, buildings varied from the elegant structure built for the chemists, which sported glass partitions, battleship linoleum, and an overabundance of florescent lighting, to the beaverboard chicken-coop built for the theoretical physicists" (65). She describes the Tech Area as "a confusing place from its very beginning," a place that "never achieved any real feeling of permanence and stability." However, "one quickly adjusted to it. What is more important is that its purpose was clear throughout and therefore its remarkable tone remained intact, too" (66).

Beginning in 1942, following President Roosevelt's Executive Order 9066, which demanded the removal of 110,000 Japanese people and their children living in the western United States, the desert West would also be the designated location for a different kind of military enclosure—the ten concentration camps that each housed 10,000 to 20,000 Japanese Americans and their families (Matsumoto 258). Both types of planned and hastily built communities challenged their residents to work in buildings poorly designed for their intended use and established rigid boundaries between insiders and outsiders. During the war Otowi Bridge functioned as an appropriated space, with the constitution of the group shifting from its original Pueblo people to Hispano and Anglo settlers and then to international scientists. Los Alamos and the internment camps, by contrast, developed as dominated spaces, the first fully created by technology and both controlled by military surveillance. Japanese Americans were imprisoned at Tule Lake and Manzanar, California; Gila River and Poston, Arizona; Topaz, Utah; Minidoka, Idaho; Granada, Colorado; Jerome and Rohwer, Arkansas; and Heart Mountain, Wyoming; barbed wire and monitored guard towers marked the limits of their freedom. The fences that enclosed the prisoners were simultaneously symbols and facts, "a deadly border that demarcated the free from the unfree" (Myers and Okihiro 203). Although the scientists at Los Alamos were united by a clear and common purpose and had the freedom to experiment, create, and destroy, their physical mobility and that of their families was limited and their trips down the Hill monitored. Both types of community operated through the doctrines "of secrecy, disenfranchisement, control, obedience, [and] limitation" not operative at Otowi Bridge (Hales 154). In 1943, Warner's tearoom closed to the public but opened for dinner to selected scientists working up the Hill, thanks to a special arrangement with Oppenheimer, who had met Warner while exploring Frijoles Canyon on horseback with his sister and brother. Many couples from Los Alamos came under assumed names to eat there regularly with Oppenheimer and his wife Kitty; other prominent scientists, like Niels Bohr and Enrico Fermi, appeared occasionally. As Jennet Conant describes the meals Warner served, "simple, nourishing stews arrived steaming hot on big terra-cotta plates and the fresh corn, salads, sweet relishes, and five varieties of squash all came from her garden." Afterward, Tilano "served the strong black coffee in big pottery cups" (Conant 157). In 1945, Phil Morrison wrote an extensive letter to Warner, thanking her for her work and hospitality: "Evenings in your place by the river, by the table so neatly set, before the fireplaces so carefully contrived, gave us a little of your assurance, allowed us to belong, took us from the green temporary houses and the bulldozed roads. We shall not forget. . . . I am glad that at the foot of our canyons there is a house where the spirit of Bohr is so well understood" (qtd. in Bird and Sherwin 267).

From 1921 to the end of the war, the house and tearoom at Otowi Bridge provided hospitality for an unprecedented network of communities developing in this part of the Southwest. Peggy Pond Church noted the resemblance to Ghost Ranch in the Piedra Lumbre basin to the north, where Georgia O'Keeffe began to live and work in 1934: "Like Edith Warner and her tea room at Otowi Bridge, the Packs and Ghost Ranch became a refuge for those working on the first atomic bomb" (Poling-Kempes, *Valley* 208). In 1942, several strangers arrived to investigate the Ranch and the people working and staying there, just as Oppenheimer had investigated Warner's teahouse. Dorothy McKibbin, office manager of the Manhattan Project, reviewed the reports and approached Arthur and Phoebe Pack with the idea of turning their Ranch into a summer retreat for the scientists. In the summer of 1943, the Packs agreed to close Ghost Ranch to all but close friends and family and host the government workers, aware that they needed to protect the scientists' privacy and maintain conversations on neutral topics. According to Leslie Poling-Kempes, the scientists were treated like "extended family," sharing the Ranch's horses for trail rides and "the cool stream-fed swimming pool," drinking mint juleps on the supper porch, and eating "dinner served family style at the small Mexican leather-topped tables" (*Ghost Ranch* 156). The fellowship that they shared at Otowi Bridge and Ghost Ranch extended through the time of the first nuclear test at the Trinity Site near Alamogordo on July 15, 1945, and, to some extent, after the war's end in August of that year. Several men returned to Ghost Ranch, discussed the implications of their research, and sought measures to avoid nuclear war in the future. However, whereas Ghost Ranch expanded in the late 1940s to become a year-round lodge and retreat that catered to servicemen, Otowi Bridge lost its function as a cultivated site of refuge. When the army resolved to build a new bridge in 1947, bypassing the old site, people from the pueblo and scientists from the Los Alamos Laboratory helped Warner and Montoya to rebuild their house and start a new garden on the other side of the road, but even this collaborative effort could not sustain their unofficial network of cultural exchange. Warner died a few years later in 1951.

In the view of writers and artists, Los Alamos and Otowi Bridge came to constitute a single historic landscape integrated through Warner's perspective. Waters's Gaylord explicitly links "the myth of the project on top of the mesa" with "the myth at the foot, at Otowi Crossing," explaining that in retrospect he understands that "they were two sides of the same coin." Together they formed "perhaps the only true myth of these modern times" (*Woman* 74). In both *The Woman at Otowi Crossing* and *In the Shadow of Los Alamos* (Warner 2001), edited by Patrick Burns, Warner stands at the boundary of the unknown, functioning as a figure for the convergence of nature and culture, spirituality and science. Burns writes about the many worlds meeting at Warner's tearoom: "Edith was not only living at the bridge, she was the bridge between the ancient communal lifestyle of the San Ildefonso Pueblo and the new community of scientists and engineers soon to bring about a new era in the history of mankind" (xii-xiii). Thomas Lyon, too, emphasizes Warner's symbolic potential, explaining that her location at the bridge placed her in a cultural borderland: "Who could have been more representatively located, at the crossing of the river, precisely between the San Ildefonso Pueblo on the east and Los Alamos to the west?" (Waters, *Woman* xv). Such representations of

Warner as the embodiment of Otowi Bridge situate the potential for social and historical meaning in her position between cultures and prefigure the uneven development of the new West. With disproportionate growth concentrated around urban, military, and technological centers, the spaces in between, though appropriated by those who lived there, would be left for reification, contamination, or obliteration.

Through textual representations of Warner, Otowi Bridge has developed a mythology of mystic convergence and come to symbolize the cultural values of hospitality and tolerance threatened by the invention of the atomic bomb. Looking at Otowi Bridge's natural and appropriated landscapes through Warner means looking beyond the moments of inevitably significant risk and destruction that defined the beginning of the Atomic Age and cultivating visionary models of domestic beauty and cultural tolerance. The possibility that the foundation of civilization, symbolized by a well-tended garden and a welcoming shelter in the desert, might be permanently destroyed was of great concern to Oppenheimer. The Reith lectures he delivered in England in 1953 especially reveal his dark thoughts about the human costs of atomic progress. "Uncommon Sense" begins with the stern reminder that "this house, this earth in which we live will one day be unfit for human habitation." Then Oppenheimer continues to meditate on how humans are part of the process of history and seem to require two kinds of thinking: "the way of time and history and the way of eternity and timelessness." He proposes that these approaches are "complementary views, each supplementing the other, neither telling the whole story" (*Atom and Void* 52–53).

Warner claimed for herself a unique ability to feel connections between the belief systems she encountered and to produce a new kind of space. To some extent, Waters and Burns simply extend those claims. Although *The WPA Guide to 1930s New Mexico* identified her as a writer, Warner labored too hard on her garden, her house, and her tearoom to produce more than a few articles and journal entries. Between 1942 and 1950, she circulated an annual "Christmas Letter" that described her impressions of the seasons and everyday tasks and joys, such as discovering Mariposa lilies in spring, the demands of the harvest, the feel of summer's dry heat, and long hikes up the mesa in fall. Though she realized that others considered her house "a landmark" or "an experience," in a letter from 1947 she explained the meaning of the place as the cultivation of understanding: "For me it was two decades of living and learning. I had hoped to live out my life 'where the river makes a noise'" (*In the Shadow*

101). Even her account of "that August day when the report of the atomic bomb flashed around the world" remains grounded in the daily routine that allowed her to connect with the land and to provide for others—"It seemed fitting that it was Kitty Oppenheimer who, coming for vegetables, brought the news" (96).

Rather than asserting a public identity, Warner's writings articulate the need for responsible use of the Pajarito Plateau's natural spaces, her desire to serve its native residents, and her commitment to provide refuge for strangers to the area. Her work in her garden and in her house, which she considered a "war job," allowed for regular contact with local women who supplied her with eggs and milk in exchange for produce, with Montoya's family and cacique, and with the scientists at the laboratory up the Hill. It also gave her time to witness dances at San Ildefonso and Santa Clara and to explore the mountains around her. A passage from her journal on March 2, 1933, reveals her openness to her environment: "I go out into the sunshine to sit receptively for what there is in this stillness and calm. I am keenly aware that there is something. Just now it seems to flow in a rhythm around me and then to enter me—that something which comes in a hushed inflowing." A few months later, on May 21, she wrote, "I am I and earth is earth—mesa, sky, wind, rushing river. Each is an entity but the essence of the earth flows into me—perhaps of me into the earth." Then she observed, "The detail of life becomes the scaffolding" (162–63). Each of these passages conducts an experiment with the body, feeling both space and a rhythm of experience. Warner invokes material elements in order to leave them behind, thus privileging the process of moving toward some immaterial, all-encompassing truth over the truth itself. Working dialectically between material and philosophical experience, and between the body's engagement with physical labor and its senses, her writing suggests the kind of "rhythm analysis" that Lefebvre proposes in his conclusion to *The Production of Space* as a means of overcoming alienation and restoring the "total body." In his effort to move beyond theory, Lefebvre conceives of the body's senses as layers of experience that "prefigure," or function analogously, to "the layers of social space and their interconnections" (405). He claims, "The genesis of a far-away order can be accounted for only on the basis of the order that is nearest to us—namely, the order of the body."

Warner's heightened awareness of seasonal rhythms, a response at once private and shared with her neighbors at San Ildefonso, apparently contradicts the strenuous efforts at scientific mastery occurring simultaneously in Los Alamos. The comfort she finds in the recurrence of things seems proof of the power of secular ritual, not scientific discovery. Yet Oppenheimer himself developed his love for the area through repeated summer visits, often with his brother, Frank (*Letters* 134–36). He had long wished to combine his "two great loves," which were "physics and desert country," and with the founding of Los Alamos he succeeded (Rhodes 451). He also valued the "fraternity" of the international scientific community, concluding his 1945 speech to the Association of Los Alamos Scientists with an admonition to his audience: "remember that the value of science must lie in the world of men, that all our roots lie there." To Oppenheimer, the "strongest bonds in the world" were those "that bind us to our fellow men" (*Letters* 325). J. B. Jackson similarly responded to the "long and immobile" New Mexico summer by feeling that the daily afternoon storms connected him to ancient rites, "some myth made visible for the millionth time" (*Sense of Place* 17). Each of these Anglo residents of mid-twentieth-century New Mexico learned to imagine a world beyond the visible landscape by looking deeply into the present material world.

   The Woman at Otowi Crossing further dramatizes Warner's private experiences of re-emergence and interconnection in order to create imagined spaces of cultural and even global convergence at Otowi Bridge. Although the novel juxtaposes the site's multiple histories, these histories meet under extreme pressure in the figure of Helen Chalmers, Waters's name for Warner. A critical episode pairs her discovery of ancient pottery with an atomic explosion to show how she transformed material and atmospheric ruin into new creation. Chalmers rides into the mountains with Facundo (Tilano), reaches into a hollow, and finds the rim of a bowl painted with a plumed serpent and imprinted with the mark of a woman's thumb. Then she hears "a muffled report from Los Alamos" and immediately feels a "strange sensation as of a cataclysmic faulting of her body, a fissioning of her spirit, and with it the instantaneous fusion of everything about her into one undivided, living whole." Waters prolongs this experience of "unbroken continuity," explaining that in this moment Chalmers felt that nothing "could ever alter this immemorial and rhythmic order. Not the mysterious explosions on the Hill, nor the ever-increasing mechanism and materialism of successive civilizations. . . . With this reassuring conviction, the fierce proudness and humble richness of her life at Otowi Crossing rushed back at her with new significance and challenge" (124–25). In this imagined space of pure sensation, different temporalities, cultures, and natures meet, and deep ecological rhythms triumph over the new science of atomic destruction. Such scenes exemplify the novel, described by Lyon in his introduction to the *Frank Waters Reader* as "the story of Helen Chalmers's coming into a timeless, intuitive, regardful view of existence, not dissimilar from that of some of her Indian friends" (xxvi). Building on Warner's own writings, Waters's novel, too, aims to reconnect lived experience with the natural order. Both texts display reverence for local tradition, an effort to link scientific and spiritual understanding, and a utopian longing for peaceful, ecological integration.

For Chalmers, the return down the mountain to the Crossing also means that everyday life and the local landscape will assume new meaning through the body. Even her later awareness of her own cancer, also described as a "cataclysmic explosion," will yield a new inner reality made meaningful through writing, a reality that "dissolves into eternal meanings" (Waters, *Woman* 21). Whether or not Warner's own visions were delusions, or Waters's narrative mythic in its own way, both accounts imagine a unified space of feeling through the body. Just as Willa Cather created the character of Bishop Latour from Bishop Lamy in *Death Comes for the Archbishop* to mediate physical, spiritual, and historical experiences in New Mexico's desert landscapes, so too does the fictional Helen Chalmers mediate and reconfigure the relation between local experience and imperial ambition.

The centrality of Warner's consciousness, her body, and her house to the novel that intervened to tell the imagined history of Otowi Bridge suggests how women's experiences in modernity, especially within the domestic spaces of private life, do the work of resisting the official histories of regional conquest and global domination.[3] At the time that Waters began his literary reconstruction of Warner and Otowi Crossing, the conceptual opposition between an imposed masculine and militarized scientific community and a native, ecologically aware one was just emerging. This is also roughly the time that Jackson published his first essays in the journal *Landscape* and Lefebvre began to inquire into the social and political significance of space.[4] Waters showed that the figure of a woman's body like Warner's might symbolically heal the divide. At the end of his study, Lefebvre, too, imagined a body that could migrate and produce its own space, "establishing itself firmly, as base and foundation, *beyond philosophy*, beyond discourse, and beyond the theory of discourse" (405–7). Despite the apparent optimism of this vision, he realized that it was not a project for science or even for theory, and he despaired of realizing any "*science of space*" that could produce new knowledge. He admitted that "work in this area has produced either mere descriptions which never achieve analytical, much less theoretical, status, or else fragments and cross-sections of space" (7). Instead of an idealized body or a science of space, Waters gives us the poetics of a historical body—and thus suggests a new praxis for re-inhabiting haunted spaces at the boundaries of physical and metaphysical experience.

Opening Edith's House

The title of the exhibit *Critical Mass* "refers ambiguously to the assemblage of physicists at Los Alamos—literally to the amount of fissionable material necessary to sustain a nuclear chain reaction and more generally to a coming together of cultures and traditions" (Davidov, "Narratives of Place" 42). One of its central pieces was a collection of nine prints Rubenstein displayed as "Edith's House" (fig. 13) that keep opening Warner's domestic interior space to the outdoors, thus mixing environments and states of being. While the viewer is encouraged to focus on the central, grounding images of the hearth and Warner braiding her hair, the surrounding images pull her out into the landscape, whether built or natural. The roof seems to be made of sea, plants, and sky, providing only the shelter of immersion in nature. Like the series of chambers that constituted the exhibit as a whole, "Edith's House" contradicts the very notion that a house or a tearoom could be a private and separate sphere. It gestures instead toward the idea that in the Atomic Age our understanding of home will depend on how we imagine our position in space and on our relation to many natural, cultural, and spiritual worlds. Recall Ellen Meloy's description of the atom: "Atoms are matter, but they also consist of a great deal of empty space." The smallest spaces between electrons are called "deserts." Consequently, "Home is both the mass and the space, the red-boned rock and the places where one tries to shape belief around mystery" (*Last Cheater's Waltz* 223).

Rubenstein displayed many of her photographs for *Critical Mass* in house-like structures, both memorializing and reconfiguring the intimate, cross-cultural community that Warner nurtured. Instead of preserving the house as a space of domestic refuge, the exhibit deconstructs the notion, repeatedly breaking it down and rearranging it according to the complex natural, scientific, and political forces that created it. A photograph of Warner superimposed on "Fat Man"—the bomb detonated over Nagasaki, Japan, on August 9, 1945—similarly creates an eerie juxtaposition of

Figure 13. Meridel Rubenstein, "Edith's House," from the exhibit Critical Mass, 1993. (Courtesy of Meridel Rubenstein)

domestic and technological forms. To Davidov, "this photograph seemed to suggest more than a shattering of the domestic world with its rituals of tea and sympathy"—she also finds "a troubling sexual ambiguity that implies an enigmatic connection" ("Narratives of Place" 46). The image may preserve the capacity for tolerance and spiritual knowledge that Warner symbolized—but only as long as the viewer's gaze rests on her face. Once the viewer looks away, toward the cup and saucer that represent

Figure 14. Meridel Rubenstein, "Fat Man with Edith and Tilano," from the exhibit Critical Mass, 1993. (Courtesy of Meridel Rubenstein)

the comforts of Warner's teahouse, and then back again to apprehend the entire shape of the weapon, she has already begun to follow a path of irreversible destruction and confront a knowledge of the future that Warner only intuited. In another image, Rubenstein superimposes a photograph of Warner and Tilano sitting together on their step on part of the weapon, suggesting the fragility of their companionship and hospitality— and indeed of any human activity in this atomic landscape (fig. 14). The image's central panel shows a hand offering a traditional Pueblo water jug, and its third panel reveals Otowi Bridge and the desert that surrounds it. Each part of the image projected onto "Fatman" is truncated and distorted by the weapon's shape, proving the local culture and landscape of Otowi Bridge to be already transformed by the bomb's existence.

With these photographs and other arrangements of images and voices in *Critical Mass*, Rubenstein and Zweig show "the worlds of scientists and Native Americans as they intersected at the home of Edith Warner during the making of the first atomic bomb in 1944 in Los Alamos, New

Mexico" (Rubenstein, *Belonging* 76). First installed at the Museum of New Mexico in Santa Fe in 1993, their project combines Rubenstein's framed arrangements of still photographs with Zweig's video works "Archimedes' Chamber" and "The Dinner," thus assembling the people and symbols that converged at Warner's house: Oppenheimer, Fermi, and Bohr; Einstein and Archimedes (the Greek mathematician said to have abandoned theory for weapon design late in life); the Pueblo potters Blue Corn and Isabel Atencio, along with other native people and their children; food; the house and bridge at Otowi Crossing; and hand tools and atomic weapons. In "The Meeting," a panel composed of forty pictures of people and artifacts stretching across two walls with a video "hearth" in the corner in between, each portrait is the same size and exerts the same degree of influence. Isabel Atencio, Tilano Montoya's niece, displays her pottery, while physicist Edward Teller clutches his notes. An ear of corn, a pie, the "Jezebel" reactor, an Awanyu pot, and the "Fat Man" all occupy equal, adjacent squares, presenting artifacts, private people, and public figures as potential and contingent symbols for the site's human history.

Rubenstein and Zweig put the figures and artifacts that met at Otowi Crossing into new spatial relations, juxtaposing them, allowing them to observe and speak to one another, and thus "re-creating a sense of the collision of cultures" at this site (Davidov, "Narratives of Place" 59). The organization and mixed media of the installation open the possibility for ongoing, collaborative narration and include the viewer in the process. Like poststructuralist historians, the artists present their project as a means of reconstructing the past from the bottom up and challenging any master narrative: "we enlarge the lives of ordinary people, we strip the mythic characters of history down to their ordinariness, and we replace the usual metaphors about historical figures with images of fallibility and their connection to place."[5] As in Rubenstein's earlier portraits of New Mexican lowriders, the photographs in this exhibition have narrative components, but they tell no official story. With its multiplicity of voices, images, and media, *Critical Mass* creates a seemingly infinite combination of chance encounters. Rubenstein simply assembles the elements that *could* tell a story or become symbols—if the viewer chooses to take the responsibility for performing such interpretive work.

While the exhibit's visual technologies provide one strategy for exploring a landscape's conjunctions of space and time, myth and history, the printed images in *Critical Mass* test the capacity of still photography to transfer moments of seeing into occasions for historical inquiry. Because they arrest, magnify, and call attention to people or details embedded in objects and landscapes we might otherwise overlook, photographic images disrupt our usual patterns of looking at monuments. While Otowi Bridge might initially lure observers with the hope of a personal connection to the past and promise access to knowledge yet to be articulated, images of its ruins can also reveal the decay of meaning, what Jackson calls "the negative image of history" (*A Sense of Place* 23). Along with the remains of buildings and artifacts and the poetics of the body, we need to excavate the complex history of ideas about such places as symbols of global connection or domestic enclosure. Among the many representations of Otowi Bridge, Rubenstein's photographs of Warner most radically reconnect this figure to the social and natural spaces through which she defined herself, and they reconfigure the relation between person and place in ways that allow viewers to imagine Warner's expansive inner life. By alternately opening Warner's body, mind, and house to the surrounding desert in "Edith's House" and projecting them onto the convex surface of "Fat Boy," Rubenstein invites her viewers to imagine the physical experience that shaped everyday life at Otowi Bridge and inhabit the past's many moods.

Breaking and Entering Manzanar

At Manzanar and the other camps built to house Japanese Americans thought to threaten national security during World War II, many prisoners planted gardens, wrote poetry and songs, and drew pictures to keep their imagination and their community alive despite the hard labor and the physical deprivation they endured. Among the literary works produced from the experience of incarceration were Miné Okubo's *Citizen 13660* (1946), Yoshiko Uchida's *Desert Exile* (1982), Jeanne Wakatsuki Houston and James D. Houston's *Farewell to Manzanar* (1973), texts that describe such artistic production and reflect on individual and communal strategies for survival at Manzanar and the other camps. Uchida recalls how people at Tanforan, in California, "all worked constantly to make the windswept racetrack a more attractive and pleasant place" (93) by growing vegetables and flowers. When forced to leave for the Topaz camp in Utah, she remembers feeling that she was being uprooted again: "it had only been a crude community of stables and barracks," she wrote, but because everyone worked to make the space their own, within months it had come to seem like home (103).

As with many aspects of women's wartime experience, outside observers and photographers provided the first and often lasting impressions
of the camps' historic significance. Uchida recounts the importance of
family photographs when she lived in Berkeley before the war; her father
took formal portraits to celebrate every occasion (19). Like many Issei,
first-generation Japanese immigrants, he wanted to document his new
life and share it with the friends and family he continued to visit in Japan.
Photography was another privilege withheld during the period of imprisonment. Government photographers Dorothea Lange, Clem Albers, and
Russell Lee, along with Ansel Adams, visited the camps to document
conditions—and, according to many critics, to make political statements.
According to Davidov, making photographs of the prisoners was very
difficult for Lange. Whereas her work for the FSA allowed her to fulfill
"her sense of her obligation [to the poor] and her ability to disclose and
communicate the truth," as an employee of the War Relocation Authority she worked under "debilitating ambiguity" and constant surveillance.
Davidov reads her images as "rich in content demanding an emotional
response that seemed to . . . insist upon the viewer's sharp recognition
of the fact that war is a contest in which human bodies are the tokens of
victory" ("'The Color of My Skin'" 229).

In contrast to Adams, who published his photographs of Manzanar
almost as artistic landscapes in *Born Free and Equal*, posing prisoners
"against the familiar redeeming mountain terrain to suggest the mythic
possibility of transcending adversity," Lange worked hard to document
"the extraordinary thing that was happening to ordinary people" (Davidov, "'The Color of My Skin'" 233–34). Melody Graulich acknowledges
the "sincerity" of government photographers like Lange, who "recognized
that the Nikkei were indeed victims of racism and of a government eager
to consolidate support for the war effort," but she argues that many of the
images "use Japanese Americans and their experiences as props to support an ironic political statement about American hypocrisy" (224–25).
Both assessments hinge on reading the relation between bodies and their
environment in photographs made under difficult and politically complex
conditions. With the exception of Toyo Miyatake, a photographer and
prisoner who made a camera with smuggled materials and recorded his
own experience from the inside, camp photographers were outsiders who
scrutinized the facades of people and speculated about how the communities worked (Davidov, "'The Color of My Skin'" 236–40). As with other
ruins of this period, gaining any access to the inner lives of internment

camps and of the people incarcerated there required retrospective and collaborative reconstruction.

Engaging in just such a reconstructive project, Joan Myers worked with historian Gary Ohikiro to gather personal narrative, historical background, and visual encounters with the camps' physical remains. In the "Author's Note," Okihiro confessed his initial reluctance to work on the project. As a Japanese American, he had long felt the power of the camps: "The camps, like all traumas, loomed large upon our collective memory. They told us that we mattered little, we were disposable, we were vulnerable and powerless" (Myers and Okihiro 221). Having already written about the period of internment from a historian's perspective and well aware that the subject had received extensive critical treatment, he resisted writing what Myers requested: "a text that is personal and alive with the daily activities, hopes, and tragedies of those who were incarcerated" (9). As he proceeded with the project, however, he began to realize that a text "layered" with many histories could reveal "a deeper stratum in my excavation of self and history" (10). Describing his essay as "interwoven" with "strands and fragments of personal memory, history, and the accounts of historical actors," he expresses his hope that this hybrid form "purposefully explores the borders and interstices of subject and object, subjectivity and objectivity" (10). He suggests that readers think of the photographs and the essay not as comments on each other but as separate texts that "have converged upon a space and time" (10).

Indeed, the texts and images he and Myers produced approach the reconstruction of the past from different directions. When Myers first pulled off the road to explore the camp at Manzanar in 1981, she discovered "a small historical plaque" in the parking lot, crumbling buildings, abandoned gardens, and "small bits of construction debris and household trash: nails, scraps of pine lumber, tin cans, glass and china shards" (13). The site's official marker offered no explanation of the events that had taken place there, but the bits of trash and other material traces of Manzanar's history seemed to demand that the stories of this largely forgotten place be excavated. In fact, it was one of the most useless objects that drew Myers in and urged her to photograph all ten relocation camps: a rubber toy car buried in the sand and cracked from the sun. "Who pushed this palm-sized car around in the sand fifty years ago?" she wondered, reaching toward the vanished, traumatized subject: "Did that child behind barbed wire remember a time when he rode in a real car with a favorite uncle to a family dinner?" (14). The car began to stand for the domestic lives that the Japanese prisoners at Manzanar created for themselves and provided access to feelings and everyday rituals otherwise lost within official or politicized photographs.

Myers's photographs of the camps' remains were presented as a touring exhibit sponsored by the Smithsonian Institution Traveling Exhibition Service and published with Okihiro's text in 1996 as *Whispered Silences*. The photographs resist the explicit impoverishment of the site's official history with the implicit but unrepresented richness of the prisoners' personal experience, and in the process they begin to construct "countermemories": images of unintelligible detail that, unlike remembered scenes, refuse to be integrated into coherent stories. We could place them in a history of war photography, beginning with Matthew Brady's Civil War album and continuing through Lange's internment camp photographs. But in these images, Myers exposes war's destruction and waste through things rather than bodies. Like the photographers associated with the New Topographics, the Rephotographic Survey Project, and the Atomic Photographers Guild, she has, in Mike Davis's words, "recognized the oracular and critical potencies of the commonplace, the discarded, and the ugly" (*Dead Cities* 39). Davis writes about the way that Richard Misrach manipulates the aesthetic qualities of his photographs of nuclear test sites like the writers of Latin American political fiction, "reveal[ing] the terrible, hypnotizing beauty of Nature in its death throes, of Landscape as Inferno. We have no choice but to look" (38). Myers works on a smaller scale: she negotiates the complex aesthetic, political, and personal histories of her sites through precisely framed scenes. But she too turns the aesthetics of western landscape photography against a century's habits of seeing.

The abandoned entry station at Manzanar and the other things Myers finds at the camps function as historical traces whose specific human connections cannot be recovered. In the absence of inhabitants, she tests the capacity of inanimate materials to articulate possible pasts to viewers who did not share them and forges an emotional connection by playing with point of view: some discarded objects she photographs up close, in complete isolation, against neutral black or white backdrops; some ruins are all middle ground, shown in their natural overgrown state; remnants of official structures rise before grander vistas of desert and mountains. Each approach plays on the viewer's knowledge of photographic, cultural, and national histories as it frames junk as art, documents once-cultivated landscapes to suggest their former living state, and displays the futility of controlling nature through constructing fences and buildings.

For example, Myers presents case studies of three ordinary vessels: an empty glass medicine bottle; a Royal Crown cola bottle broken at the neck, label still attached; and an assortment of china shards. None of these generic objects betrays personal history, just proof of general use— medicine was needed, soda was consumed, food was served. By displaying these things in all their mass-produced inscrutability against blank backgrounds, Myers challenges her viewers both to produce meaning for them and accept their status as waste. While the china shards surely evoke a prized ritual of tea drinking and the value art historians place on ancient ruins, again their isolation returns them to plain materiality. The other objects bear no marks of national or ethnic identity and thus might refute the threat of foreignness that ostensibly justified the camps. These images play instead with the fear that the debris of the past will remain unmarked, unclaimed, and meaningless. If we do not pay attention, it will remain trash, the by-product of any cycle of migration, any act of consumption, any repressive legislation.

Whispered Silences also tests the tension between the historical burden of reconstructing the landscape as a prison camp and the aesthetic joy of perceiving form or natural beauty. Consider Myers's photograph titled, "Entrance guard station, Minidoka, Idaho" (fig. 15). The varied textures and tones of the shrubs, rocks, and ground cover in the long foreground engage the viewer's eye first and claim the viewer's attention. Though the still-solid tower and wall of the guard station loom on the horizon, here nature has again become the strongest presence in the landscape. Another view—of the entry station at Manzanar—takes the reverse perspective, setting the massive ruins of the tower's foundations against the grander background of snow-covered mountains (fig. 16). Both ways counter symbols of enclosure and structures of authority with natural expanses, revealing the futility of human ambition to control life in the desert. With photographs of the gardens that prisoners planted, Myers balances man-made ruins with nature's cultivation (figs. 17 and 18). In the images of gardens at Gila River, Arizona, she controls the scale of her images, showing enough of the gardens to suggest their overall design and enough of the surrounding landscape to suggest the natural forces of entropy that the gardeners worked against. The rocks that mark the garden's boundaries seem to become natural gravestones, commemorating the deaths of the prisoners and the life of their artistry at once. Unlike Adams's photographs of the camp nearly a half-century earlier, Myers's images do not imply that natural beauty counters or corrects human suffering. Instead, they

Figure 15. Joan Myers, "Entrance guard station, Minidoka, Idaho," 1996. (Courtesy of Joan Myers)

Figure 16. Joan Myers, "Entry station, Manzanar, CA." (Courtesy of Joan Myers)

show that when we look at the desert we have the choice to see beauty, but such pleasure must also encompass historical knowledge. Visitors to the Pajarito Plateau and the area around Otowi Bridge faced the same challenge of reconciling what they saw with what they knew. In both cases, the viewer's investment in reconstructing the past derives from social or environmental interests made personal through contact with the objects that have survived.

Instead of reconciling these contradictory views, the collection of photographs Myers has arranged emphasizes the importance of remaining attentive to and curious about the landscape, whether driving along ordinary highways or visiting designated historic sites. While we may never know who played with the toy rubber car, who quaffed the elixir, who drank the cola, who planted the gardens, who gazed at the view—much less what they thought—we can notice the features of the object or place we still have in front of us: its streamlined design, its restored ecology, its topographic contours. As Myers invokes modernism's celebration of the mass-produced object and the romance of ruins, she suggests that aesthetic perception is just the beginning of a more complete, historically informed

Figure 17. Joan Myers, "Garden, Gila River, Arizona," 1996. (Courtesy of Joan Myers)

Figure 18. Joan Myers, "Gardens, Manzanar, CA," 1996. (Courtesy of Joan Myers)

response to places once claimed as home. Rather than the aggressive aestheticism of Misrach's photographs, images that produce fascination and horror, Myers's work cultivates an awareness of the ambivalent provenance of ordinary objects and their wayward or unstable aesthetic charges. The photographs show us the beauty of what exists—and the ongoing difficulty of imagining the bridges that could connect us with an increasingly remote past.

Whereas Myers probes the meanings of objects and physical landscapes, Okihiro explores the meanings of inner geographies. Both types of investigation, concrete and psychological, are necessary to connect generations, ethnicities, and locations and to begin the creative reconstruction of a people's "desert exile." Okihiro articulates the relation between the diverse Japanese people who came to America and the generations of Japanese and other Asian Americans who had to find their homelands—"in the stories of our parents and grandparents, in their voices, in their language" (Myers and Okihiro 95)—by orchestrating a wide range of oral narratives. He tells the private histories of the prisoners through the sensations of their bodies, their perceptions of "cold," "hot," "dark," and "light." These opposed and extreme physical states speak directly to the harsh conditions the prisoners endured and indirectly to their inner perceptions and emotions. The camps were located in the kinds of places that would soon become nuclear test sites, "land so desolate and forbidding that no one had tried to develop it" (Davidov, "'The Color of My Skin'" 224). Conditions inside the camp were primitive, with living quarters often improvised from "animal stables given a coat of paint and flimsily constructed barracks—which were to be their protection from extreme weather conditions—blistering summers, freezing winters, dust and sandstorms" ("The Color of My Skin'" 224). Living in barns or barracks without insulation and lacking blankets, imprisoned Japanese Americans struggled to keep warm and to keep faith. Still, Okihiro intersperses evidence of resistance and creativity with the facts of hardship throughout his essay. "Only those who defied the darkness could dare to dream," he explains (Myers and Okihiro 204), "For many, the act of creating restored a semblance of self-control and self-definition. Inscribing one's tracings upon the 'hard earth' helped to dispel the darkness" (205). He then recounts many creative acts, from planting cactus and flower gardens to writing haiku, conducting tea ceremonies, painting, calligraphy, and composing poetry. Such "artists continued their work in the camps and inspired a resurgence of culture and a restoration of cultural identity among a bruised and battered people," he asserts (207).

After gathering all of these artifacts, oral narratives, and personal recollections as evidence of collective strength and creativity, Okihiro evokes the suffering of both his people and Holocaust victims as he utters the following declaration, dedication, and prayer on behalf of the living and the dead: "We will never forget as long as the haunting memories of lonely desert gravesites pursue us still. We will never forget as long as the wind blows cold and hot and the dark gives way to light. We will never forget as long as the grass grows green and the splashing raindrops on stone find their way to the sea. For with commemoration, we define ourselves as human, and with the inscriptions of the past, we reconfigure our destiny" (244). The collective pronoun in this passage refers specifically to Japanese Americans like Okihiro who have struggled to overcome prejudice and shame as twentieth-century citizens of the United States. It also affirmatively links those who survived these camps and others with the generations that followed, forging a collective and enduring memory through the act of speaking. Finally, it widens the scope of the promise not to forget to include all of humanity, suggesting that we all endure suffering and thus share the responsibility for alleviating it, just as we all inhabit a natural world defined by elements, cycles, and seasons. When Okihiro concludes *Whispered Silences* with an appeal to his readers to acknowledge their shared history, making the process of reading ruins and listening for ghosts a matter of patriotic pride, he may well be echoing Uchida's statement of national purpose at the end of *Desert Exile*. Uchida claims to have written the book "for the young Japanese Americans who seek a sense of continuity with the past." She goes on to say, "But I wrote it as well for all Americans, with the hope that through knowledge of the past, they will never allow another group of people in America to be sent into desert exile ever again" (154). For these writers, as for the artists who struggled to represent the environmental legacy of the Atomic Age, the meaning of the twentieth-century Southwest could not be detached from traumatic encounters with the desert's haunted ruins.

The Desert

Black Places and Irradiated Icons

> Revivals and new forms of piety continue to recur, and, whenever
> the existing spatial order proves too restrictive, new sacred groves
> or their equivalents will be discovered and used. Each such
> episode will reveal the link which has always existed between
> various forms of religious belief and the manner in which space
> and time are perceived.
> —J. B. Jackson, *The Necessity for Ruins*, 88

In 1941, during a flight from Albuquerque to New York, Georgia O'Keeffe
wrote to Maria Chabot of the "breathtaking" view below. As she gazed
over the desert, she saw the arrangement of water, mountains, and earth
as a work of art, like a "marvelous rug" or "abstract paintings" (Chabot
and O'Keeffe, *Chabot–O'Keeffe* 12). Such a perception of intricately organized natural patterns also rendered the desert a sacred space that offered
refuge from the struggles of O'Keeffe's life and the tumult of the Depression. Mircea Eliade distinguishes sacred from profane space in just such
terms—whereas profane space lacks differentiation, sacred space has a
composite organization that allows those who cross its threshold to imagine approaching a spiritual center. O'Keeffe explained the New Mexican
desert to Chabot similarly: "The world all simplified and beautiful and
clear cut in pattern like time and history will simplify and straighten out
these times of ours—What one sees from the air is so simple and beautiful
I cannot help feeling that it would do something wonderful for the human
race" (*Chabot–O'Keeffe* 12).

The New Mexican desert has long made visible "the dramatic confron-
tation between the new and mobile and optimistic human installation on
the one hand, and the overpowering 'timelessness' of an ancient landscape
with its cosmic chronology on the other" (Jackson, *A Sense of Place* 25).
While outsiders from the earliest colonizers to the Gold Rush pioneers

viewed the desert as a forbidding place full of famine and cruelty, "a hellish landscape of useless sandy sweeps and lava cones" (Wild 1), more recent settlers, freed from the practical constraints of mere survival, have looked to the desert's apparent emptiness for personal fulfillment. Taking advantage of modern technologies such as irrigation, easy transportation, and air-conditioning, many twentieth-century desert dwellers deliberately rejected civilization in favor of what seemed to be a more authentic natural world.[1] In *Savage Dreams*, Rebecca Solnit articulates the desert's psychological and spiritual dimensions for outsiders and natives in the twentieth century:

> Solitude, emptiness and silence, the forbidding climate and scale of the land, the slender margin for survival—all these things affect a mind used to a more crowded, lusher world. . . . Here in the silence, voices that cannot be heard elsewhere, the voices of one's own fears and dreams and the voices of the geologic earth, the sky, the wind, and death, murmur to the traveler. For those in pursuit of such spiritual knowledge, the desert is the best place to hear the voice of the whirlwind; for those who aren't, it is a terrifying place.(62)

Peter Wild explores the irony of seeking spiritual truth in this land of hardship in *The Opal Desert*, explaining that in the twentieth century, "old ideas about exploitation became mixed with new ideas about beauty, spirituality, and notions of regaining our pioneer heritage" (2).

The choice to build Los Alamos in northern New Mexico followed from an understanding of the desert as an unclaimed and potentially spiritual space, but the first nuclear test at Alamogordo in southern New Mexico on July 16, 1945, further complicated the modern desert's contradictory meanings. Many writers have noted that J. Robert Oppenheimer selected New Mexico as the place to develop the atomic bomb because of its austerity, grandeur, and beauty. Los Alamos made the desert a refuge for scientists; the Trinity Site made the desert a place where utter destruction was realized. Those who witnessed the first nuclear explosion at Trinity seemed to see a sun of their own creation and responded with their own forms of worship. While Oppenheimer reportedly claimed that at that moment physicists suddenly knew sin, others interpreted the sight as proof of redemption. "Victor Weisskopf said he thought instantly, as he watched the orange fireball levitating amid its electric-blue halo, 'of Grünewald's Christ ascending in the *Resurrection*'" (Johnson n.p.). Solnit proposes that the bomb's invention changed the world's cosmology as profoundly as the defining biblical events of the expulsion from Paradise, the Flood, and the Resurrection. With the detonation of "Fat Man" and "Little Boy" over Hiroshima and Nagasaki, Los Alamos at once became the origin of a new science of destruction and the center of a new kind of profane world. After the bombs, after the buildup of radiation from decades of nuclear testing, after the incomplete burial of toxic waste, the boundary between sacred and profane spaces dissolved. While still holding its appeal for outsiders as a landscape that offered refuge or reinvention, the desert also became a place whose pervasive and invisible contamination challenged human attempts to assert hierarchies, draw boundaries, and create sanctuaries.

The era that preceded Trinity—the Depression—defined trauma in terms of wounds to a national body. The people who suffered needed work and new places to live, practical demands that could be substantially met by New Deal programs. Marginal figures, like the "Forgotten Man" in Busby Berkeley's delirious musical number in the film *42nd Street*, the Joad family in *The Grapes of Wrath*, and Maria in *People of the Valley*, celebrated physical vitality as they embodied the social problems wrought by unemployment, migration, and urbanization. The war marked "the end of an era as the nation turned outward, from contemplation of its own wounded body politic during the Great Depression, toward the defense of ideologies in which *other* wounded bodies would figure as signs of this nation's restored health and power" (Davidov, "'The Color of my Skin'" 223). In the Atomic Age, social and global ills began to take physical forms more difficult to represent and resolve.

In this chapter, I show how representations of the Southwestern desert produced just before the Trinity Test and in the last decades of the twentieth century make visible the mythic and environmental threats of the Atomic Age and begin to transfigure the iconography of the desert.[2] I begin by looking at how Georgia O'Keeffe made the New Mexican landscape into a kind of sacred space through her aesthetic organization of nature and through her rituals of visiting, naming, and painting distinctive sites. As Ann Ronald observes, O'Keeffe "taught us . . . to interpret the high New Mexico desert landscape more evocatively than before," and she did so by focusing "on the primordial shapes and colors that lie beneath the foreground of our visual awareness." O'Keeffe "turned the earth inside out, interiorized the exterior, somehow saw behind the strata"—and thus opened the surface of the landscape (*Ghost West* 155–56). I focus on the transformation of O'Keeffe's persona after leaving New York and on her studies of the Black Place, arguing that her relocated life and painted landscapes created a precedent for writers in the post-Atomic Age who pursued the desert's environmental, spiritual, and philosophical knowledge through similar rituals of contact, immersion, and articulation.

In the rest of this chapter, I consider a variety of texts that open the boundaries between bodies exposed to radiation and the contaminated worlds they inhabit, including Leslie Marmon Silko's novel *Ceremony* (1977), Terry Tempest Williams's memoir *Refuge* (1991), Carole Gallagher's documentary *American Ground Zero* (1993), and Ellen Meloy's naturalist narrative *The Last Cheater's Waltz* (1999). These texts alternately narrate the experience of the body and represent the gap between the surface of the protagonists' desert homeland and its hidden contamination. Akira Lippit has proposed that the nuclear detonations at Hiroshima and Nagasaki irrevocably "exposed the fragility of the human surface"; afterward, the constitution of the human body could no longer be taken for granted, and "new *phenomenologies of the inside*: psychoanalysis, X-rays, and cinema" aimed to expose such interiority (*Atomic Light* 4, 5). In the post-Atomic Age, I argue, the permeability of both body and landscape becomes a means of figuring a world where human and natural realms can no longer be divided, nor sacred space contained.

The Black Places of O'Keeffe Country

By the beginning of the Atomic Age, O'Keeffe had already claimed the area around Ghost Ranch in the Piedra Lumbra basin as her chosen home, having visited regularly during the summer of each year beginning in 1936. According to Barbara Lynes, leaving New York allowed her "to define herself to the American public in her own way and on her own terms and to craft a public persona that not only countered, but also ultimately replaced, the one Stieglitz, as impresario of her career, had established" ("Identity and Place" 39). O'Keeffe's letters provide ample evidence of the affinity she felt with the landscape. In 1929, on a trip to Taos and through the Southwest with Dorothy Strand, she wrote to Henry McBride, "You know I never feel at home anywhere like I do out here. I finally feel in the right place again, I feel like myself again and I like it" (qtd. in Lynes, "Identity and Place" 41). If, as Eliade explains in *The Sacred and the Profane*, "to settle somewhere, to inhabit a space, is equivalent to repeating the cosmogony and hence to imitating the work of the gods" (65), then O'Keeffe's decision to settle in New Mexico after a nervous breakdown in 1933 can be understood as a personal and religious decision to re-center and apotheosize herself within a sacred space. To feel "right" and like herself meant to feel at home—and to occupy a place where she could open her body to the environment. Sharyn Udall describes O'Keeffe's relation to her new landscape as exploratory and sensuous. "Her geography was one of expansiveness and release," Udall explains. "Where other artists might have risked the loss of self in this territory beyond mapping, she embraced the distance as a means of nurturing and sustaining the self" (196). After studying Hopi kachinas and witnessing the Hopi Snake Dance, a Zuni Shalako night ceremony, and a Navajo healing ceremony, O'Keeffe learned to approach the landscape reverently, too. Just as for the natives of the desert Southwest, for O'Keeffe the "holy places" became the mountains, canyons, water, earth, and air that surrounded her (Udall 239).

Such a conception of the desert as a multilayered aesthetic and religious space informed O'Keeffe's extensive work in the Southwest. It also allowed her to shift public attention from her isolated body to the natural subjects of her work. In the 1920s, O'Keeffe's body, as photographed by Stieglitz, represented a modernist ideal.[3] A decade later, however, O'Keeffe used Southwestern materials and landscapes to create icons of her own: luminous cow's skulls and pelvic bones set against brilliant turquoise skies; the White Place north of Abiquiu; and, notably, the Black Place, the subject of the "last great series" of landscapes she painted at least twelve times (*Georgia O'Keeffe* 478). From the early 1940s until the end of her life, these iconic subjects both derived from her intimate knowledge of desert places and revealed new experiments with abstraction. At the same time, by moving to northern New Mexico and immersing herself in its land and cultures, she helped to produce a public identity "as a courageous, self-disciplined pioneer, whose artistic success was the result of self-imposed isolation and hard work" (Lynes, "Identity and Place" 47). Christopher Merrill ventures that she became "a cultural icon" because, in an era that seemed to require male artists to choose between a complete life and their profession, "she made her life an integral part of her work"—viewers admired her "as much for how she lived as for her paintings" (*From the Faraway Nearby* 1). Her public persona became increasingly entwined with the austere images of the desert and the houses she lived in, a connection that she promoted in interviews, produced on canvas, and staged in photographic portraits. When O'Keeffe expressed the hope that "the human race" would find something wonderful in the formal arrangement of the New Mexican landscape, she spoke to the possibility that her ability to open herself to the desert and thus gain redemption could extend to people who saw it, like she did, as sacred ground. Ronald describes exactly this difference in perception when she confesses that she sees the Piedra Lumbre as "a trickster mountain discolored by the smog. Georgia O'Keeffe saw a sacred place, its outline crisp and clear, its silhouette a solemn source of energy and myth" (158).

The place that O'Keeffe named simply the Black Place seemed to resist realistic depiction and to test her ability to orient herself in her chosen home. Located 150 miles west of Ghost Ranch, it was dramatically void of trees and vegetation, not easily accessible, and subject to harsh weather. O'Keeffe discovered it while taking a guided tour through Navajo country in 1940. Each return journey required substantial planning and a camping companion—usually Chabot, an aspiring writer who took care of Ranchos de los Burros (the house at Ghost Ranch that O'Keeffe first stayed in as a paying guest of Arthur Pack's family and then bought in 1940) during the summers from 1941 to 1945. Working beside O'Keeffe, Chabot raised vegetables, cooked, and organized painting expeditions. She came to love the landscape as O'Keeffe did, explaining that "the Piedra Lumbre is the best thing I've ever known in New Mexico—the closest thing to God, I guess."[4]

In the summer of 1941, the two women visited the White Place twice and, in early November, made two trips to the Black Place (*Chabot–O'Keeffe* 11). When they returned in October, 1943, Chabot reported on the excursion to Stieglitz, describing how they witnessed the "magic" of the beginning of winter, the new movement of bushes and trees, and the "miraculous blue" of the sky. Even when the north wind began to blow and clouds appeared everywhere, O'Keeffe kept painting. "You off there in the city cannot know what clouds mean when you are 150 miles from nowhere," she explained, "—with only a narrow strip of road connecting you with four walls and a fire in a stove." She described their rustic camp, their collapsing tent, the difficulty of keeping the fire going, and her confidence that O'Keeffe's single painting, not yet started, "will be the best thing yet of the black country" because of their powerful encounter with the place and the sky itself. After a summer of working the bean fields, culminating in this trip, Chabot had "an utterly new respect and awe of the sky" that she believed only her companion could communicate visually (125). O'Keeffe's own narrative of this trip makes the weather seem much less inspiring. It focuses on the wind and heavy rain that caused one corner of their tent to collapse and produced "a pale dawn, as dismal as anything

I've ever seen—everything grey; grey sage, grey wet sand underfoot, grey hills, big gloomy-looking clouds, a very pale moon—and still the wind" (*Georgia O'Keeffe* 60). Under such conditions, she could not drink a full cup of coffee, much less paint; she "finally painted it from memory—red and later green."

Black Place III (fig. 19), painted in 1944, depicts a formation of hills that seem to project vertically rather than recede toward the horizon. Bisected by the irregular zigzags of a stream flowing deep in a blackened canyon, the landscape consists of cliffs that could not be climbed and surfaces that could not be traversed. The sharp, dark edges of the cliffs face the viewer, and the surface contours beyond create slippery bulges or recesses so deep they seem to plunge the eye down to the stream below. A white band of hills in the distance appears at first like a bank of clouds, but it is a false horizon, with more grey rocks extending to the edges of the canvas. The stream flows between the white hills, too, with no point of origin in sight. The painting blurs conventional separations between near and far, surface and depth, and even black and white. Located at the intersection of seeing and feeling, this Black Place represents an otherworldliness, a desert space whose meaning resists enclosure and easy interpretation.

Whereas O'Keeffe's first studies of the site, like *Grey Hills* (1941), "were rather straightforward descriptions of the rise to a high horizon, a geological oddity of low gray hills crowned with black and banded with pink" (Eldredge 114), her subsequent work paid closer attention to the formation's deep recesses, exaggerated its verticality, and explored the process of organizing the landscape. Lynes has observed that when O'Keeffe "emphasized the V-shape of the canyon's entrance" in her paintings of the White Place, she was continuing her exploration of an abstract form evident in her early work in more literal terms. Lynes calls *Black Place III*, by contrast, a painting that aims "to summarize, not specify visual experience" because it is a "synthesis of forms that may have been extracted from several sites" (*O'Keeffe and New Mexico* 45–46). In a review for *The New York Times* on January 28, 1945, Edward Alden Jewell called this third painting "the true climax of the series"—even, he hazarded, "one of the climaxes of O'Keeffe's career."[5] As O'Keeffe became more familiar with the Black Place (she painted it at least twelve times between 1942 and 1949, creating the later canvasses from memory), she simplified its design, revealing a typical working process of "ultimately 'possessing' a motif through its distillation to barest essentials, and then moving on to new pictorial

Figure 19. Georgia O'Keeffe, *Black Place III*, 1944. (Copyright Georgia O'Keeffe Museum)

challenges" (Eldredge 116). Meanwhile, each visit to the site became part of a ritual pilgrimage, which rewarded the artist's close attention, as changes in angles of light and the intensity of shadow precisely conveyed shifts in a season. When she was elsewhere, knowledge of it gave her sustenance. "I have been working on a pastel of the Black Place," she wrote to Chabot from New York on December 3, 1945. Though it seemed far away, "It is fine however to think of it all alone and windblown and lonely—all out there in the sun and the stars—without us—Oh—it is good to know it is there—" (*Chabot-O'Keeffe* 298).

O'Keeffe's series of encounters with the Black Place coincided with the scientific experimentation at Los Alamos and the release of the atomic

bombs over Japan to end World War II. Both aesthetic and atomic inves-
tigations in the desert led to intense reflection on the meaning of human
aspiration and religious experience. As witnesses to natural processes that
seemed to elude full human control, artists and scientists bore responsibility for the knowledge they gained, and they aimed to communicate this
knowledge. Poling-Kempes explains that even though the details of atomic
development at Los Alamos were not fully revealed until the United States
dropped a bomb on Hiroshima on August 6, 1945, "the presence of an
ultraimportant, top-secret, war-related project on the Hill was common
knowledge" to the rural residents of northern New Mexico, who could not
help but notice the sudden arrival of military personnel, scientists, and
equipment on the Pajarito Plateau (*Ghost Ranch* 153). Through their own
experience in the region and especially through their association with the
Packs at Ghost Ranch, where many scientists came to relax, O'Keeffe and
Chabot surely knew a great deal about the potential of the Manhattan
Project. In fact, in the next paragraph of the same letter that describes
remembering the Black Place, O'Keeffe mentions "the 'Bomb' men" at Los
Alamos, including a man named Mike she knew had been part of the project for two years. Chabot had just written about a function she attended at
the Laboratory of Anthropology in Santa Fe, where the scientists involved
with the Project "showed a colored movie of the Hiroshima bombing—a
beautiful and frightening thing." These "thoughtful men" also reflected
on their responsibility for the destruction, just as Einstein did in an essay
published in November of that fateful year in *Atlantic* magazine. "There
seems no question that we must abandon the primitive idea of boundaries
and sovereignty," Chabot concludes in the letter (*Chabot–O'Keeffe* 297).

O'Keeffe's sustained meditation throughout the 1940s on a place she
defined through its absence of color seemed to test her ability to organize the desert into aesthetic patterns and maintain boundaries between
types of space. Her many trips back to the site and her repetition of the
title, varied only by the addition of a number or article, suggest that she
sought to understand the meaning of "blackness" and its association with
the unknown.[6] Mary Douglas observes in *Purity and Danger* that ritual
"can come first in formulating experience. It can permit knowledge of
what would otherwise not be known at all. It does not merely externalise
experience, bringing it out into the light of day, but it modifies experience in so expressing it" (79). O'Keeffe's repeated returns to the Black
Place constituted a kind of secular ritual that allowed her to expand her
iconography of the desert to include encounters with the unknown. Like

all rituals, it involved contact with a symbolic form of death in order to break down old categories of identity and make way for new forms of art. If the desert light served to purify O'Keeffe's life and her aesthetic vision, leading her toward a series of studies of bleached bones and of the White Place, the Black Place paintings remained her signification of the desert's yet-unrealized threat.

Contaminated Homelands

While O'Keeffe was thrilled to see the patterns of the desert from above, writers like Leslie Marmon Silko, Terry Tempest Williams, and Ellen Meloy sought to represent the desert's forces of creation and the human legacy of atomic destruction from below. As they delved deeply into places that had been and would continue to be sacred to their communities, families, and themselves, they discovered the devastating effects of uranium mining and nuclear testing. In response, they constructed narratives that both reveal the land's hidden history of contamination and seek to reconcile evidence of ruin with new acts of faith. In an essay on desert cultures, Roger Dunsmore argues that "there is a human way of the desert that fulfills the desert, every bit as much as there is a desert way of the human that fulfill the human being" (104). Each of the writers discussed here explores a reciprocal process of fulfillment, one that originates in their native faith and then moves beyond their culture's traditional religious practices. These stories thus profess the necessity of internalizing the "local, external world" in order to survive in the desert with "power and beauty" (Dunsmore 113).

Ceremony reimagines Silko's storied homeland after the horror of the atomic bomb. The novel revolves around the journey of Tayo, a mixed-blood man from Laguna Pueblo who returns from serving in World War II with nightmares about the Japanese men he refused to kill; his cousin and fellow soldier, Rocky, who died; and his uncle Josiah whom he imagines he killed. The novel enacts an intricate series of rituals to heal Tayo's trauma and that of the Laguna people. Although Silko begins the novel at sunrise, with Tayo returned to his ancestral land, she immediately indicates that while her protagonist may have returned home physically, he has not yet integrated his interior landscape, or "the internalized place world of the mind," and the exterior landscape, which includes the pueblo's relation to the nation and the world. Unable to sleep, wracked with nausea, inarticulate, haunted by memories of battle and death, and filled with guilt about betraying his family, Tayo "experiences ultimate deterritorialization" (Arnold 72). Only by restoring deeper memories of his uncle and his sensory connections to the landscape will he succeed in reimagining his homeland and becoming fully human.

By figuring Tayo's alienation through his body and reinforcing it through his uncontrollable flashbacks of soldiers and civilians destroyed by warfare, Silko locates one source of his deterritorialization in the development and detonation of nuclear weapons. At the veterans' hospital, Tayo feels like a mere "outline" of a body, like a *hibakusha*, the Japanese term for a person whose body was penetrated by radiation at Hiroshima or Nagasaki. Doctors, nurses, and other patients "saw his outline but they did not realize it was hollow inside" (Silko, *Ceremony* 13). He walks through the hospital's disinfected hallways like a zombie, living in a seemingly perpetual twilight. As he realizes later, in the hospital he was outside of time and able to see only death in the future: "He inhabited a gray winter fog on a distant elk mountain where hunters are lost indefinitely and their own bones mark the boundaries" (13). Once home, he still has "the feeling that there was no place left for him; he would find no peace in that house where the silence and the emptiness echoed the loss" (30) of Rocky and Josiah. Whereas in the jungle it was the rain that seemed endless, at home the desert seems to be suffering an endless drought caused, Tayo fears, by his own malevolent prayers.

Over the protests against "Indian medicine" voiced by his aunt and the Army doctor, Tayo's grandmother seeks the help of Ku'oosh, a traditional medicine man. Ku'oosh smells and speaks like the past, his skin redolent of "mutton tallow and mountain sagebrush," his language "the old dialect full of sentences that were involuted with explanations of their own origins, as if nothing the old man said were his own but all had been said before and he was only there to repeat it" (31). He provides Tayo with powerful reminders of sacred places and an important lesson about the fragile nature of the world. In her essay "Interior and Exterior Landscapes," Silko presents her understanding of landscape as a delicate web that encompasses "[t]he land, the sky and all that is within them," including humans. "Interrelationships in the Pueblo landscape are complex and fragile," she writes, and "[s]urvival depended upon harmony and cooperation not only among human beings, but also among all things" (7). This is the understanding that Ku'oosh presents to Tayo. He, too, states, "this world is fragile." Then he slowly explains the nuances of the notion of fragility and the intricate connections between words and the stories that give them meaning. However, despite his wisdom and his experience in promoting healing and restoring the balance in his native landscape, Ku'oosh lacks the ability to confront—and even to imagine—the horrors of "the white people's war." Traditional wars could not be conducted without direct combat, but the white warfare Tayo witnessed involved "killing across great distances without knowing who or how many had died," a monstrous affair that "the old man would not have believed" even if he had seen it (Silko, *Ceremony* 33). Tayo realizes, "Ku'oosh would have looked at the dismembered corpses and the atomic heat-flash outlines, where human bodies had evaporated, and the old man would have said something close and terrible had killed these people. Not even oldtime witches killed like that" (33–34). Later, Tayo's grandmother confirms the inability of the older generation to comprehend nuclear weapons when she remembers seeing the white light from the explosion at Trinity: "So big, so bright even my old clouded-up eyes could see it. It must have filled the whole southeast sky. I thought I was seeing the sun rise again, but it faded away. . . . You know, I have never understood that thing I saw" (227–28). Silko suggests that if modern white warfare lies outside the Pueblo imagination, seeming "monstrous" in its inhumanity, nuclear warfare lies beyond tribal—and perhaps any human—comprehension. Attributable only to the worst witchery, the sudden transformation of humans into "outlines" can be reversed by neither traditional healing methods nor Western medicine.

Ku'oosh's failure to imagine a nuclear landscape provides the initial and imperative reorientation of Tayo's consciousness. As Cherokee scholar Sean Teuton argues, "Until he reconsiders his supposed hallucinations in Laguna terms, as informative religious experiences, Tayo struggles against the forces that encourage him to grow and to become part of a dynamism that not only reveals the inherent balance of the living world, but also weaves humans into the web of relations that sustains it."[7] It is essential that Tayo understand first the boundary that divides Pueblo and white consciousness so that he can begin to reconstruct his tribal identity; the release of the atomic bombs over Hiroshima and Nagasaki confirms that boundary. Ku'oosh presents a compelling example of how Pueblo people chose to live and sustain their humanity before their coerced involvement in World War II. The teachers Tayo seeks during the rest of his journey, including Betonie and Ts'eh, show the way toward adapting and developing new means of survival in the post-atomic world.

It will take the inventive and inclusive ceremony devised by the Navajo healer Betonie to raise Tayo's consciousness of the origin of his loss in the white people's theft of Pueblo land and to restore Tayo's ability to feel his environment with all of his senses. Cherokee scholar Daniel Justice explains, "Rather than conforming to the Eurowestern philosophy of dualism that splits the cosmos into differentiated fragments that can be designated, as per religion historian Mircea Eliade, either 'sacred' or 'profane,' most Native spiritual traditions (and thus literary traditions) draw upon a perspective that experiences *all* existence as sacred" (172). After Tayo leaves Betonie, he begins to feel this integration again. Rather than riding in a truck, he wants "to walk until he recognized himself again" and notices how sounds like the buzz of grasshoppers and the crackle of dead sunflower stalks surround him (Silko, *Ceremony* 143). His friends Harley, Emo, and Leroy cannot forget the overwhelming and alienating sensations of being in cities and fighting with weapons—as Ts'eh explains to Tayo, "Only destruction is capable of arousing a sensation, the remains of something alive in them" (213). Tayo, however, begins to replace his own recent memories with the more powerful feelings of re-immersion in his homeland. Gradually, as he realizes the deceit of the white people who told him lies, claimed his cattle, and stole his land, he can sing again and feel that "the instant of the dawn was an event in which a single moment gathered all things together" (169). By the time he returns to the ranch to take care of Josiah's cattle, he is certain that despite his losses, "nothing was lost; all was retained between the sky and the earth, and within himself" (204). Because of this internal conviction, Tayo can look at the mountainside, feel its motion from within, and know that "the world was alive" (205).

In both her essay and the novel, Silko addresses the way the U.S. government's "decision in the early 1950s to begin open-pit mining of the huge uranium deposits north of Laguna, near Paguate village has had a powerful psychological impact upon the Laguna people. Already a large body of stories has grown up around the subject of what happens to people who disturb or destroy the earth" ("Landscapes" 21). The mining destroyed land where people used to cultivate gardens and orchards, and after the miners dug out the uranium they abandoned the site, leaving behind deep pits, barbed wire fences, stripped shacks, and dead cattle. In *Ceremony* Tayo observes that "[t]he sandstone and dirt [the miners] had taken from inside the mesa was piled in mounds, in long rows, like fresh graves" (227). As Teuton notes, many environmental critics read the end of *Ceremony* "as an allegorical call to practice vigilance for destructive ecological actions," and others read it as a cautionary tale specifically aimed to raise awareness about the dangers of nuclear weapons (140). Tayo's understanding that the ambition to destroy land and people can be an even more powerful unifying force than belief certainly supports these interpretations, but I agree with Teuton's view that Silko simultaneously invites environmental allegories and inscribes Tayo's story within larger mythological patterns, thus combining "mythic and material" elements in ways that sustain a tribal understanding of human experience (140). While standing on the abandoned uranium mine, Tayo finally connects the warfare in Japan with its technological origins in his desert homeland just one hundred miles from Los Alamos and three hundred miles from the Trinity Site. He realizes that all humans could be understood as "united by a circle of death" or by the white witchery that spanned twelve thousand miles (Silko, *Ceremony* 228), and at this point he finally grasps the urgency of resisting a conception of his home as contaminated with the lived experience of his body and the sacred stories he has learned.

Williams's memoir *Refuge* also layers descriptions of natural catastrophe to narrate a process of healing. As Williams tests the resemblance between two kinds of disaster—the flood that threatens bird habitats around the Great Salt Lake and nuclear fallout—she explores the significance of the birds' habitat and the power of the desert to restore spiritual health to her mother and herself. Organized around the behavior and fate of different species of birds, each chapter of *Refuge* traces the relation between natural phenomena, which can be observed, and human sickness and loss, which can only be felt. Each stage of spiritual recovery requires the body's presence, whether imagined through her mother's physical suffering or experienced through her own senses. As Douglas explains in *Purity and Danger*, the body "provides a basic scheme for all [religious] symbolism"; its persistence reminds us that no part of our experience can be "rejected outright" (202).

Williams repeatedly insists that she belongs fully in the natural world, first to claim protection from the trauma of her mother's death and then to write it into the landscape. She compares herself to the vulnerable creatures that inhabit the Bear River Migratory Bird Refuge and represents her own body as coextensive with their endangered habitat: "The birds and I share a natural history. It is a matter of rootedness, of living inside a place for so long that the mind and imagination fuse" (*Refuge* 21). Walking along the "wrackline" of the Great Salt Lake, she finds a landscape of ruins that corresponds to the breakdown of her mother's body and her family: "a bleached narrative of feathers, bones, occasional birds encrusted in salt"

(120). Williams explains that usually if one place becomes flooded and uninhabitable, birds seek a home on higher ground. Now, hemmed in by roads and an ever-bigger airport, there is no new habitat to be found. "Without these places of refuge, successful migrations would cease for millions of birds," she warns (264); without the refuge of family and faith, she, too, could lose her emotional home and be forced to abandon her migratory pursuit of spiritual understanding and healing.

Williams searches hard for the spiritual insight that her mother discovered through accepting her sickness and immersing herself in the desert. When Diane Tempest first battled cancer in 1971, her mother Mimi described the surgery that would remove the tumor in her breast as "one of the most spiritual experiences you will ever encounter." After the operation, Diane confessed to her husband and her children that she had "felt the arms of God around [her]" (282). When she discovered a new tumor after her previous battle with cancer twelve years before, she chose to continue with her trip down the Colorado River in search of healing and peace. She explained to her daughter, "In the long run I didn't think one month would matter. In the short run, it mattered a great deal. The heat of the sandstone penetrated my skin as I lay on the red rocks. Desert light bathed my soul. And traveling through the inner gorge of Vishnu schist, the oldest exposed rock in the West, gave me a perspective that will carry me through whatever I must face. Those days on the river were a meditation, a renewal" (29). By distinguishing between the inevitable arrival of death and the present satisfaction of "bathing" the soul with rock, light, and heat, Diane argued for the necessity of spiritual revelation to counter and transcend her body's physical decline. In nature she found "my peace, my solitude" (86) and "the intimacy of all that is real" (87).

When her mother dies, Williams tries to deepen her own ecological and spiritual awareness by rendering the desert's inner life. One day, she discovers a dead whistling swan. She finds no evidence of human intervention such as a gunshot wound, but rather a single, fresh corpse. Barely aware of the passage of time, Williams prepares the bird for burial, covering its eyes with stones and washing its bill and feet with her own saliva. Then she lies down next to the bird's body and imagines herself inside it.

> I imagined the great heart that propelled the bird forward day after day, night after night. Imagined the deep breaths taken as it lifted from the arctic tundra, the camaraderie within the flock. I imagined the stars

seen and recognized on clear autumn nights as they navigated south. Imagined their silhouettes passing in front of the full face of the harvest moon. And I imagined the shimmering Great Salt Lake calling the swans down like a mother, the suddenness of the storm, the anguish of its separation.

And I tried to listen to the stillness of its body. (121–22)

Here Williams reconstructs what she could not have seen: the interior of the bird, its rhythmic breaths, and its feelings of fellowship. She conjures voices that she could not have heard: the lake's maternal "calling" and the bird's sounds of silence. This episode reenacts the paradox of evoking meaning from absence and human community from death that she faced in narrating her mother's cancer—and that writers in the post–Atomic Age continue to confront. It reconfigures an individual death as ecological trauma, both extending the range of human relations to include all living things and articulating experience that can be known only non-rationally, through faith or imagination.

As her narrative complicates the desert's visual signification, Williams also engages in her own private rituals, such as the process of purifying herself through writing about her imagined immersion in the dead bird's body. Afterward, Williams declares renewed faith in the desert and repeats her creed: "I believe in walking in a landscape of mirages, because you learn humility. I believe in living in a land of little water because life is drawn together. And I believe in the gathering of bones as a testament to spirits that have moved on." She claims "it is here," in the salt flats, that "I find grace" and "remember the sacred" (148). The official funeral for her mother, by contrast, seems empty and grotesque. She and her grand-mother Mimi carefully prepare the body, bathing it with perfume and dressing it with a white French cotton gown, satin stockings and slippers, and a green satin apron hand sewn by a great aunt long ago. Williams had admired her mother's beauty and elegance when they shopped together at Bloomingdale's. This final ritual seems to secure the consistently exquisite appropriateness of her mother's appearance. It also confirms their final separation and reveals her inability to control her mother's social repre-sentation. Though she tries to dress the body properly and remove the ghastly makeup applied at the funeral home, the mortician overrides her efforts. Arriving early to the funeral to meditate, she finds "The face paint was back on." Her response is outrage "at our inability to let the dead be dead," and she weeps "over the hollowness of our rituals" (235).

Afterward, Williams explains, she needed "a celebration to move me from death to life" (276). She decides to go to Mexico, to the village of Tepoztlán, on the eve of el Día de los Muertos. First she wanders through the market and buys marigolds and an owl mask. Then she follows a man who had bought many masks and asks him what she should know about the Day of the Dead. He directs her to an adobe shrine up the hill with a turquoise door where she finds other villagers waiting and praying. In the company of fellow worshippers, Williams feels that her "individual sorrow was absorbed into a sea of collective tears" (277). She sees the spirits of the dead enter two women and a child, possessing them and then releasing them from grief. "Their stories were not so unlike my own," Williams realizes. "It was the reverberation of tone I recognized, like a piece of music you return to again and again that awakens the soul. The voices of my Dead came back to me" (278). At night, she joins the village's celebration and processes to the cemetery, where survivors offer food, photographs, flowers, and candles at family graves. When one woman explains that on this day "the Dead are among us," Williams realizes that fundamental boundaries have dissolved; through making contact with the dead and accepting contamination, the ritual creates a new community. Although she struggled to find peace and acceptance in her native landscape, immersing herself in Mexico and its folk tradition allows her to release her anger, celebrate her mother's life, open herself for healing, and return home whole.

The narrative ends with a declaration of militancy, gradually replacing the disordered patterns of loss with descriptions of rituals of reinvention and acts of political protest. The epilogue speaks directly against the Mormon culture of obedience, which, in Williams's view, "ultimately killed rural communities in Utah during atmospheric testing of atomic weapons." The deaths of her mother and grandmother lead Williams to "question everything, even if it means losing my faith, even if it means becoming a member of a border tribe among my own people" (286). Fighting her isolation and her recurrent nightmare of nuclear explosion, she describes a dream of women gathering from all over the world, pledging to adopt Native perspectives, honor nature, and celebrate "the witch inside themselves" as they sing an old Shoshone song. "They would reclaim the desert for the sake of their children, for the sake of the land" (287), the dream seems to promise, echoing and feminizing Ácoma poet Simon Ortiz's subtitle to *Fight Back: For the Sake of the Land, For the Sake of the People* (1980), an impassioned sequence of poems and stories that narrates the experience of working in the uranium industry. Soon, however, the blast of a nuclear test destroys this ecofeminist utopia, scarring the earth and galvanizing the women to protest the assault on their power. Unlike natural labor, which held "the promise of birth," the "pains beneath the desert promised death only, as each bomb became a stillborn" (288). The women begin to walk toward "the contaminated country," and suddenly it becomes clear that the dream is real. They duck under the barbed wire that encloses the test site and approach the existing town of Mercury. Now fully embodied protesters, they wrap themselves in Mylar and wear masks, continuing farther and farther toward ground zero until soldiers arrest them. Having endured a nightmare of loss and grief that could not be healed by her Mormon faith alone, Williams writes herself into a new dream of solidarity with mothers who "have come to reclaim the desert for our children" (289). She confesses that she herself was among those who "crossed the line" at the Nevada Test Site, and explains that this transgression finally led her home to a community of "women who recognized the sweet smell of sage as fuel for our spirits" (290).

Irradiated Icons

Photographers and writers in the post-nuclear West have continued to experiment with strategies for representing the contaminated desert. Often rejecting fiction and abstraction for the more explicitly hybrid modes of documentary, natural history writing, and memoir, they approach toxic landscapes as sites of trauma that cannot be redeemed entirely through art. They render these sites either visually, through auditory and tactile senses, or symbolically, by rewriting the dangers of radiation in iconic terms as black forms or magical bodies. Cathy Caruth writes in *Unclaimed Experience* that trauma produces a series of intricate separations and reconnections—between past events and present experience, between dead bodies and living ones, between knowing and unknowing. It is "the narrative of a belated experience"—one that does not escape the past but "rather attests to its endless impact on a life" (7). Trauma yields historical understanding only through violent disruption of rational thought or of monologic discourse. Like a traumatic event, a nuclear landscape functions "as a kind of index of historical reality"; it resists being placed "within a coherent mental, textual, or historical context in ways that would allow it to become part of lived experience and subsequent memory" (Baer 11, 10).

Narratives of the nuclear Southwest are indeed stories of trauma that confront the difficulty of reconciling necessarily incomplete knowledge of the vast scale of destruction with private and belated acts of witness and mourning. These narratives lie at the intersection of the public (and largely masculine) discourses of national "security," cultural sovereignty, and science and the private languages of encounter and sensory experience. They recognize that historical reconstruction is engaged in "a deeply ethical dilemma" (Caruth 27). Organized around enclosed spaces and surfaces that the writer aims to penetrate, these texts seek both ecological literacy and new languages of ruin.

One way of telling the story of ground zero might be through monuments and artifacts, which "carry the news of history in a kind of code of remembrance," according to Meloy. We have seen such an approach to narrating traumatic landscapes in Edward Weston's photographs of abandoned cars and ruins of Rhyolite and in Joan Myers's photographs of the debris left at Japanese-American internment camps. Deciphering the "code of remembrance" for nuclear test sites is not easy, however: access is restricted, fallout is invisible, dust conceals radioactivity. As Meloy writes in *The Last Cheater's Waltz*, "Everything is out of sight, yet nothing is hidden" (33).

In 1986, Robert Del Tredici organized the Atomic Photographers Guild with the premise that "everyone is a downwinder" and with the commitment to reveal the secret landscapes of the nuclear West (Davis, *Dead Cities* 38).[8] Carole Gallagher was among the international guild's original members, and her study *American Ground Zero* reveals the breakdown of bodies exposed to nuclear testing. The project probes the fragile surfaces of people and communities affected by radiation released during above-ground detonations at the Nevada Test Site between 1951 and 1963, documenting the experiences of survivors in black and white portraits and through a text composed mainly of first-person narrative.

The first portrait in the collection shows "Atomic Cowboy" Ken Case holding a framed photograph of a mushroom cloud in front of his chest. Case's job for the Atomic Energy Commission required "riding a herd of cattle and horses over ground zero after a nuclear detonation so that the effects of radiation on wildlife could be measured by scientists at Los Alamos" (3). Gallagher explains that his exposure to radiation caused cancer that required him to have a substantial part of his intestines and his spleen removed—when she interviewed and photographed him, most of his body's organs were cancerous. This first portrait immediately reveals the new function of the irradiated body: to dramatize the contradiction between the explosion's external creation of spectacular light and its internal destruction of life, thus allowing its devastation to be seen in human terms. The portraits that follow show atomic veterans and widows in various states of dying, mourning, and fighting. Herman Hagen, member of the pipefitters' union at the Nevada Test Site, was once 227 pounds. Gallagher depicts him as she encountered him: shriveled arms enclosing an emaciated belly, dying from myeloma (cancer of the bone marrow). Another portrait shows Alden Roberts, Mormon schoolteacher and outdoorsman, who developed cancer around his heart and could barely speak after the many operations that paralyzed his vocal chords (202). Betrayed by his body despite a lifetime of healthy living, Roberts sits calmly on a woodpile while the brilliant sun reflects off the leaves of the lush trees behind him, palms pressed together between his knees, the right side of his face substantially missing.

In the narrative segment accompanying each portrait, Gallagher describes the subject's life and records his or her oral history. She also notes her own struggle to do justice to her subject's courage: "One could never be sensitive enough in the delicate situation of asking to photograph a man whose cancer had so obviously eaten him alive. . . . A man so firm in his belief in God reduced me to thinking of any such deity as a cosmic sadist, yet Alden Roberts was far stronger than I in this situation" (204). Her study of Elmer Pickett presents a man who worked as a mortician in St. George and "had to teach employees new embalming techniques" to treat the bodies of children wasted by leukemia after the onset of atomic tests. The caption reads: "Elmer Pickett, who lost 16 in his family to cancer, with his panoramic view of Snow Canyon, site of many Hollywood westerns. 'John Wayne's two sons I got to know real well. Susan Hayward's twins, we took them fishing, we took them hunting. . . . As you know, that cast [for *The Conqueror*], the majority of them died of cancer'" (149). In this case the photograph of the legendary and now toxic canyon bisects his body. Though seemingly empty, the ground is full of radiation dispersed far beyond both photographs' frames. Throughout Gallagher's documentary, the bodies and the voices of veterans and survivors speak for the dead and for the ruined landscape.

Many photographs in *American Ground Zero* depict widows or mothers holding pictures of the husbands or children sacrificed to nuclear testing. Pat Proudy hugs a portrait of her dead husband in his Marines uniform, looking straight at the camera while the sun descends to the horizon glowing in the dusk like a nuclear explosion (90). When her husband suddenly developed terminal lymphoma in 1976 and died several years later, she filed a lawsuit against the government and organized the National Association of Radiation Survivors to represent the 250,000 people exposed to radiation through nuclear testing. Gallagher's photograph juxtaposes the couple's happy past (conveyed through Chuck Proudy's smiling, youthful face) with its desolate present (conveyed through the empty landscape in the background and the lines of grief around Pat Proudy's eyes). While Pat may not feel the effects of radiation directly in her own body, the photograph of her that Gallagher created suggests that she has shared her husband's suffering, internalized it, and made it her own.

Another powerful portrait depicts Winonah Shah, who poses with two snapshots of her son-in-law, Jim, and her two grandchildren at her chest. She and her husband, who worked for a mining company in Tempiute, Nevada, always used to go see the mushroom clouds that rose from nuclear blasts, just as other people would go to see fireworks. "We never missed a time when they set a blast off, and after a while it got commonplace," she recalled (129). Although sometimes government officials warned them to stay inside, no one in the 1950s really knew what fallout was, and many people in the town shared Shah's faith that the government would protect them. One day her daughter, in eighth grade at the time, missed the warning and walked over a mountain nearby. She immediately developed an "eruption on her face." A little more than ten years later, at age twenty-four, she died of leukemia. Three years afterward, Shah's husband also died, in his case from lung cancer. "I don't know how I made it through," Shah confessed to Gallagher. "I wanted to die, I didn't want to live" (131).

Because many of the women who lost their families to cancer had professed faith in the military or in the Mormon church, confronting the source of the sickness and suffering they witnessed and shared also meant confronting the fallibility of the institutions they had trusted and questioning the beliefs that defined them as Mormon women. Judith Neilson spoke to Gallagher about her frustration with the Mormons' refusal to engage with the world outside their own community and with their "sheeplike" adherence to an image they would like to project as "so clean and so fresh and so patriotic" (217). Even Neilson's mother urged her to accept her lot and refuse the interview. Her own struggle with her son's condition, however, led her to speak out against the testing and the Mormon church. Born at two pounds with some organs incompletely formed or located outside his body, deaf, and legally blind, Sean survived, but at great cost: Neilson's husband abandoned the family, leaving her to find a way to support herself and her son's expensive medical needs. She confirmed to Gallagher that despite the official denial of "direct proof" of widespread cancer in St. George, "if you interview every family, every family will tell you [their] health problems. The percentages are way too high not to be recognized" (218).

The story told by Darlene Phillips is similar. When she was younger, part of a patriotic Mormon family, she never wanted to miss the spectacle of a nuclear test over Bryce Canyon just before dawn: "It would be kind of chilly, and we would count down with it because we knew what time it was to go off. Then you would see the whole sky light up as if the sun were coming up backward, and even the shadows of the trees would be wrong, casting their shadow in the other direction. And I should have known then that the world was upside down, that it was wrong, but I didn't" (302). Later she camped beneath the thick dust of a fallout cloud in Arches National Monument. On both occasions, Phillips saw effects of the blasts without knowing what they were or what suffering they would cause—only through her retrospective narration as witness to nuclear testing are her memories revealed and made coherent. Fighting against the claims of the Mormon church that the people of Utah proved their loyalty to the United States by allowing the testing to continue, the belittling diagnoses given by the doctors Phillips consulted for her chronic hepatitis and severely compromised immune system (one chart explained her symptoms as "housewife syndrome"), and the universal disapproval of her family and neighbors for her decision to protest, Phillips speaks her own history of extensive contact with radiation and its brutal consequences. Bearing the effects of radiation within her own body, Phillips presents herself directly to the camera. Gallagher photographs just her face, as if encouraging viewers to look into her eyes and through her skin, to penetrate the surface of the body and find its inner truth. As in all of the portraits, the photographic image, oral narrative, and documentary history collaborate to reconstruct the human legacy of atomic testing. While any one of Gallagher's subjects might be capable of telling his or her own story, the narrative of the book connects individual testimonials into a composite narrative of suffering and partial redemption.

The study ends with portraits of toxic landscapes void of people. In the second-to-last section, "Downwind," Gallagher includes Dorothea Lange's majestic image of St. George, Utah, from 1953 with the comment, "These fallout rich fields . . . were grazed by Boots Cox's herds of cattle, loading their milk with toxic amounts of radioactive isotopes" (252). Gallagher explains, "the hidden secret of each and every one of these landscapes is the presence of radioactive toxins that are certain to be there" (xxiv). In this new context, Lange's image seems not so much untrue as inadequate. Although full of visual information, from the texture of the bushy grasses growing along the curving and even dirt road to the state of the irrigated fields, the architecture of the Mormon temple, and the contours of distant mountains, the photograph remains fixed in time, unable to anticipate the future and incapable of revealing contamination's invisible threat.

Gallagher's own landscape photographs appear in the book's final section, "Contaminated Lives and Landscapes of the West." Following so many portraits and stories of disease and death, the photographs that emphasize the sky—whether full of white clouds extending deeply to the horizon or dark with ominous storm clouds—restore the dominance of open spaces and communicate a new awareness of the environment's toxicity. Geneal Anderson, chairperson of Utah's Paiute Indian Tribe, already spoke of the need to have the protests of indigenous people heard and to restore the health of the people and their home places (229–30). Gallagher's photographs of a land and sky seemingly unable to sustain life echo that plea. In many cases, Gallagher puts old icons or signs to new symbolic uses. She titles an image of the shores of the Great Salt Lake at Saltaire "Wrong Way" (410–11), referring both to the road sign rising out of the water and to the path of environmental destruction she has traced through the book. Finally, with its handmade memorial, "A cross in the atomic breeze, Pine Ridge Reservation, South Dakota, 1984" conveys a desolation in the landscape that seems to correspond to the grief of the unpictured survivors. The title of Gallagher's photograph, however, disperses the loss through the landscape and carries it beyond the photograph's frame; a form of fallout, the "atomic breeze" will eventually merge with and contaminate the air the viewer breathes.

The preceding combination of text and portraits taught viewers not to trust their eyes, nor to rely on conceptions of natural beauty that have become irrelevant and dangerously misleading. Although working within the powerful documentary tradition of an earlier era, Gallagher also shows how that tradition falls short in representing trauma and tragedy because it fails to probe beneath the visible surface. Photographs provide testimony, but their testimony can be false. As Neil Campbell writes of Richard Misrach's portraits of test sites, "the camera has lied to us, showing nature, but nature poisoned" (*Cultures* 60). By themselves, the photographs cannot bridge the gap between seeing and knowing what traumatic events like nuclear testing precipitate; they require the supplement of writing. Ulrich Baer argues in his analysis of photographs of the Holocaust that both photography and trauma "mark crises not of truth but of reference. The images considered open questions not about their facticity but about the ways in which some events attain full meaning only in retrospect . . . and how this belated registration may facilitate or block remembering or forgetting" (181).

While the bodies of the survivors in Gallagher's text seem vulnerable—scarred by operations required to remove cancer, supported by crutches, emaciated, deformed by genetic abnormalities, or stooped with sorrow—the landscapes reveal their injuries and thus their full meaning only belatedly, if at all. Gallagher structures her text like a narrative in the sense that she attempts to control how readers and viewers begin, engage with, and end the story of ground zero, but she also builds temporal gaps into this narrative structure: The people who live show portraits of the dead and tell about what their lives with the dead and dying were like; the photographer shows how she sees images from a previous generation; the reader takes the information provided and projects it into the future to anticipate the extent of destruction to come. *America Ground Zero* cannot be read from cover to cover in one sitting; the evidence it accumulates is too devastating for readers to process at once. However, by returning and reading in fragments, readers come to realize the risks of nuclear testing and to recognize that they may not find again an uncontaminated homeland or a "sacred grove."

Sacred/Profane: The Post-Nuclear Desert

In an essay that explores the contradiction between claiming the desert as home and desiring the cool refreshment of turquoise swimming pools, Meloy describes what she sees from her twenty-fifth floor room at the Bellagio Hotel in Las Vegas, one of the desert's most flamboyant artificial places: "[The room] overlooked a spectacular view of Mt. Charleston and the craggy slate and mauve ridge that held it. Subdivisions spread to the northwest, nearly to the lip of the Nevada Test Site. The window was thick and tightly sealed. . . . The late afternoon sun played on the mountains, taut and glowing. Mark and I put on our matching terrycloth courtesy bathrobes and posted our chairs in front of the glass" (*Anthropology* 57).

Playing the tourist and ironically mocking the recreational practice of gazing at the nuclear explosions that had only recently ceased, Meloy records this desert's uneasy mixture of natural beauty and unnatural construction. Only the boundary, or "lip," of the Nevada Test Site seems to contain the sprawl, suggesting that the site may be, paradoxically, the last and best defense against unchecked development. Viewed from such height and distance, the contradictory elements of the contemporary landscape, sacred and profane, merge.

In *The Last Cheater's Waltz*, Meloy attempts to map such merging of profane and sacred worlds in the Southwest's irradiated deserts. At the beginning, she feels threatened by the presence of "alien pebbles" of uranium in her familiar Tsé Valley and by the dissolution of the boundary between known and unknown universes. Sensing that she had "lost all frames of reference" and perhaps "forgotten the point of consciousness," she knows that a journey back must involve touching the things she feared (4). She writes, "To reinhabit my own body I had to traverse, again and again, the desert's cruel and beautiful skin" (8). Note the repetition—"again and again"—and the attribution of "skin" to the desert: both details announce how thoroughly the text links the wounds of body and landscape and uses the body to transgress the desert's fragile surface. Like Silko and Williams, Meloy shows that any representation of the desert landscape after its repeated exposure to nuclear tests also requires an investigation of its inner life and its partly visible past.

In the center of her narrative is a description of her visit to ground zero at the Trinity Site. Meloy stares at a photograph of the explosion brought out for the tourists in her group attending the semiannual open house and tries to reimagine the scene as a symbol of new life. She proposes that the cloud "looks like a jellyfish. A breast. Or a zygote" (69). Then she tries to translate the visible light into the almost unimaginable heat generated by the bomb, described by many eyewitnesses as a "sheet of sun" (70). She considers the possibility that "[t]he sterilization of landscape allows its reinvention; only at zero can there be a beginning, a blank slate to fill, even if the story that fills it—an apocalypse—itself becomes nothing again, in an instant" (29). Yet she keeps confronting the difficulty of either reversing the image's inevitable association with destruction or reconnecting the image with its place and occasion of origin. She compares it with similar photographs of Hiroshima and Nagasaki, which seem even more detached from the ground and the human destruction beneath it, and finds the visual exhibit to be an unsatisfying way of figuring the site's toxic history.

We may continue to "tell the story, in fragmented images and abstractions or in mantras of copious technical detail and meticulous analyses of historical context and policy making," but the existing forms of representation offer us only the illusion of knowledge, she concludes. They "sanitize nuclear weapons," "buffer despair," or transform horror into comedy (70). How else, she asks, might the history of ground zero be told? How might its spiritual and philosophical meanings be recovered?

At Trinity, Meloy gazes at the "obelisk-shaped cenotaph" and wants "to lie down on the seam," linking the imprint of destruction with the landscape that surrounds it. She hopes that by rupturing the surface of the landscape with her body she will break through the trauma of the bomb's secret history and find a sensory route that "leads to meaning, then understanding" (36). Her complex response to Trinity reveals her emerging understanding of the desert's beauty through sustained contact with its profane elements. Stephen Tatum describes this "forensic" ritual as "(1) a particular kind of sensuous encounter with the material objects in the world and (2) the special handling of such objects or artifacts so as to produce a redemptive sacred experience" ("Spectral Aesthetics" 139). Here at Trinity, Meloy struggles to create sacred space at the point of bodily contact with ground zero and to imagine what it would be like for contamination to enter her own body. Soon, however, she reveals the limits of her imaginary transgression when she sees a man standing very quietly next to her who might have been a real survivor of Hiroshima. She writes, "Without expression he watched the cenotaph. He was Japanese. It is possible to feel at once hollow and aflame, like a ghost burning." At this moment, standing on the original site of catastrophe, she imagines herself as a glowing sacrifice that might be able to bring two alien experiences together. Unable to speak, she gestures with her chin "to the nighthawks in the sky above us, cutting the pale dawn air in great swooping arcs" (223). With the boundary between her inner body and the external world dissolving, Meloy looks up at the sky, seeking a new spiritual hieroglyphic that could allow both survivors to transcend their earthly histories.

Meloy's inability to speak across cultures shocks her into recognizing her disorientation and accepting the only redemption this earth can provide: the beauty of surrendering one's identity and dissolving into the natural environment—or, as Meloy quotes José Saramago, the happiness that exists in "sea, light, and vertigo" (*Anthropology* 155). She finds a similar joy while traveling through the waters of the Yucatán Peninsula. Meloy finds layers of blue ocean as intricate as Navajo sandstone, the remains of a jack fish eaten by a shark, the "complicated landscape" of a coral reef, and rich indigo paint. However, the more she immerses herself in this foreign place the less articulate she becomes. She understands people who speak to her in Spanish, but both on the reef and at dinner with Mexican hosts she feels "tongueless, mute, lost without a verbal map to nuance and detail" (*Anthropology* 140). She learns that the Maya have more than nine words for blue; if these words are lost to history, they can never be replaced. "If language is frozen, if I am mute in this part of the world, then it will be a synergy of senses that saves me" she concludes (144). Although initially she relinquishes her desire to know the names of things and accepts the "exotic, wholly liquid place" that "lies outside words but well within the realm of the sensual," (152) gradually she comes to accept the necessity of verbal expression, even if words fail to convey all of her new knowledge.

In both memoirs, Meloy tests the relation between the external landscape and the body's interiority, exploiting the body's symbolic potential to link sacred and profane spaces and continuing in literary terms the post-nuclear feminist activism practiced by Williams, Gallagher, and Solnit, among others. Nuclear contamination has always been a "women's issue," Solnit argues in *Savage Dreams* (96). Some of the first protests against nuclear testing focused on the dangers radiation posed for children, prompting many women to write letters of opposition to President Eisenhower in 1957, organize the Women's Strike for Peace in 1962, and lead anti-nuclear movements in the 1980s. More recent protests by the "Princesses of Plutonium" and others in the late 1980s involved women who walked as far toward Ground Zero at the Nevada Test Site as they could before being arrested for trespassing. Meanwhile, many Western Shoshone people who live in the Yucca Mountain area with the Southern Paiute and Owens Valley Paiute "simply disregarded the fences and signs and continued to walk across the land, visit traditional sites, and hunt and gather on it" (Solnit 17). By calling public attention to testing the military still kept secret, women and native Shoshone and Paiute people focused new attention on the symbolic potential of the body to make "the landscape of national sacrifice" visible, to resist enclosure, and to mobilize political resistance to the "internal nuclear colonialism" the military practiced when they chose to conduct nuclear tests on traditional homelands and sacred grounds.[9]

Women photographers and writers in the post-Atomic Age have extended this legacy of protest through challenging and revising the desert's iconography. Although acutely aware of the limits of art to transform perceptions of the world and of the difficulty of their quest to represent a natural world that has been permanently damaged by human ambition, they continue to seek new visual and verbal languages that could bear witness to the desert's inner life and secret histories. For these artists, survival is like a condition of grace that demands continued expressions of faith and penance, the kind of fundamental rituals that all religious cultures enact. To live in the desert Southwest in the late twentieth century, Silko, Williams, and Meloy show us, means not just staging protests but also confronting innumerable "Black Places" where the histories of sacrifice still need to be felt by the body, spoken by the people who inhabit the region, and written into landscape. "Purity is the enemy of change, of ambiguity and compromise" (Douglas 200). Black Places or contaminated landscapes might then represent the limits of our ability to confine civilization's ruins within an enclosed site and the necessity of sharing the spiritual costs of global "progress." To transgress the limits of rational, human, and historical knowledge, we, too, must open our bodies to the desert's mixture of the sacred and the profane, share the entwined risks of beauty and radiation, and fashion our own icons.

The Border
Imagining Transnational Homelands

There have not been many frontiers like this one, I imagine.
An abstraction, a Euclidean line drawn across the desert, has
created two distinct human landscapes where there was only one
before. Much of the frontier is river, and rivers are meant to bring
men together, not to keep them apart. The rest of it is a straight
scientific line inscribed in sand, no more related to the terrain, no
more part of the view than are those groups of letters which maps
show to the north and south of it: Chihuahua and Texas and New
Mexico.
—J. B. Jackson, *Landscape in Sight*, 43

So begins one of the first essays J. B. Jackson published, in 1951. His subject
is the immediate sources of the visible differences between the United
States and Mexico, from shifts in property ownership after the Mexican
Revolution to growth in mining, which concentrated development in a
few towns and encouraged the architectural display of newfound wealth.
But Jackson also uses the border as an opportunity to explore the meeting of European ideals of rationality and American notions of freedom
and power. He writes that he wishes the Latin faith in reason, rather
than power, "had spread northward into our country before the line was
drawn." North Americans could have used more rationality and enlightenment, he believed.

But [the border] was drawn a hundred years ago, and now there are
two nations, two landscapes, two ways of looking at the world and of
living in it. In time, the Southwest will lose its identity, but the aspects
of it that we value and try to keep alive hark back to that large, undivided region; it is Chihuahua which represents the original even now.
Chihuahua is what we once were: a sun-struck landscape full of bright
plans for the future. (Jackson, *Landscape in Sight* 53)

Writing in the middle of the twentieth century, Jackson presents the border as a neat, if unnatural, dividing line between nations and cultures. In a later essay, he defends the border's meaning in broader social terms, arguing that the boundary paradoxically works to create collective identity and "binds us all together in a group." Taken by itself, a border separates insiders and outsiders, natives and strangers, citizens and aliens. Taken as a system, however, it becomes a "network of boundaries, private as well as public," which "transforms an amorphous environment into a human landscape" (*Landscape in Sight* 309).

This chapter analyzes recent representations of border landscapes to see whether photographers and writers in the United States still look to Mexico for the origins of the greater Southwest's common culture and for "bright plans for the future." The short answer, I think, is yes, however tempered these representations may be by the realities of border and cultural politics. The longer answer, which this chapter seeks to provide, is that artists project very different experiences of migration and exile into the borderlands and differ as to the personal, cultural, and social transformations that border crossings make possible. I focus on selected depictions of the border from the perspectives of photographers Geoffrey James and Peter Goin and writers Cormac McCarthy, Alberto Alvaro Ríos, and Arturo Islas, artists who live in Canada or the United States, and thus approach the transnational boundary from the north, like Jackson did. Their work, alternately realistic and philosophical, confronts the difficulties of seeing a landscape that discourages steady habitation and communal formation. Their representations of the border, accordingly, keep testing which aspects of its culture can be seen, which must be felt or thought through, and which can serve transnational affiliations.

It is often the body—whether imagined in motion, in contact with the dead, or resurrected as a spirit—that articulates the border's ambivalent, hybrid culture and bears the responsibility for sustaining it. In the next chapter, I look at *The Hummingbird's Daughter* by Luis Alberto Urrea, a novel written from the point of view of Mexican protagonists who live in Sinaloa and Sonora and cross into the United States only at the novel's end. Written in the mode of magical realism and invested in re-enchanting Mexico's indigenous culture, Urrea's novel imagines life in the borderlands not, perhaps, as it once was, but as we can now imagine it to have been. These final chapters of my study ask what difference nationality makes—and what it means to reconstruct a homeland defined originally by an official, physical boundary and reconfigured over generations of crossings.

Salman Rushdie elegantly poses the problem of returning to one's homeland from a place of exile through a photograph that hangs on his wall. "It's a picture dating from 1946 of a house into which, at the time of its taking, I had not yet been born" (*Imaginary Homelands* 9). The photograph reminds him that he lives in a present that is foreign, far away from the past that is his home, "albeit a lost home in a lost city in the mists of lost time." He explains that it was his return to this house in Mumbai that gave him the idea for *Midnight's Children*. He discovered that the reality of the house and the city was intensely colorful and disordered, whereas the photographic memory was limited to a two-dimensional, black-and-white picture. His physical alienation from his homeland produced both a sense of loss and the realization that he and his fellow exiles would "not be capable of reclaiming precisely the thing that was lost; that we will, in short, create fictions, not actual cities or villages, but invisible ones, *imaginary homelands*, Indias of the mind" (10). Being "out-of-country and even out-of-language" is a cultural and physical fact. Rushdie's novels, accordingly, cannot be "about" India, but rather about the process of remembering his native place and constructing his own version of it among many possible ones.

Since its violent demarcation following the Treaty of Guadalupe Hidalgo in 1848, the border between the United States and Mexico has been highly politicized. Two icons have stood for this official boundary: the fence that the United States built to deter illegal immigration, now a permanent spatial reminder of national and economic division; and the Rio Grande/Rio Bravo, once a symbol of natural and imagined power, now proof of industrial pollution and a source of real disease. Claire Fox points out that both types of boundaries have appeared in films, novels, and photographs as "border establishing shots," views that immediately locate the action for the viewer or reader. They "invoke the border both literally and metaphorically" (*The Fence and the River* 11). With increases in migration following NAFTA and the persistence of gross economic disparity between Mexico and the United States, the fence as a physical barrier surely matters less than the movement of people, resources, and cultural traditions across it. Yet the boundary fence and other physical markers of the border still function for photographers and writers as sites of resistance to official declarations of cultural difference. Goin, James, and McCarthy work with the physical evidence and material ruins of the border they see before them in order to test its power and imagine how to reconfigure it as a zone of contact.

Following the example set by Américo Paredes in his conception of "Greater Mexico," Chicano/a poets and novelists from Ríos to Urrea, meanwhile, tend to blur the line separating the nations to emphasize the region's shared social histories and to claim the borderlands region as a productive cultural site. The region has been, of course, the birthplace of Gloria Anzaldúa's *la nueva mestiza*; Néstor García Canclini's exemplary hybrid postmodern space; and the site of what Debra Castillo calls "shadowtexts," discursive locations simultaneously "inside/outside dominant discourses."[1] The instability and ambivalence of the border celebrated by each of these writers suggests that they have looked to the national boundary not only to understand multiple ways "of looking at the world and of living in it," as Jackson puts it, but also to imagine a less repressive transnational culture defined by a network of allegiances. As Castillo explains, for scholars the border area "offers an alternate space featuring a flexible and mutating set of social and cultural arrangements" because it "sets up a position for both living and thinking, one involving a sense of place as well as implicit displacement" (Castillo, "Borderlining" 18). The characters in the border stories I consider here, however, seem less willing to leave the past behind and less optimistic about the border's utopian potential. As much as they try to distance themselves from the histories of their families and the border, the material landscape intervenes to limit their imaginary movement. The persistent trope of the open grave, for example, refuses to keep the dead buried and resists the pursuit of progress and assimilation. Voices, spirits, and magical bodies keep returning from the dead, reminding the living that their memories can never fully be their own. Both images and texts produced in the late twentieth century imagine borderlands full of human stories of loss and lacking the bright future that Jackson hoped for. At the same time, they also reveal the origins of the region's shared history of migration, abandonment, and reconstruction more fully than any "original" Jackson could have projected.

Tracing the Line, Running the Fence

Peter Goin's commitment to "trace" the entire length of the border in the early 1980s resembles the heroic effort of the American West's first generation of survey photographers—and indeed Goin chose to print his images in a rare folio edition, just like William Henry Jackson. He consulted United States Geological Survey maps, though outdated; state highway and county maps; National Park maps; and, when these failed, relied on

Figure 20. Peter Goin, "Rio Grande," from *Tracing the Line,* 1987. (Courtesy of Peter Goin, *Tracing the Line*)

the expertise and permission of Border Patrol as he followed first the Rio Grande and then the 276 permanent monuments erected to divide the territory. He also used every means of transport available to him, traveling by "light truck, 4–wheel drive vehicle, light aircraft and helicopter" as well as on foot ("Following the Line" 25). Simultaneously an explorer of the border zone and an observer of its cultural remains, Goin produced a photographic survey in *Tracing the Line* (1987) that "introduces new visual images of a landscape previously avoided, neglected, or fenced with 'no trespassing' signs" (*Tracing the Line* n.p.). The images alternately reveal the border to be an agent of destruction and a social space capable of healing abstract division.

The first stretch is marked by the broad curves of the Rio Grande, which Goin depicts from the causeway at the Falcon Dam between Laredo and McAllen (fig. 20). This photograph, which bridges the United States

Figure 21. Peter Goin, "Last International Ferry at Los Ebanos," 1987. (Courtesy of Peter Goin, *Tracing the Line*)

and Mexico, shows viewers how powerfully the river flows and sustains the land on either side. Because the river keeps moving, this stretch of the border seems to lack permanence. Subsequent images reveal footprints migrants have left at the river's edge, or the paths they have followed to cross it. For example, "Last International Ferry at Los Ebanos" (fig. 21) is one of the rare images that includes people, in this case the men waiting for the few customers who choose the ferry over the more convenient bridges built to connect the fifteen "sister" cities that straddle the border. The ease of the men conveys the routine business of the crossing, even if their own work seems outmoded, on the verge of extinction. Other images of the river contrast the landscape's history of use with its current abandoned state. One photograph reveals the stone foundations of Zapata, a town that flooded when the Falcon Reservoir was built. Another shows a pump station near Kinney, Texas, once used to provide water for mining

Figure 22. Peter Goin, "Pump Station abandoned near Kinney, TX," 1987. (Courtesy of Peter Goin, *Tracing the Line*)

operations, now a favorite hiding spot for migrants (fig. 22). A third shows a railroad tunnel built by Chinese laborers near Amistad Recreation Area, used for ten years, and then abandoned. A fourth shows the hot springs and ruins of a spa in Big Bend, and a fifth asks the viewer to contemplate an overgrown (and probably rarely visited) cemetery. At times the Rio Grande itself is shown eroding its banks or at a standstill because of silt or overgrown trees. Clearly, this is an unstable line.

The photograph of the beginning of the land boundary shows how dramatically "[t]he geometry of a boundary conflicts with the natural order of the landscape" (Goin, *Tracing the Line*). In the foreground, we see dirt, empty bottles, and other debris. Although there is a stone fence and some barbed wire, these enclosures appear hastily constructed and neglected, with the official marker nearly hidden in the trees. On the left, on the Mexican side, one car is parked in the shade of a tree, while a man stands next to the open trunk of another vehicle. A couple walks toward the camera, but their features are blurred, as is their purpose. They would probably not be just visiting a place like this that lacks shelter and beauty, but we cannot determine either their origin or their destination. Hills rise into the background on the U.S. side, accessible but uninviting. This stretch of desert landscape is unremarkable except for the marker that splits it in two and declares its official status. Goin writes in *Tracing the Line*, "Instead of being simply an anonymous stretch of land, the landscape derives identity from the structure imposed on it." Images such as this one emphasize the process of marking and naming the land that transforms it from desert to borderland.

A photograph taken farther on, at a "drive through" a quarter-mile west of the port of entry at Naco, Arizona, focuses on a more popular site for crossing. The upper coils of barbed wire are intact, but the chain-link fence has been pulled apart in the center to provide easy access to and from the open road on the Mexican side. The viewer looks in from the United States, over the tire tracks and footprints in the sand, to see an ordinary street, parked cars and trucks, and modest houses; only the broken fence marks the significance of the site to people on both sides. Elsewhere the border appears more forbidding and seems to create greater pressure on the people who live near it. Goin calls the "Tortilla Curtain" near El Paso, Calexico, and San Ysidro an "impenetrable fence" and shows its solid construction; the reinforced boundary, combined with abandoned land on either side, creates an eerie sense of emptiness.

Goin's images of the area approaching Tijuana, by contrast, reveal Mexican settlements or abandoned, stripped cars that crowd up against the line, as if revealing the urgent desires of their inhabitants to gain access to the United States. Along this strenuously policed stretch of the border, empty land can be the most menacing. Whereas the line of cars waiting to cross between San Ysidro and Tijuana might provide safety in numbers, anyone who tries to cross the "Soccer Field," one of the most dangerous areas of the border, takes his or her chances (at the time of Goin's writing, 200 to 2,000 people tried to cross into the United States every night at this point). One of the last images of *Tracing the Line* depicts the view from Spooner's Mesa, looking east over "Smuggler's Canyon," site of innumerable violent crimes, many perpetuated by coyotes, who prey on migrants and smuggle them illegally over the border for a fee. Taken in daylight, the photograph shows "the stage, not the participants. Yet the stage reveals the presence of the actors by how they have changed and charted the character of the landscape" ("Following the Line" 24).

   Canadian photographer Geoffrey James also tested the meaning of
the border fence in Tijuana and organized his images to dramatize the
economic inequality between the two adjacent countries. His work along
the border began almost by accident after he had traveled across the
United States and into Mexico and noted "the sadness and decay of most
American cities." He decided to photograph the fourteen miles from the
Pacific Ocean inland that separates San Diego and Tijuana. The result
was *Running Fence*, an exhibit that opened in 1998 and traveled across
North America for the next two years and then a book "dedicated to
those who cross with hope, but without papers." As a series of images, it
constructs the border as a contradictory space: a site of potential contact
but producing primarily isolation, integrated by capital but separated by
inequality. As in the collective portrait Goin created in *Tracing the Line*,
James's border is a place where hopes, bodies, and buildings are more
often abandoned than transformed.

   James's work also contributes to the rich critical history of the border,
focusing on Tijuana. García Canclini called the city a place to formulate
"strategies for entering and leaving modernity" and "one of the biggest
laboratories of *post*modernity" (*Hybrid Cultures* 233). For the Argentine-
born intellectual, the quick growth of Tijuana from 1950 to the mid-1980s
due to migration from nearly every part of Mexico produced a metropolis of exuberant cultural hybridity.[2] Saldívar and Castillo, among others,
have also taken Tijuana as a test case for conceptualizing the U.S.–Mexico
borderlands. In "Tijuana Calling," Saldívar lucidly analyzes the way that
Beverly Lowry and Luis Alberto Urrea deploy rhetoric that perpetuates
the imperial relation between the United States and Mexico and the way
that Rubén Martínez, Richard Rodriguez, and Guillermo Gómez-Peña
seek to rewrite that relation through their auto-ethnographies. Regina
Swain and María Novaro note that much of the discourse about Tijuana,
which they call a "hyperdetermined geographic location," engages "the
most common stereotypes that each of these dominant cultures [the
United States and central Mexico] has created about the other" and thus
creates "the discursive equivalent of the no man's land" ("Utopia" 190, 217).

   The factual basis of James's project, however, resists postmodern play
and retrospective recovery. Rather than idealize a discursive location,
the photographs show the places that most migrants desperately want to
leave behind. James's study of the border deliberately preserves national
and cultural differences, perhaps to show how the real landscape resists
transformation into an imagined hybrid space. It is committed instead to

representing a series of sustained divisions: between nations, between ways of building houses, between order and disorder, between empty policed space and inhabited landscape. It insists on a critical and impenetrable distance from its human subjects, who seem to have nowhere to go. What James "establishes" in his still photographs is the difficulty of imagining how to remedy the economic inequality in this borderland. He explained in an interview, "My feeling is that photography, as a tool for social persuasion, is very inefficient. It's much more effective to make a film. The argument can be much more coherent in a film. The interesting thing is that people don't look at photographs until they are ready to" (*Past/Present/Future* 18). The people who look at *Running Fence* are unlikely to be inhabitants of the U.S.–Mexico border—after opening in San Diego, the exhibit of this project traveled to Vancouver, Calgary, Oakville (Ontario), Montreal, and New York. Because of their distance and relative privilege, when they look at these photographs James expects them to be prepared to see the border's beauty and to take responsibility for the economic and social problems it reveals.

The book's first plate juxtaposes a typical roadside sign urging "Caution" with evidence of why the sign is necessary. It shows adults running across the road, pulling their children behind them. In the photographs that follow, however, the fence itself seems the most active being. Viewed from its origin at the Pacific (fig. 23), it seems to divide the sea and climb over rocks and sand. When set behind an overly sanitary house, it provides an athletic, graffiti-covered contrast to the new construction and the city's more established culture. The fence's vital presence is surely what James had in mind when he named the project. When we put more pressure on the title, we find an allusion to Christo's 1976 installation from Bodega Bay to Petaluma in northern California, as well as the ironic opposition between the fence's free extension across space and the migrant's experience of pursuit and capture. At no point does the fence seem more free as where it seems to run across Tijuana's hills and entice us to admire the glittering lights of San Diego (*Running Fence*, Plates 6 & 7). We could also interpret "running" as meaning elusive, always moving just out of reach. What remains visibly fixed in James's images, meanwhile, is the differential development of the land adjacent to the fence. Whereas the United States has designated the land for industry and border patrol, Mexico uses the land for roads, houses, and restaurants. Spooner's Mesa, on the U.S. side, is eerily empty at dusk, while the low lights of Tijuana gleam in the near distance (Plate 12).

Figure 23. Geoffrey James, "The Beginning of the Fence at Playas Tijuana," from *Running Fence,* 1997. (Courtesy of Geoffrey James)

Another image shows how an American quarry ravages the land, while Mexican houses domesticate the landscape (fig. 24). The imperial imperative—the provision that designated the federal land within sixty feet of the border in California, Arizona, and New Mexico as "no-man's land"—allows just enough space for viewers to see how access to resources and the use of space is defined by a nation's economic status and official policies. The difference is too stark, as James's photographs show us; the two sides of each image cannot be assimilated into a common state of "hybridity." Perhaps because James believes that too often "photography aestheticizes the world" and "renders everything safe and manageable," in this project he dramatizes such irreconcilable differences. The irony is obvious in his revision of a famous Robert Frank photograph from *The Americans,* "Covered car–Long Beach California" (1959). Whereas Frank documented the fastidious care Californians seemed to lavish on their

Figure 24. Geoffrey James, "Looking towards Mexico, Otay Mesa," 1997. (Courtesy of Geoffrey James)

automobiles, James reveals the necessary protection Mexicans give to their equivalent resource: the supplies needed to "cross over" (fig. 25). Both images situate their respective valued objects within a landscape dotted with palm trees, but in James's image the background is the border, not a single-family house.

Running Fence reveals the pressures that national policies and global economic ambitions exert on migrants and on the spaces that migrants create. Studies of the borderlands led by Chicano/a historians similarly argue for revising fixed images of the fence and the river to account for the mobility, cultural hybridity, and violence of life "on the line." They, too, acknowledge a powerful counter-history to border crossing: the often-futile effort to establish stable communities. James's viewers will find little to celebrate in his images of life on the border and may learn to give up migration's romantic fiction, especially as the concluding images

Figure 25. Geoffrey James, "Crossing supplies tent, Avenida Internacional, Tijuana," 1997. (Courtesy of Geoffrey James)

in *Running Fence* confirm the border to be a zone of division rather than contact. One photograph barely catches a few migrants preparing to cross the border, but their presence is only part of the story (Plate 41). From the viewer's slightly elevated perspective, every built element of the landscape creates another layer of enclosure: the low and open wire fences along the edge of the road, the dirt pathways worn to a cluster of houses, the long stretch between telephone poles, and the mountain ridge in the distance all serve as fences. The three white crosses erected just against the official border fence seem more solidly grounded than the few people about to walk out of view. This is an ambivalent scene—settled, perhaps, but probably at great human cost. James's viewers, meanwhile, remain uninformed, left to speculate about the past and the future.

What will be the fate of these "dwellings" (a term Jackson used to describe the kind of American homes that are merely temporary shelters, ready to be abandoned for new opportunities)? Where will their inhabitants go? Writing on "The Moveable Dwelling and How It Came to America" in 1984, Jackson imagined the future for inhabitants of such provisional structures in the United States:"[W]hen we know America well, we find nothing really sad in the spectacle. The deserted house, nine times out of ten, is a chrysalis from which its inhabitants have happily escaped to some brighter or more alluring prospect. Only in the Old World, with its dream of permanence, does the deserted house or the deserted field invariably speak of human tragedy" (*Landscape* 97). On the U.S.–Mexico border, many productive settlements never took shape, and many "escapes" were neither happy nor bright; there, the aesthetics and the politics of permanence as understood by people in the United States are challenged. James makes the case that looking at the border means confronting landscapes in the process of abandonment and ruin and seeing how dreams of mobility and permanence collide. Other photography projects, notably the collaborative and mostly anonymous "Border Film Project" (2007), provide more evidence that the U.S. border policy needs radical revision.[3] Meanwhile, it takes novelists and poets to tell the human tragedies of migration—and thus to reclaim the borderlands as a landscape that articulates how Mexico's Old World origins, familial histories, and cultural riches combine to create the contemporary experience of exile in the southwestern United States.

Crossing the Line

We have seen in chapter 2 how village stories in New Mexico stylized rural life before World War II. Borderlands fiction stylizes the experience of Anglos, Mexican Americans, and Chicano/as through the end of the twentieth century in a different way: around patterns of crossing and return and tropes of the open grave. With these formal strategies, among others, the genre constitutes a powerful literary response to what José David Saldívar calls "the culture shocks of the modern Southwest in late capitalism," the experience of cultural loss and marginalization shared by migrants and their descendants throughout the region.[4] This fiction articulates the way identity develops alternately through attachment to place and exploration of other cultures located across the border or back in time. It follows protagonists across spatial, political, and temporal boundaries and in the process works to reconstitute individuals and communities.

Cormac McCarthy writes border novels as belated Westerns—or, rather, as "anti-Westerns." Whereas standard Westerns "approach and retreat from a contested center" and produce "a similar pattern of address and withdrawal in their readers," in Forrest Robinson's classic definition of the genre, anti-Westerns often find themselves "unable to escape the very thing they seek to dismantle."[5] Their location on the border is essential to this anti-imperial process. As Tatum explains, "writers deploy geographical tropes associated with . . . the circulation of bodies across borders in order strategically to represent and then critique, and sometimes parody, the colonizing imagination's desire for mastery, stability, and containment" ("Topographies" 313). In *All the Pretty Horses* (1992), *The Crossing* (1994), and *Cities of the Plain* (1998), McCarthy tells the stories of young cowboys who constantly crossed the border on horseback between the late 1930s and the early 1950s, seeking meaning and honor in places that were not only distant from home but could barely be mapped. In all the novels, the landscape directs the action of the Anglo protagonists, whose local and individual experiences repeatedly resist their culture's efforts at mastery and historical containment.

The Crossing, the trilogy's central novel, begins with a family settling a "new" New Mexican landscape:

> When they came south out of Grant County Boyd was not much more than a baby and the newly formed country they'd named Hidalgo was itself little older than the child. In the country they'd quit lay the bones of a sister and the bones of his maternal grandmother. The new country was rich and wild. You could ride clear to Mexico and not strike a crossfence. He carried Boyd before him in the bow of the saddle and named to him features of the landscape and birds and animals in both spanish and english. (3)

As Susan Kollin observes, "Billy becomes Adam in the garden, living in a state of wonder that is temporarily outside the encroachments of history" ("Genre and the Geographies of Violence" 578). One could argue that it is the loss of that newness that motives Billy Parham to leave his home in pursuit of a wolf his father ordered him to trap; he seeks the wildness and exhilaration experienced by explorers and western heroes so often lost to the next generation, or simply to maturity. Through Billy's wanderings across the border, first in the name of returning the wolf to her homeland, then in the name of recovering his own family and its honor, the novel interrogates Anglo claims to the land north of the border and animates its local Mexican and Native American cultures. Each journey, however, leaves the novel's hero less certain of the border's meaning and his place in this territory's violent and incomprehensible history.

In Book I, the wolf stands as a figure for pure, instinctive movement and for the unknowability of the natural world and its historical cycles. Billy observes the tracks wolves have left in the gravel and then catches a glimpse of them leaping "in a silence such that they seemed of another world entire" (4). An old man whom Billy consults about how to trap the wolf confirms that "no man knew what the wolf knew" (45). In order to get closer to that knowledge, Billy traps the wolf and then frees her so that she can return home and give birth. From that point on, the two different beings gradually become intimate, first through their common journey and then through Billy's care of her body. For example, he gives her water and "touched the pleated corner of her mouth. He studied the veined and velvet grotto into which the audible world poured. He began to talk to her" (77).

McCarthy's description of the wolf's migration from Mexico attributes historical understanding and geographical memory to the animal: she attacks cows because their domestication seems a "violation of an old order. Old ceremonies. Old protocols"; she resists leaving visible tracks in the new territory, refusing to cross roads during the day or to "cross under a wire fence twice in the same place" (25). By contrast, Billy's sense of where he belongs is much less defined, as we see when he crosses the U.S.–Mexico border for the first time:

> When he set out across the valley to the south the grass was golden in the morning sun. Antelope were grazing on the plain a half-mile to the east. He looked back to see if [the wolf] had taken notice of them but she had not. She limped along behind the horse steadfast and doglike and in this fashion they crossed sometime near noon the international boundary line in Mexico, state of Sonora, undifferentiated in its terrain from the country they quit and yet wholly alien and wholly strange. He sat the horse and looked out over the red hills. To the east he could see one of the concrete obelisks that stood for a boundary marker. In that desert waste it had the look of some monument to a lost expedition. (74)

Note the way that Mexico suddenly seems different and strange, despite its "undifferentiated" terrain. The division the border creates is not visible but imagined as a stereotypical dividing line between real and mythic space. Here, Billy transforms the landscape south of the border into a symbol of the Old World, a figure for a history inaccessible and mysterious to those who seek access to it from the United States.

The first Mexican town Billy approaches, Morelos, is "an old Mormon settlement from the century before," like a frontier town fixed in time. The townspeople there are having a fair with exhibits from an earlier era: freaks and vanishing Tarahumara and Yaqui Indians "carrying bows and quivers of arrows and two Apache boys in deerskin boots with grave and coalblack eyes who'd come from their camp in the sierras where the last free remnants of their tribe lived like shadowfolk of the nation they had been" (104). Further proof of the town's lack of development comes with its treatment of the wolf, as the animal is immediately caged, put on display, and sacrificed for sport. This scene also perpetuates stereotypes of Mexico as a place where laws are rarely enforced and women perform the traditional labors of cooking, nursing, mourning, or whoring. Later, Billy will look across the border to "where the antique world clung to the stones and to the spores and living things and dwelt in the blood of men" (331). Kollin rightly calls this "a racialized geography" that forces McCarthy's hero to experience utter disorientation and self-alienation. Billy can never claim this culture as his own and must continue his quest for contact with a past that he can integrate into his own sense of himself.

Meanwhile, McCarthy uses the wolf to introduce an alternate way of being in the world. An animal does not desire belonging, he simply exists, follows his instinct, and responds to the immediate environment. For the wolf, the notion of cultural inheritance is meaningless. Yet, Billy can choose to follow the wolf and share her territory, and the novel raises the question of how different the two species really are. Toward the end of Book I, Billy tastes the wolf's blood, and it tastes like his own—perhaps offering proof of their common origin and hope that their differences can dissolve. At the end of this book, as Billy performs a version of last rites on the wolf's dead body, he senses an overwhelming unity among all living things and thus approaches the realization of this hope:

> The [wolf's] eye turned to the fire gave back no light and he closed it with his thumb and sat by her and put his hand upon her bloodied forehead and closed his own eyes that he could see her running in the mountains, running in the starlight where the grass was wet and the sun's coming as yet had not undone the rich matrix of creatures passed in the night

before her. Deer and hare and dove and groundvole all richly empaneled on the air for her delight, all nations of the possible world ordained by God of which she was one among and not separate from. (127)

This prelapsarian imagining, located in a landscape conspicuously free of social markings, suggests how the rest of the novel will work: by moving between places that are saturated with a past that the protagonist cannot fully understand and those that lack cultural history in an effort to determine what kind of knowledge is necessary for an individual to survive in the borderlands.

Like other writers of the U.S–Mexico borderlands, McCarthy combines narrative trajectories of migration and return with tropes of burial. Billy's repeated journeys to Mexico and back in *The Crossing* teach him that "[k]nowledge of self is inseparable from a knowledge of the body's location in place," as Tatum puts it ("Topographies" 312), but his journeys also teach him to associate attachment to a single place with death. For example, in Book I he encounters in the Bavispe River Valley a group of Indians who had been working in the mines of western Chihuahua.

> There were six of them journeying overland to their village in Sonora bearing with them the body of one of their number killed under a scaffolding. They had been three days enroute and three days more lay before them and they had been fortunate in the weather. The dead body lay apart from them in the leaves upon a rude bier of poles and cowhide. It was wrapped in canvas and tied with bindings of grass and rope and the canvas of the shroud was worked with red and green ribbons and laid over with branches of the mountain ilex and one of the Indians sat by it to guard it or perhaps to keep the dead man company. They spoke some Spanish and they invited him to eat with little ceremony, such was the custom of the country. (92)

These Indians, unidentified by tribe, are carrying the body of one of their own back to their homeland. The place of burial, for them, must be the place of origin; in death, the history of work and migration will be erased. The procession home is clearly part of the ritual, as the men have decorated the shroud with colorful ribbons and consecrated it with branches. Whereas the "little ceremony" of sharing a meal with a stranger can be improvised, a burial requires that tradition be observed.

Then, toward the novel's end, Billy himself undertakes a ritual journey to rebury his brother's corpse. Boyd was shot and wounded, and despite careful treatment of his wound, he died. Boyd's death compounds the losses Billy has already endured: those of the wolf and of his parents. By Book IV of *The Crossing*, this belated western hero has no family, no romantic attachments, and no home; he has become an ordinary solitary man. He is not even the hero of a *corrido*, the Mexico folk ballad that "tells the tale of that solitary man who is all men" (386); Boyd already fulfilled that role. Billy's remaining task is to lay his brother's bones to rest in the proper ground. He approaches the cemetery outside of San Buenaventura where Boyd was buried at dusk, his own wandering in contrast with the "grooved" movement of the cranes flying overhead. Looking for his brother's grave, Billy notices cairns of rock, some already scattered on the ground, "sepulchre tablets blacked over with lichen," and smoldering trash. He finds his brother's grave by the date burned into a wooden cross; "There was no name" (389). The next day he returns under gray skies to dig with a primitive spade. "Midafternoon the blade struck the box," and by dusk he clears one end of the box. McCarthy describes the work of excavation in methodical detail, just as he described the work of releasing the wolf from the trap, as if to locate the significance of the relationship between beings in the labor required for one to free the other.

> He worked the end of the rope loose from the coffinbox and laid the rope by on the mound of loose dirt. Then he took up the spade and with the blade of it he split away a long sliver of wood from one of the broken boards and knocked the dirt loose from it against the box and struck a match and got it lit and stood it slantwise in the ground. Finally he climbed down into the grave and by that pale and fluttering light he began to pry apart the boards with the spade and cast them out until the remains of his brother lay wholly to sight, composed on a pallet of rotting rags, lost in his clothes as always. (392)

Returning with his horse, "[h]e climbed down into the excavation and gathered his brother up in his arms and lifted him out" (392–93). Billy finally aims to ride back to his home in New Mexico, carrying his brother's weightless remains.

But even this bundle of bones does not survive intact. Challenged by bandits who shoot his horse, Billy watches the bones fall and become "unshrouded" (396), fully exposed once again. After crossing the international boundary marked by white obelisks one last time and beginning to dig a proper grave, a local American sheriff appears and says, "You caint just travel around the country buryin people. Let me go see the judge and see if I can get him to issue a death certificate. I aint even sure whose property that is you're diggin in" (422). His brother's body cannot be laid to rest, for official and unofficial reasons. Crossing the border back into the United States means that law takes precedence over life and death; Billy must follow legal procedures and respect property rights. But the borders that Billy tried to cross between states of being may be even more significant. When Billy climbed into the open grave himself, he blurred the boundary between natural and sacred earth. From this act on, he inhabits a transitional space of his own making. The novel concludes with his return to a new and difficult world, not to the home Billy had left behind. At the end, standing in darkness and silence, save for the wind, in the middle of the road, Billy bows his head and weeps. "He sat there for a long time and after a while the east did gray and after a while the right and godmade sun did rise, once again, for all and without distinction" (426). McCarthy concludes his novel with the powerful image of a man simultaneously broken and emerging into a more integrated existence, like someone who has completed a religious ritual by wandering in the desert, encountering death and contamination, and thus purifying his body and his spirit. We have seen similar rituals in the post-atomic desert, and in fact McCarthy's more recent novel *The Road* could be read explicitly as the spiritual remapping of a landscape ravaged by atomic explosions and fallout. Here McCarthy's hero has neither gained access to the cultural mysteries of the Old World nor created a bright future. He has, however, seen enough of life on both sides of the border to return humbled, without illusion, and in a condition of permanent exile.

"All the Earth Is a Grave"

Asked in an interview whether *Mexicanos* are preoccupied with death, novelist and Stanford literature professor Arturo Islas first replied defensively, "What's wrong with that?" Then he elaborated, "[T]he culture I come from is not afraid of death in the sense that it's not afraid to talk about it, it's not afraid to pay it homage, it's not afraid to pay it tribute. That doesn't mean we are mournful grieving people. It means that you can't have life without a sense of your mortality" (Burciaga, "Conversation" 164–65). For Alberto Ríos, death is the condition for poetry in the borderlands because it marks a definitive shift in states of being. A writer who brings back the dead asserts his power to flaunt rational expectation and to define a community through stories and imagination rather than political and economic reality. The emphasis that Islas and Ríos give to human mortality announces the affinity between them and the Mexican- and Latin-American cultures that substantially shape their identities. By imagining encounters between characters in the United States and mythic or familial figures from their Mexican past, they interrogate the limits of national demarcation and the collective meaning of migrant experience.

For these authors and for other writers of borderlands fiction, graves function as both symbolic resting places and sites where buried stories are excavated. Within the transitional topography of the cemetery and the gravesite, the open grave plays a special role. At an open grave, the miracu- lous or the historical—or the absence of either—must be confronted and explained. Throughout the borderlands, the nature of such sensations and their resolution reveal a great deal about a person's cultural identity and his or her relation to history. In *The Crossing*, McCarthy describes an actual grave and the work of excavating the body within. For Ríos and Islas, "open graves" take many forms, from the mouths of spirits to people talking from hospital beds to a disembodied wind. As Saldívar argues, it is the spatial contradiction between the extended physical line of the border and the immaterial space of the spirits that defines Chicano border stories (*Border Matters* 84–85). In the process of figuring such borders between life and death, these writers animate and give voice to the mul- tiple and conflicting histories that the dominant cultures of each nation have suppressed.

Cultures define themselves through their burial practices, and allow- ing a grave to remain open usually violates fundamental beliefs in the importance of separating the living from the dead. James Griffith has studied cemeteries in Nogales, a city that straddles the border, focusing on how Mexican families in Sonora work harder to decorate the graves of their dead relatives with elaborate paper flowers in observance of All Souls' Day than the Mexican-American or Anglo families north in Arizona. The Mexican women who make artificial wreaths start taking orders in September; by October, planted flowers (especially yellow mari- golds) begin to be harvested and brought to the gates of the cemetery; and on November 1, families are busy clearing gravestones, re-lettering nameplates, and painting wrought-iron crosses in preparation for the next day's festivities. On the Anglo side, families also bring flowers to the graves as decoration, but there are more fresh bouquets, and the colors seem to be more subdued. Few trucks in Arizona sell decorations and food at a cemetery's entrance, and the Catholic church directs an official procession. Griffith attributes the difference to the continuities with Baroque culture still important to Mexican identity: "Profusion of detail; richness and complexity of color, form, and meaning; a fascination with miniaturization, movement real and implied, and dramatic contrast" (*A Shared Space* 24).

Several critics have noted the many ways that Ríos blends and crosses boundaries, deliberately mixing metaphorical and realistic descriptions; his burial scenes heighten such fluid poetics.[6] Ríos himself sees his writerly role as that of a guide between worlds and ways of being. He has spoken often of his desire to represent the voice of a community in his writing, as well as of his acceptance of indeterminacy: "Community itself becomes a kind of character in much Latino writing; it has energy and is a player. . . . Also it's characterized by an openness to the idea that we don't have an answer or explanation for all things. So there are ghosts, all kinds of escapades that a coldly scientific perspective would dismiss. But somebody who's lived through it says, 'But it did happen; it happened to us. We all went through it'" (Interview by William Barillas 122–23). He explains, "I think I take readers to places *and* I bring them back. But I set up my own laws, my own set of rules and boundaries. I try very hard not to let go of your hand" (qtd. in Jenks 120).

Ríos's story "Nine Quarter-Moons" in *The Curtain of Trees* integrates many of these elements as it connects the real and the surreal and makes the border difficult to fix in place and in time. In fact, it transforms the borderlands into wind—not just an occasional, random wind, but a wind that blows across the centuries. Even as the people in this unnamed border town want to forget, the wind reminds them: "Townspeople who had been through this before had to remind everyone, and had to warn the children especially, as the bully air barged into town after being away. They had so much wanted to forget that they did, in fact, forget" (3). The wind lives and even behaves like a person, specifically like "a distant, barely tolerated second cousin whose uneven presence and irritating laughter through the years of occasional visits caused some tension, even if out of politeness everyone laughs" (3). Ríos calls this wind "a parable for what might happen in this town" (4). It is also a parable for the border's history of cultural miscommunication and idealization, set against the continued rhythms of everyday life. The story's title comes from the prosaic appearance of the baker's hands, which prove their hard work with flour packed under his nine nails (the tenth finger he lost when he was a butcher, and the town considered that he had sacrificed it for them).

Ríos's wind brings fragments of news from Mexico, but the voices do not speak clearly. His narrator explains that the wind had in it old radios suddenly brought to life, "echoes of conversation from other towns" and "the occasional cat and mesquite branch and swirling parrot" (5). Like the barely welcome cousin, the wind's voices fail to restore any desired connection with distant places and people, reminding the town instead of its isolation. Then the wind becomes an "outlaw," then a "circus wind," and finally a whirl of smells and colors:

> In a smell of cotton candy, which was really orange blossoms and jasmine, with perhaps some honeysuckle and chicken with rosemary that had been cooking; in a dappled light, which had to filter through all the things swirling in the air, and which got turned left and right, and which sometimes filtered through colored glass or cellophane, turning blue and red and violet; in a taste of rain, not so much because rain was imminent but because so many bottles of water and apple soda had been opened by the wind, along with so many cartons of milk and tins of gasoline and barrels of beer, which became a wet gold in the air; in an aura of Neapolitan ice cream strategies, a taste of watermelon wedded as well to a taste of rabbit stew; and in a roar, but a roar at once taken back as too amateurish and easy, so that all that was left was quiet: in this quiet, the wind found its moment and disappeared. (6)

Shifting its status from representative of the extended Mexican family to the "outlaw" of popular American culture to an unruly "circus" that deliberately invokes the socially disruptive potential of the carnival, the wind finally takes sensory form as air—air in constant independent motion, air saturated with the combination of smells familiar to people in this locality. Once the wind passes, the people start cleaning up, filling the atmosphere with the sounds of their labor: "It was the sound of ancient work. Fix the fence, sweep the floors, paint the door blue again" (8). Everyday life resumes, perhaps more quietly than usual. And then, Mr. Calderón's second cousin really does arrive, unannounced and still not really wanted. This time, the townspeople are prepared—they will not accept the stranger and his assumed familial connection without questioning him. "[I]f it is you, what is the name of our grandfather?" Mr. Calderon asks—and the story ends.

The wind in the story takes us to the limit of physical knowledge without relying on the abstract geometry of the border line, the explanations of a mystical past, or the consolations of private religious belief. Ríos's work thus extends the poetics of dissolution and reconstruction that characterized Southwestern literature in the modernist period, especially in Willa Cather's "anti-Westerns" *The Professor's House* and *Death Comes for the Archbishop*. Cather's novels figured the landscape's native history as a partly articulate sensation, dissolving the feeling of the past into the air and leaving the work of reconstruction deliberately unfinished. Cather's Anglo and European protagonists pursued their desire for regional knowledge but persistently came up against the limits of their ability to claim mastery of it. Ríos encodes such a condition of unknowability into his depiction of the air that moves perpetually across the border. More circular than linear but always open and in motion, this ambivalent wind might stand for the persistence of a never fully represented past.

In the story "What I Hear from the Bear," Ríos describes burial rituals as embedded in everyday life. He distinguishes the proper clothing and decoration for a child who died (white lace garments, often adorned with daisies, sweet peas, or lilies; a crown of flowers) from the clothing appropriate for an adult. He conjures the smells and sounds of burial rituals: marigolds and roses; the rosemary and pine used for wreaths; "sweet bread and coffee, and sometimes rain, which in turn raised the passionate but quiet scent of the creosote in those hills"; the voices of those people hired to announce deaths to the town in the days before radio, television, and daily newspapers, people often dressed as clowns or bears (*Curtain of Trees* 41). These sensory memories of burial practices confirm his identity as a member of this borderland community and provide material for fictional evocations of his family and his neighbors in mid-twentieth-century Nogales in *The Curtain of Trees, Capirotada*, and *The Smallest Muscle in the Human Body*.

In *The Rain God* (1984) and *Migrant Souls* (1990), Islas imagines the borderlands around El Paso and Ciudad Juárez through the reflections of several members and generations of the Angel family who migrated from Mexico at the time of the Revolution, dispersed to various cities in the United States, and returned to confront the deaths of the family matriarch and several of her beloved sons and grandsons. As Saldívar has argued, Islas's great subject is the return to the border cities of El Paso and Ciudad Juárez after the migration north and then out, across north America. His characters all struggle to define themselves as Mexicans and Americans through their understanding of family and cultural histories that originated in Mexico and may not survive into the second generation. Organized around memories of witnessing natural and unnatural deaths, *The*

Rain God and *Migrant Souls* reconstruct the double lives of second- and third-generation migrants and meditate on the effects of death, violence, and loss on those who remain in the United States. The novels locate those meditations alternately in enclosed domestic spaces (studies, gardens) and open ones (the desert, the ocean), liminal spaces that bring together different generations, cultures, states of being, and sexualities. By narrating the memories of many characters, Islas creates voices that link physical and spiritual realms. Roberto Cantú observes that *The Rain God*'s narrator "appears to be speaking through the mouths of dead family members while, simultaneously, allowing them to speak through his 'words' and his 'blood' (read both in its ancestral and sacrificial resonances)" (148). Saldívar calls Islas's strategy "chronological dislocation: the free wandering flow of mind, back and forth in time, over names and events at least known to the narrator but not to us on a first reading" ("The Hybridity of Culture" 166). It is also the monological mode of magical realism, as we will see in the next chapter.

Representing "the very ideals of the border-crossing intellectual," Islas moved fluently between city and academic life and between American, Anglo, European, and Latin American literary traditions (Saldívar 74–75). Born in El Paso, he taught at Stanford from 1971 until he died of HIV/AIDS in 1991. In 1992, Carlos Fuentes named "Islas's novels exemplary of the 'boom' in U.S. Latino/a literature—an emergent transnational writing." Islas's role in the study of border literature continues to grow.[7] Saldívar goes as far as to claim that "*The Rain God* and its companion novel, *Migrant Souls* . . . manage to encompass some five hundred years of U.S.–Mexico border space and time, of the geography, history, and psychology of *la frontera*" (75). In an interview conducted in 1987, Islas explained the way that his origins in El Paso shaped his identity and his ways of looking at other places. "The entire bicultural, bilingual *ambiente* is extremely important to my work," he explained. Though his second novel (*Migrant Souls*) is set in several cities, from San Francisco to New York, Islas insisted that its "perspective is still the same because the eyes through which I view those places are the eyes that come from El Paso. I transplant the desert into San Francisco, the desert into Washington, D. C., and then look at those places from that point of view. . . . [T]he Mexican and American reality that I carry around with me is the Mexican and American reality we find here in El Paso. Mexican and American realities in Mexico City are different" (Interview with Aguilar Melantzón 3–4). The Galarza lecture he delivered at Stanford in 1990 drew parallels between his family history and Galarza's, noting that although he did not grow up in Mexico and his teachers never spoke of Mexican history, in El Paso he never felt far from his family's country of origin. He still considered himself located on the bridge, "a child of the Border" defined by the border's uneven historical awareness, its light and landscape, its people, and its cultural identity. In a later interview, he revealed that the character of Miguel Chico was closely related to himself but he claimed, too, to be "all of my characters. . . . I'm like dream figures" (Burciaga 163).

An acute awareness of economic necessity and an understanding of the fluid, often disorienting exchange between nations and cultures inform Islas's fictional articulations of borderlands subjectivity. Located in the towns of El Paso and Ciudad Juárez, renamed "Del Sapo," *The Rain God* and *Migrant Souls* reveal that people cross the line every day for work, seemingly paying little attention to the national boundary. Maria, a Mexican woman who works for the Angel family, is described as "one of hundreds of Mexican women from across the border who worked illegally as servants and nursemaids for families on the American side" (*Rain God* 13). During political campaigns, when border patrol became an issue for Mexican and American politicians, "Maria and all women like her took involuntary vacations without pay" (14). Islas's narrator in *The Rain God* describes the town as a place that does not observe national differences: "The border town where Felix spent most of his life is in a valley between two mountain ranges in the middle of the southwestern wastes. A wide river, mostly dry except when thunderstorms create flashfloods, separates it from Mexico. Heavy traffic flows from one side of the river to the other, and from the air, national boundaries and differences are indistinguishable" (113). Yet, Islas's migrant family still feels set apart, especially those characters who move away and achieve independence and worldly success. They can never fully leave behind the memory of the crossing, which often meant witnessing brutal deaths. Although Islas's border exists in real historical time, his characters' memories of crossing and returning to a landscape full of beauty and forbidding history work to reconfigure the border's material and official existence.

The story of the death of the family matriarch Mama Chona concludes the six interconnected stories that constitute an extended, migrant family saga in *The Rain God*, and her death will be a reward for her life of struggle: "It was the moment she had been waiting for all her life, a life of loss and sacrifice. . . . If there was justice in heaven, as she knew there was not on earth, the angels were preparing to welcome her with songs and jewels in their hands as offerings for the scars on her soul" (174). She always had faith that she would ascend to heaven, leaving the suffering of the world behind, and join the many members of her family who had already died: her first husband, Carlos, who died traveling toward the border; her second husband, Jesus; her sister Cuca; her first son, Miguel Angel, killed by a bullet in San Miguel de Allende that could have been fired by someone in the government or a revolutionary, as no one claimed responsibility in this early stage of the Revolution; her twin daughters, drowned due to a servant's neglect; a stillborn child; and, most significantly for the novel, her son Felix, murdered in the desert by a young man who rejected Felix's sexual advances.

After such loss, in Mama Chona's Catholic reckoning, there should be redemption. As death comes closer, Mama Chona begins to smell rain in the desert and imagines that she can see profuse desert flowers:

> She longed to see the yucca and ocotillo in bloom, to breathe in their fragrance and praise them for their thorniness and endurance. If only human beings could be like plants. In one of her daydreams, she sees the desert sand filled with verbenas and blooming dandelions, and with the first Miguel by her side, she discovered wild roses. The mourning doves accompanying them were the color of twilight. "Look," she said to her son, "look!" She opened her eyes and saw that she was still in that strange room with all the family waiting for her to die. (179)

Suddenly, Mama Chona—and perhaps the entire family—senses the presence of her dead son Felix, who embraces her like a Rain God himself, "smell[ing] like the desert after a rainstorm." Here Islas does away with the grave, allowing the most powerful female character with the deepest ties to Mexico to move right from the sterile hospital bed to the fertile desert. Even as the reports of revolution in Mexico reached her in America, Mama Chona had already left her homeland behind and "had grown to love the bleak desert landscape" (*Migrant Souls* 39). Now, at death, she fulfills *her* dream of migration: she will leave the physical world and its ruins for utter freedom of movement.

For her children and grandchildren, however, such dreams will be more difficult to realize. They are still trapped in the hospital room, distinctly unfree. What distinguishes the family matriarch, a first-generation migrant, is not only her embrace of death and her acceptance of a new homeland but her knowledge of Mexican culture and her pragmatic historical consciousness. To the end of her life Mama Chona held fast to Catholicism and to pre-Columbian myths, non-rational beliefs that she thought would protect her from the border's social and historical realities. Islas's narrator explains, "In Mama Chona's eyes, theology was much more important than history." Other members of the Angel family, however, "led double lives and followed the rules of both cultures as best they could" (42). She always kept with her a copy of a poem allegedly written by Netzahualcóyotl, King of Texcoco, and transcribed by her beloved first son, Miguel Angel. The poem's importance to her lay in both its personal association and its transcultural meaning. It begins, "All the earth is a grave and nothing escapes it; nothing is so perfect that it does not descend to its tomb. / Rivers, rivulets, fountains and waters flow, but never return to their joyful beginnings; anxiously they hasten on to the vast realms of the Rain God. / As they widen their banks, they also fashion the sad urn of their burial" (164). Netzahualcóyotl's poem promises that "the written page" will recall the grand, if doomed, accomplishments of past generations; the novel's epigraph, from Pablo Neruda, also promises to give voice to the dead. The poem evokes the power of men to create their own government, to conquer others, and to amass wealth, but also asserts the poet's power to record such accomplishments. Poetry alone can record nature's "joyful beginnings," Netzahualcóyotl proclaims. Cultures may vanish, but the "written page" of the poem will remain.

While these textual allusions to Mexico's pre-Columbian past and to Neruda, the great Chilean poet of the twentieth century, seem to promise literary riches and provide consolation for Mama Chona, they fail to be fully integrated into the worldview of the next generation. Miguel Chico's formal education in American schools led him to reject his Mexican past and conform to academic expectations for scholarship in the United States, and his familial education, conducted primarily by Mama Chona, taught him to behave politely in public and to indulge in the pleasures of oral tales, or cuentos, only in private. The translation of "All the earth is a grave" in The Rain God also indicates the difficulty exiles face in recovering the culture of their lost homeland; for Miguel Chico, the poetic power of pre-Columbian and Latin American poets may not survive translation across the border.[8] Erlinda Gonzales-Berry has noted how subtly Islas uses pre-Columbian beliefs throughout the novel, especially those beliefs that are commonly over-mythologized. In her view, Mama Chona's death and the allusions to Neruda and Netzahualcóyotl both work to construct a hybrid mestizo worldview, rather than a traditional Mexican one. By privileging neither pre-Columbian nor Judeo-Christian beliefs, neither contemporary Latin American nor historic Mexican poetry, she argues, Islas's fiction engages in a productive play of religions and cultures. Daniel Cooper Alarcón has observed that several writers of Chicano/a coming-of-age stories, like Luis Valdez and Sandra Cisneros, feature protagonists who deliberately reject their parents' displays of Mexicanness, announcing their generational difference through acts of assimilation or hybridity (Gonzales-Berry 258–61). By using the same poetic text to signify differently for each character, Islas may be exploring the process by which migrants construct their own imaginary homelands, both within and against the collective experience of their generation.

We see this complex and highly individual process of reclaiming the past through memory and literature in both *The Rain God* and *Migrant Souls*. In the first novel, Miguel Chico clearly reaches the limits of his intellectual achievement when he struggles to reconcile his present accomplishments with his family history. His father travels from El Paso to Berkeley and appears in his study, seeking forgiveness for his affair with his mother's best friend. In the chapter "Rain Dancer," the memory of his uncle Felix travels, too, from the borderland desert to Miguel Chico's Berkeley garden at twilight, filling it anew with loss and longing. Miguel Chico knew his uncle "loved those quiet moments at dusk as much as the smell of the desert just before and after a thunderstorm when the sky, charged with lightning, became fresh with the fragrance of the mesquite, greasewood, and vitex trees" (Islas, *Rain God* 114). This doubled twilight and the memory of the desert signify temporal and spatial sites of transition, marking scenes of death and their incorporation into the bodies of those who witnessed them. It confirms the truth of the words attributed to Netzahualcóyotl through the feeling of the body, without inquiring into scholarly matters of origin.

In Islas's fiction, the border landscape becomes a grave of cultural history, an archaeological site whose largest spiritual and cultural meanings must be brought to the surface through repeated excavations. According to Islas's colleague José Antonio Burciaga, *The Rain God* "gave the magical realism of Latin American literature 'a distinct desert flavor . . .'" (qtd. in Aldama, *Dancing with Ghosts* 43). What Islas translates from pre-Columbian poetry into his fiction is not its history of scholarship but its aesthetics of feeling. Noted for its "beauty and delicacy," Aztec poetry such as Netzahualcóyotl's also implicitly responds to a brutal political reality.[9] The figure of the flower, thought to stand for poetry itself, and the heart, often a symbol of ephemeral life, appear in *Migrant Souls* to express the longing for a desert homeland and the emptiness of family tradition felt by second- and third-generation migrants. While we might consider these motifs "universal," it is worth remembering Rushdie's claim that a migrant's "physical fact of discontinuity . . . may enable him to speak properly and concretely on a subject of universal significance and appeal" (12).

Miguel Chico also draws from other cultural traditions in telling stories to his family. When he visits his nieces Hanna and Rebecca in Los Angeles, he tells them about a Japanese prince who wanted to see a morning glory. The prince sent a messenger to a lord who was expert at growing them and announced that he would appear on a certain day to see the flowers. When he arrived, he encountered "field after field of trampled vines and broken trellises," an empty great hall, and, on the table of the main room, "a single, perfect morning glory floating in a simple peasant's bowl" (195). Hearing the story, Hanna starts to cry, recognizing that her uncle had tried to explain to her the nature and cost of beauty. The following day, Miguel Chico's cousin Josie picks a gardenia from the bush outside as her final gesture before returning to Del Sapo and "left it floating in a paper cup by the kitchen sink." However, "[s]he could not bring herself to destroy the bush. She felt it would haunt her in a desert too dry to offer her gardenias" (196). In a sense, Josie translates Miguel Chico's story, feeling its truth as her daughter did and re-expressing it in her own environment. Both story and act use flowers as symbols for beauty that cannot last, just as Aztec poets used flowers to indicate the ephemerality of life.[10] As he layers the images of flowers and evokes their aesthetic and cultural resonances, Islas gestures toward a synthesis of poetic traditions and everyday experience and suggests that any intellectual recovery of the past must be complemented by faith in both history and art.

Migrant Souls continues to explore the economic pressures that kept the border permeable and the emotional pressures that keep migrants in motion. The novel begins by describing the childhood of another branch of the Angel family, the Salazars. Struggling to provide for her husband Sancho and her three daughters, Ophelia, Serena, and Josie, Eduviges raises her own chickens and pigeons. Once "she even bought a live duck from God knows where and kept it until the Garcias next door began complaining about all the racket it made at night" (20). So she kills it and serves it in a *mole poblano*, which Josie refuses to eat because she liked the duck alive. Then, Eduviges decides to make a proper American turkey for Thanksgiving, despite her husband's preference for enchiladas, his offer to bring "a nice, fat pheasant from the Chihuahua mountains," and his resistance to turning his daughters "into little *gringas*" (22). She knows that meat is always cheaper across the border, so the entire family travels to Mexico to buy the bird. This is a comic episode in many ways. It reveals Eduviges's determined and crazy driving; depicts the stupidity of the turkeys themselves, said to drown in the rain because "[t]hey stretch their necks, open their beaks wide, and let it pour in" (27); describes the absurd image of Serena sitting "like a *Virgen de Guadalupe* statue on her yellow plastic-colored throne" gobbling with the turkey; and concludes at Don Luis Leal's Famous Tex-Mex Diner, where the cultural hybridity of the borderlands is depicted in real, everyday terms: everyone drinks Coke with their *menudo* and *gorditas*.

For Josie Salazar, though, the episode constitutes a serious encounter with what it means to live on the border. She and her sister ask her father if they had arrived yet so many times that he threatens to "leave them in the middle of nowhere." They laugh and ask him where they can find "the middle of nowhere," and together they hazard some answers: the deep bottom of the sea or the Sahara Desert, Sancho says, or "the space between the stars and no planets around" or the top of Mount Everest, according to Serena (26). However, Josie keeps her attention on the place where she lives, insisting that the middle of nowhere is Del Sapo, Texas. Then she revises her claim, saying it is in her own heart. By imagining parallel sites of absence, Josie maps her lack of cultural rootedness within both her body and the external landscape. Tatum suggests that "[t]he space of the heart can be said to identify an *internal* topography of transitions, a rendering of human consciousness itself as a paradoxical space of conjunction and division, arrival and departure" ("Topographies" 329). The emptiness of Josie's heart identifies a space of absence from which her new homeland must be imagined. Though she was "brought up on deportation stories as fairy tales and family legends," the reality of witnessing the other borderlands feels different. She notices the young Indian women with children and the old Indian women begging in Ciudad Juárez, and she sees herself in the dark-haired mothers and her sister Serena in the elderly beggars. She asks her father what it means to be an "alien," as the newspapers and her classmates called her, causing her father to pull off the road and declare with great seriousness, "We are not aliens. We are American citizens of Mexican heritage. We are proud of both countries and have never and will never be that word you just said to me" (29). When her mother confronts the immigration officer and pushes him away from her father's car, Serena imitates the turkey's gobble and Sancho laughs, but Josie trembles, sensing the persistence of the dangers her family has faced. Only later in the novel do we learn that Mama Chona left Josie's mother and her aunts and uncles in Chihuahua so that she could give birth to her son Miguel Grande in relative safety. Eduviges, Jesus Maria, Mema, Armando, and Felix all saw the brutality of the Revolution firsthand—one morning they woke and "watched the early light through the corpses of men, women, and children scattered like straw on the street below" (Islas, *Migrant Souls* 229). In response, Jesus Maria vowed never to return to Mexico. Although Mama Chona reached Ciudad Juárez and gave birth successfully, she did so just as her husband Jesus Angel was dying, "struck by the train that had brought us to Juarez" (231). Mama Chona recalled, "The first labor pain came when I saw him sprawled on the ground" (231). For the first and second generation of migrants in the family, crossing the border meant risking death.

Perhaps because she identifies with the Indian women in Ciudad Juárez who could not possibly cross the border as Americans and assimilate, Josie struggles to leave her family and her Mexican heritage behind and to fill her empty heart. She loses herself in *Jane Eyre* and considers imitating characters in *The Charterhouse of Parma*. She marries a gringo man, Harold Newman, and at the wedding Miguel Chico "felt he was inside a heart on fire with joy and sorrow" (102). Again, the figure of Josie's heart expands to include her closest cousin, her family, and the guests at the wedding—the borderlands community Josie cannot yet accept as her own. She tries to fill the emptiness with the intensity of her joy and sorrow, feelings that carry her as far as Los Angeles. Her oldest sister, Ophelia, chooses to marry "a decent man of Anglo-Mexican background," stay in Del Sapo, and teach her children "to follow Mama Chona's rules" (104–5). Serena chooses to teach P.E. at "the same high school her parents and cousins had attended" (105) and later lives with a woman she meets at the school. However, like Miguel Chico, Josie returns to Del Sapo when Harold leaves her, a few years after her passionate affair with one of his friends.

In a prose poem Islas wrote in 1970, "Cuauhtémoc's Grave," he uses an epigraph from Octavio Paz's *The Labyrinth of Solitude*. To discover the location of the Aztec warrior's grave "would mean nothing less than to return to our origins, to reunite ourselves with our ancestry, to break out of our solitude. It would be a resurrection," Paz wrote. In the poem and in his fiction, Islas refuses to abandon the search for origins, even as he struggles to articulate the experience of exile in the borderlands.[11]

Islas's fiction shows how the spaces of the borderlands are carried inside the bodies of those who migrate away and then come back, like Miguel Chico and Josie Salazar. In its natural form, all the earth is a grave; the border observes no national difference. As a landscape inhabited by both natives to the United States and exiles from Mexico, however, the border has neither stable meaning nor sacred status. When Miguel Chico longs for home, he "longed to return to the desert of his childhood, not to the family but to the place" (5). This borderlands desert is the open grave that both divides and connects Mexico and the United States.

6

Magical Regions

We are never free of the history of our home.
—Ellen Meloy, *The Last Cheater's Waltz*, 71

This study of the poetics of Southwestern homelands has assembled a range of texts as perspectives on the kinds of places that have produced new cultural affiliations in response to dislocation, environmental destruction, or exile. Each chapter has demonstrated the necessity of reading across genres, media, and cultures in order to reconstruct the deep cultural and affective histories of regional landscapes. While writers, photographers, and painters in the middle decades of the twentieth century worked with a fairly clear set of generic expectations, including an acute awareness of their (often limited) audiences, those who returned to the Southwest's ruined, contaminated, or abandoned landscapes late in the century began with the assumption that any adequate aesthetic representation would require the mobilization of hybrid aesthetic forms and multiple historical perspectives. To move beyond the limits of location, these Southwestern artists experimented with mixed-media texts and installations, interdisciplinary histories, environmental politics, and transnational theories. By connecting their knowledge of local places with research into other cultures and contemporary artistic, cultural, and political movements, they integrated their own explorations of the meaning of regional landscapes with ongoing critiques of the effects of globalization on their environment, culture, and structure of belief.

Writers of magical realist fiction have also succeeded in reaching global audiences interested in accounting for the gap between the promise of worldwide modernization and the persistence of tradition—interested, that is, in reimagining the relation between seemingly incompatible rational and spiritual worlds. In an essay on magical realism, narrative, and history, Ato Quayson defines magical realism in terms of the equal relation it establishes between real and fantastical elements. If the Enlightenment opposed traditional conceptions of time "saturated with ghostly or spiritual significance" with the rational "disenchanted time of history," magical realism promised a formal means of dissolving such hierarchical divisions and rendering both senses of time equally valuable (Quayson 726–28). Other distinguishing features of the genre include "the general instability of the perceived world, and the nature and range of the blurring of boundaries between the animal and human worlds" (Quayson 730). Like many cultural historians, Quayson identifies the origin of the term "magical realism" in the 1925 work of German art critic Franz Roh.[1] He notes that Roh seemed to derive his imagery from scientific inquiries into invisible matter, especially into the structure of the atom, and that he advocated close aesthetic scrutiny of the object world in order to gain access to the still-miraculous knowledge described by science.

The true origins of a popular literary form are always suspect, especially considering the various sources consulted by writers of magical realism in the Americas. Other relevant precedents for magical realist fiction of the late twentieth century include the work of Arturo Uslar Pietri from Venezuela, Miguel Angel Asturias from Guatemala, and especially Alejo Carpentier from Cuba—Latin American artists who adapted the idea of magical realism in the late 1940s. It was Carpentier who wrote about "*lo real maravilloso*" in the prologue to *The Kingdom of This World*, claiming that while European writers strained to "invoke the marvellous" in their fiction, anyone who walked on the streets in Haiti in 1943 could be "in daily contact with something which might be called *marvellous reality*," the reality of collective faith in miracles (qtd. in Moretti, *Modern Epic* 234). The original Spanish version of the term "marvelous reality" expresses the extent to which this fictional mode was conceived, for better or worse, as congruous with the experience of everyday life in the Americas. "Not a poetics—a state of affairs," as Moretti puts it (234).

The dates, national origins, and terminology of magical realism are important for several reasons. First, they mark the period of high modernism in Europe and North America within (and against) which this fictional mode developed. Second, the postwar development of the practice constituted symbolic resistance to Western domination that united writers in the Americas against what they perceived as oppressive modernization and thus led the way for other postcolonial writers. By the mid-twentieth century, magical realism's mixture of "real" and "unreal" realities effectively articulated a Latin American worldview to

North American and European readers through a "stereoscopic vision that would see the layers of pre-columbian, colonial, and postcolonial histories simultaneously" (Aldama, *Postethnic Narrative Criticism* 9). The fiction of Latin American writers embraced an "oral based, folkloric *mestizo* spirit," according to Frederick Luis Aldama, and became a hybrid mode attractive to writers and readers who sought to fight against scientific rationality and the global penetration of American capitalism and Anglo-European culture.

In this chapter I reflect on the genre's articulation in the southwestern United States and in Mexico's northwest as a significant development in the history of the novel, which provides a rich fictional form for articulating the conflict between mobility and attachment to place that has defined the greater Southwest's regional imaginary in the past century. Considering borderlands fiction within the broad category of magical realism runs the risk of equating diverse fictional practices as blandly as the proponents of the so-called world novel, a category rightly criticized by Michael Denning as a marketing device contrived to unify "distinct regional and linguistic traditions into a single cosmopolitan 'world beat'" ("The Novelists' International" 703). Southwestern fiction continues to perform distinct cultural work, however. Magical realism in the borderlands restores the voices of the region's indigenous people and values traditional wisdom as strongly as the modern desire for mobility, thus revealing and resisting the region's legacy of conquest. Because indigenous traditions rely on intimate knowledge of natural and animal worlds, the integration of human and non-human experience in this fiction signals both a recovery of native worldviews and a challenge to Enlightenment conceptions of progress. As it reconstructs earlier eras in regional history, magical borderlands fiction uses the bodies of migrants and figures of the border to re-open cultural routes between Mexico and the United States and explore competing conceptions of time. Instead of creating an idealized and atemporal fictional world, it makes the variously documented but repressed experiences of the past vividly present—and posits the instability of historical knowledge as the condition for gaining access to new states of physical and spiritual being. It thus rewrites the tragic struggle of migration into a kind of postregional romance that reimagines the regional landscape as both saturated with history and a place where cultural and political hierarchies continue to be challenged.

In the contemporary Southwest, magical realism also constitutes a literary adaptation to the conditions of survival in the borderlands, as Alberto

Alvaro Ríos's recollection of his divided childhood and his fictional imaginings attest. Ríos recalls, "Growing up in a multicultural household and neighborhood and world was always like having binoculars" because it allowed him to bring "two lenses together" to see things in the distance close up. Revising Salman Rushdie's slanted perspective on his imaginary homeland, he calls using two names in two languages "to binocularize" (Interview with William Barillas 121). Whereas many of the early practitioners of magical realism developed their literary techniques as a means to convey a common Latin American subjectivity and to articulate political resistance to dominant Anglo-European culture, Ríos here insists that his hybrid perspective both connects him with history of fiction writing in the Americas and serves to articulate the specific experience of second- and third-generation Mexican migrants in the American Southwest.

Magical realism "exists at the intersection of two worlds" and involves "the repudiation of the metropolitan paradigm" and "the affirmation of the local."[2] Luis Alberto Urrea's *The Hummingbird's Daughter* (2005) exemplifies how magical realist fiction of the greater Southwest offers new strategies for invigorating the genre and animating the complex history of the borderlands. Like the novels by Arturo Islas discussed in chapter 5, *The Hummingbird's Daughter* engages mythic and fantastic elements to tell a family saga in which indigenous belief, collective memory, and individual sensation collide. Throughout each character's migration across regional borders, from one type of homeland to the next, the memories of abandoned landscapes follow and the feeling of lost people and places permeate the air, the room, the house, or the railroad car. Each fictional reconstruction of a lost homeland restores the power of the culture that migrants were forced to leave behind, provides new cultural routes to the past, and sustains a sensory openness to the utopian possibilities of the future, often figured through the body's perpetual movement and its permeability. Such magical realist novels test the power of local structures of feeling against and within global networks of communication and exchange.[3] As practiced by Urrea and other Southwestern writers, magical borderlands fiction explores *both* the experience of the physical subject and the relation between "the megaspace of hemispheric migration and the micromappings of rooms, parlors, and kitchens" (Saldívar, *Border Matters* 78). It articulates a poetics of the smallest individual and the largest collective bodies in motion, in collision—and, finally, perhaps, in dispersal.

Urrea's nonfiction writings confirm the "truth" of Mexico as a privileged site of "the marvelous real," continuing the tradition initiated by

Asturias and Carpentier of locating the materials for magical fictions in the history of the Americas. In his collection of autobiographical sketches, *Nobody's Son* (1998), Urrea explains, "Students of magic realism in graduate school today need only to live in a small Mexican town for a few weeks. They will soon see that this mad literary genre is based in truth. My father's memories were full of ghosts, natural catastrophes, demons, miracles, weird sex, weirder pranks, floods, appalling deaths, flying saucers, Indian spirits, and tall tales" (31). Even Urrea's own childhood in Tijuana seems to him, in retrospect, "a place of magic and wonder" (65) where the power of love between the couple who cultivated a beautiful garden and took care of him as part of their family is perfectly revealed at Mamá Chayo's funeral, when her husband Abelino "reached into the coffin and put his palm against her cheek. His big, iron, calloused worker's hand. It trembled slightly, and it landed on her flesh as delicately as one of her butterflies. Just a second, no more. But all the love in the world was there, in his palm" (151).

The Hummingbird's Daughter (2005), based on the history of Urrea's distant cousin Teresa Urrea, also insists on the fantastic truth of Mexican history. The Author's Note at the end of the novel cites "hundreds of articles" about this "real person" that supplemented the folklore and tape-recorded oral histories that circulated through Urrea's family. Research for the novel took over twenty years, leading Urrea into archives containing microfilms of journalist Lauro Aguirre's writings and documents proving all the "miracles" Teresa performed, into long conversations with a Mayo *curandera* and a Chiricahua medicine man, and into published scholarship about "la Santa de Cabora" and newspaper reports about Porfirio Díaz's campaign to repress Teresa's popular and insurrectionary influence. The one source Urrea avoided was the text that scholar Robert Irwin calls "the most complete and authoritative text on this remarkable woman" (196), Brianda Domecq's novel *La insólita historia de la Santa de Cabora* (1990), because he did not want her fiction to exert undue influence on his. Desirée Martín also focuses on Domecq's novel, arguing that this representation most effectively embraces the contradictions of Teresa's life and "exposes the illusion of national unity" in both the United States and Mexico (188, 191). According to Martín, Urrea idealizes Teresa on his website and reinscribes the mythic opposition between sacred and human categories of experience in his novel (187).

It might be more valid to critique *The Hummingbird's Daughter* in terms of its historical accuracy if it did not incorporate magical realism's narrative techniques and epistemological challenges so thoroughly. What is important about Urrea's use of sources is not their truth but the proof they provide of multiple historical and cultural realities. As Irwin's detailed investigation of Teresa Urrea's emergence as a cultural icon on both sides of the border demonstrates, she "signified in multiple ways throughout her life and continues to signify in ever evolving ways even today" (261). By incorporating so many kinds of testimonials into his own imaginative retelling of Teresa's early life, Urrea confirms the fantastic reality of this historical female figure who was also a family legend. By conceiving of her as "the hummingbird's daughter," Urrea also connects his heroine's mythological origins with magical realism's integration of human and animal worlds. Huitzilopochtli, the "Hummingbird of the South" in Nahuatl, was a sun god, the Aztec god of war, the patron of Tenochtitlan, and the god of the Mexica people.[4] Urrea imagines the illegitimate *mestiza* daughter of a Tehueco Indian woman and a rich owner of a hacienda to be the incarnation of an Aztec goddess, thus supplementing Teresa's historical reality with mythological resonance. In the novel, the "true story" of Teresa Urrea, named "Saint of Cabora" and "Queen of the Yaquis," emerges as "not only far more complex than the family legends, but far more fabulous as well," writes Larry McCaffery in his review in *The San Diego Union-Tribune* (May 22, 2005). Urrea constructs a grand, layered edifice, like a Mayan temple, "from a disparate array of genres, sources and influences—Latin American magical realism, folk tales, the Bible, Aztec and Mayan myths, Western fairy tales and the contemporary American Westerns of Thomas McGuane and Ed Abbey, Octavio Paz, Juan Rulfo, Jorge Luis Borges and James Brown, Zapata and Zappa, Jack Kerouac and Carlos Fuentes, and many others," McCaffery claims, suggesting through this list the domains and temporalities the novel engages.

Urrea's fictional realization of his heroine's many levels of signification and his mastery of magical realism's mobile and omniscient narration allows him to re-enchant the region's complex history and rewrite the violent narrative of migration from Mexico to the United States that he documented so powerfully in *Across the Wire* in terms of spiritual and imaginative motion. *The Hummingbird's Daughter* begins with three simultaneous events: A young woman named Cayeta prepares for the birth of her daughter, Teresa; Tomás Urrea travels from his ranch in Sinaloa to the Sea of Cortés to meet his friend, the engineer Lauro Aguirre, arriving by boat from Mazatlán with valuable supplies; and "the People" on the ranch prepare for the Day of the Dead. Teresa will be born in poverty and without love and her mother will abandon her to her aunt, who whips her, forces her at times to sleep with the pigs, and offers no resistance when Tomás Urrea decides to raise her himself. Yet, Teresa's curiosity and faith will allow her to connect the realms of indigenous, colonizing, and peasant cultures in pre-revolutionary Mexico and then travel beyond them. Through the teachings of the curandera Huila she will learn to work miracles on the bodies of the sick and earn the faith of thousands of pilgrims; through the education provided by Tomás, she will learn philosophy and poetry; through her own imagination and spiritual vision, she will fly to Mexico City, converse with God and the dead, project the images of another man's mind onto the wall in front of her, and emigrate to the United States on Mexico's newest rail line. She is the ideal, fantastic migrant: strong in body, unattached to a single nation, endlessly flexible in spirit. Tomás travels as far as his ingenuity and his devotion to his adopted daughter and his ranch will allow—as I will discuss shortly—and he achieves rational triumphs and worldly success. However, he lacks Teresa's magical ability to transcend class, integrate diverse cultural worlds, and extend the limits of the body. The People remain as rooted as they can, sustaining their way of life against the country's political turmoil. Throughout the richly detailed narrative of Teresa's development, the Urrea family's migrations, and the People's resistance to revolution, the narrator keeps shifting perspectives to orchestrate the historic and ongoing conflict between traditional and modernizing worlds on both sides of the border.

Urrea devotes lavish attention to the rhythms of everyday life that would be accessible to a single narrator only through modern technologies of communication and travel, and he constructs characters and plots that allow indigenous beliefs to flow from one region to another. In the first chapter, the narrator describes how all Mexicans rise to drink coffee according to their taste and dream of a common Mexico: "There was no greater mystery" (8). But only "rich men, soldiers, and a few Indians had wandered far enough from home to learn the terrible truth: Mexico was too big" (9). The truth of Mexico's marvelous variety—its fantastic plants, its regional food traditions, its thousand languages—can be imagined only by those with the privilege of mobility. The novel's narrator assumes this privilege and extends it beyond any reasonable expectation. With one voice he tells the concentric and interconnected histories of the people living in and around Urrea's ranches, the Mexican states of Sinaloa and Sonora, the beginnings of revolution in Mexico, and the trans-American spread of technology and consumer capitalism. Aware that readers will already know the macrohistory of globalization in the United States, the narrator focuses on microhistories in Mexico and the experiences of the native people of Sinaloa and Sonora, like the Mayos, the Yaquis, and the Seris. Meanwhile, directly reported dialogue brings diverse historical characters to life, preserving differences in class, personality, and culture. By maintaining a consistently defocalized narration and figuring his heroine as both a means of seeing modernization's strange marvels and a figure for articulating the power of indigenous knowledge, Urrea deftly connects the reader's awareness of globalization with his own understanding of regional landscapes, traditional healing practices, and local revolutionary movements.

Throughout the novel, Urrea's narrator conveys the privilege of distance and the exhilaration of intimacy: He can see from above the organization of the people and their wagons curling and uncurling like a spiral on their way to Cabora (144); he knows that white settlers in Oklahoma are taking Indian lands, that France claimed Tahiti, and that the telephone had been invented (139); and he notes that along with this turmoil came inventions of convenience in the United States, like packaged Thomas' English Muffins and Philadelphia Cream Cheese (139). The effect is "a special kind of defamiliarization" (Faris 50) that deliberately suspends the conflict between the real and the fantastic and renders them compatible. Because the narrator assumes such a temporally, spatially, and historically inclusive perspective, he can suggest freely that nearly any thing and any place in Mexico could be wondrous or terrifying. Often he calls on us to assume a different point of view to re-experience the modern real as marvelous by focalizing the narrative through the perspectives of peasants and indigenous people.[5] For example, when Tomás reads the foreign names of places printed on the map, his chief ranch hand Segundo finds the names "more frightening hanging in the air like wasps than writhing on the page like crushed ants" (Urrea, *Hummingbird's Daughter* 112). Teresa's first impressions of the tools and refinements of western culture in her father's house convey the fabulous nature and sensory appeal of the objects it contains, like the polished wood floor, the fluttering curtains, the thick carpet, and especially the grandfather clock, which ticks like a "muted heartbeat" and looks like a "strange square tree" (58). Teresa "put her hands upon the wood column and felt it ticking. She put her ear to it to listen to such a wondrous thing" (59). When Tomás appears, she announces, "This tree has a heart" (59). The first time she lies in a feather bed, she senses that she is floating in a cloud. Having learned from Huila that everything in the natural world, including rocks, has light and life and the capacity to talk—if one listens properly—Teresa feels connections between the domestic and the natural world that can re-enchant this overly cultivated house. Through her, readers see the past's texture of everyday life intimately as if through binoculars and can enter its reality from a new perspective.

The narrative techniques employed in *The Hummingbird's Daughter* heighten the texture of everyday life while keeping major developments, like the spread of capitalism and the Revolution, in an active periphery. Natural cycles and traditional ways of life keep coming up against pressures of economic and political change; and, as if to console the reader for these bluntly narrated, often violent losses, the novel provides full descriptions of regional speech, of the characters' bodies, of the tastes of tortillas and cacti. Here, the nostalgia is for a renewed connection to locality and to the body—and for passionate faith in God, in rationality and progress, or in revolution. As Martín explains, "the desire for lost traditions and history reflects a form of community that is specifically non-national, corresponding to fluid transnational identities that are predicated upon migration" (193). Urrea compresses the story of disenchantment that accompanied each stage of modernity and nation-building, insisting that we feel the loss of spiritual and utopian imagining with full force. The third phase of magical realist fiction "tells precisely the story of how mythical thought is reinvigorated by forced modernization, which it seeks to avoid by every means. And to oppose it, of course, not (just) by taking up explicit positions, but by means of its particular narrative techniques" (Moretti, *Modern Epic* 248). Urrea's novel extends this phase with the techniques of authorial mobility, the use of ethnographic detail, and the juxtaposition of local, hemispheric, and global histories.

Meanwhile, the People—the embodiment of the Mexican peasant class—travel little, and only when required to do so. We are shown by the narrator what the People do not know: "paved streets, streetlamps, a trolley, or a ship," the utility of stairways—the materials with which cities are built (*Hummingbird's Daughter* 3). What they do know is how to use the riches of the natural world to serve their dead: to gather offerings of green tamales; glasses of tequila, rum, rompope, or beer; "candied sweet potatoes, cactus and guayaba sweets, mango jam, goat jerky, dribbly white cheeses" (3); cigarettes; and candy skulls. These are people who resist leaving their homelands, devoting most of their energy to survival and sustaining the rituals of their faith. Even when forced to travel and settle in a new territory, they remain set in their ways. The new village that they build at Cabora "was almost identical to the one they had come from—two ragged rows of shacks in a field with thin board and paper-wall latrines stinking in back, small pigpens behind these" (169). The People thus represent the collective, rooted, and increasingly archaic power of tradition, rich in sensory satisfaction but lacking the intellectual pleasures of mobility and innovation.

As the figure of the enlightened patrón whose development would be arrested by Diaz's dictatorship and the Mexican Revolution, Tomás embodies the modern contradiction between the pursuit of knowledge and novelty and the persistent desire for satisfactions of the body and communal rituals. He gains a new relish for simple pleasures when forced to leave his home ranch in Sinaloa under political pressure. When he arrives at Cabora, he finds that his new home has already been burned. He orders the house and barn to be rebuilt, and in the process learns to revel in the pungent flavors of the People's food.

> For supper they ate caldo de ajo—garlic soup: all their stale bread that hadn't gone to the pigs or the goats floated in beef broth, salted and peppered, the garlic cloves soft in the broth like little fish. And they ate arroz con pollo, the fresh chicken mixed with prairie fowl the vaqueros had shot that day and the day before, boiled with rice and a pinch of saffron. In the morning, they would breakfast on peeled and diced beavertail-cactus pads, lard-fried beans, and their last eggs. It smelled like a festival. (159)

Following this meal and Tomás's renewed appetite for simplicity, the Urrea family begins to reconfigure itself. The class hierarchy on the ranch may not break down immediately, but familial arrangements are certainly disrupted as Tomás separates from his wife Loreto. While Loreto remains in town, he happily raises bees, accepts his illegitimate son Buenaventura and his illegitimate daughter Teresa as his children, falls in love with the young and beautiful Gabriela, and finally banishes his wife from the ranch. He also finds himself "amazed" by the natural wonders of Sonora, like the blossoming cacti and energetic toads. He admires "[t]he nasty little wind scorpions, all yellow and orange and black, like Jerusalem crickets—which he, like the People, called 'niños de la tierra'—but with immense fangs and dyspeptic dispositions," scorpions that could make "single-minded clanking progress across the Alamos road" (232). He learns that "it was a jungle in miniature," if one looked properly (192).

In Tomás's new house, we see other shifts in the established order. With the acknowledgment of her father's paternity, Teresa becomes a "doña," is expected to bathe, wear shoes and dresses, brush her teeth with a powder from London, pursue her education, refrain from any rude talk, and otherwise act like a proper lady. Huila talks freely with Tomás in the library, smoking a cigar she took from the humidor. This breakdown of hierarchies, however, also produces chaos. When thousands of pilgrims begin to arrive each day for Teresa's blessing, the plazuela Tomás built for Friday and Saturday night promenades and dances crumbles, the crowd pushes for access to the porch, and no space on the ranch remains free for exploration or contemplation. Tomás admits to his daughter, "I have lost control of everything" (403)—of his family, his property, his faith in reason. Perhaps the most dramatic example of how Teresa's gifts upset the established order and her father's rational world is the sudden appearance of an Indian boy with black feet, bloody split toenails, filthy face, and lice-infested hair at the back door one night when Teresa and Tomás are sitting together in the kitchen, eating calabaza and plum pudding, and talking about their impressions of each other and of God. The others would not let the boy approach the house in the daytime because "People say I stink too bad," (399) he explains, so he waited until night. Teresa invites him in and starts plucking lice out of his hair. Tomás helps, at Teresa's orders. "They plucked lice for so long that the boy fell asleep under their fingers. Tomás wiped so much pus on the front of his pants that they had two ugly stains. For the first time in his life, he felt—well, saintly" (403). Then Teresa falls asleep in the parlor "with her head on the boy's chest," and finally Tomás "fell asleep beside them, and that's where Gabriela found them all in the morning, dreaming together in the cool orange light of dawn" (403). From a place of banishment to the patrón's parlor, the inversion of the Indian boy's position reveals the common humanity that Tomás and Teresa now share.

Tomás's reward for seeing the possibilities for change in this real world is material success. His mines and his ranch both yield handsomely, and Aguirre's engineering projects produce successful dams and logging operations. "Thus, in a few short years, Tomás had become powerful. Truly was he a patrón, a man now, not a boy. He had his library. Thanks to Aguirre, he had water running in his white house. He had a fine life, and it would drone on exactly the way it was until he died. Little change. Few adventures" (280). The language the narrator uses to describe the protagonist's social ascent undermines the value of material success and worldly power. Indeed, having experienced a reinvigorated relation with his new homeland, Tomás seeks to sustain the energy of the collision of native and imported cultures by returning to a state of wildness, not "droning" on into the future. Whereas the People miss their "green homeland" and the "romance" of the region they were forced to leave, Tomás searches for new and extreme experiences. Though he does not understand his own urges, he wants to witness the "fabled hundred-mile footraces" of the Tarahumaras, or be attacked by a lion (280). Anything would be better than more of the same, he thinks. Particularly humiliating is Loreto's suggestion that the ranch is a rustic affectation: "this jape about the little country home, the little country cabin, was particularly pointed, and it drew blood like a paper cut" (234). When Tomás reaches the limits of rationality and European civilization, he turns toward the places that still contain what Moretti calls "the reserves of magic of the modern world-system: places of prophecies and archetypes; of apparitions, and pacts with the Devil" (*Modern Epic* 249). However, Tomás checks his own journey into the reserves of magic when he witnesses his daughter emerge from a coma following a seizure—a miraculous recovery that attracts thousands of pilgrims, produces chaos and destruction on the ranch, and results in the brutal suppression of a peasant rebellion in Tomóchic by Diaz's officers (Martín 183).

Although Teresa's reward for learning to use her powers of healing will be isolation and exile from her native Mexico, the part of her life narrated in *The Hummingbird's Daughter* emphasizes the freedom she gains through integrating varieties of knowledge. She discovered young that she could see external manifestations of internal states, such as colors surrounding people. One day she noted that "Tomás had worry leaking out from under his hat like smoke. Along with these purple clouds were some baffling vibrations that, for reasons she couldn't explain, looked to her as if they came from a lemon" (57). Gradually she realizes the power to conjure heat in her hands, to receive the breath of the hedionda bush, and to deliver babies. The warm, healing touch of her hands on women's bellies feels like the honey Tomás so carefully cultivates, and the ability to stay connected with the earth that Huila taught her makes literal and magical the notion of being rooted. She learns to use the many tools offered to her—reading and writing from Aguirre and Tomás, the healing powers of native plants from Huila and the Mayo medicine man Manuelito—and thus synthesizes the powers of perception, literacy, and indigenous tradition. Urrea figures this freedom in physical terms, too, when he describes Teresa's ability to transport her friends to locations of their choice. Realizing that she can "capture [her friends'] dreams and direct them" (253),

Teresa flies with Gaby to Guaymas to feel the sea breeze and smell the salty air. She explains to Josephina, "We were really there. . . . It was more than a dream" (254). Combining the magic of flying with the concrete reality of distant places, Teresa's night journeys extend the novel's poetics of re-enchanting Mexico's native places and anticipate her experience of crossing the border with the U.S.

One night Teresa takes Gaby and Josephina to Mexico City. The three girls leave behind their earthbound condition as "prisoners of the ground" when Teresa transforms them into states of nature, but they maintain their bodily and temporal identities. They become first water, then clouds, and then air as they drift above villages and migrating birds to the streets of Mexico City:

> Yes, streets. They saw now the carriages clopping down the boulevards. Buildings, houses, dark parks. Boats in canals.
>
> Music rose from a far plaza. Cooking smoke. Song lifted to their ears. Voices. Trumpets. They fell to earth ensnared in the scents of the city: perfume, cigars, charcoal, steam, garbage, water, horses, carne asada.
>
> Their feet touched wet cobbles. (257)

In this magical encounter, the city offers real sensory riches, if little social order. In Cabora, the girls were "prisoners of the ground"; in Mexico City they follow the dictates of their own bodies and become "ensnared" by scent. They begin to walk through the streets, "gawk" at trolley cars, explore the cathedral. Finally "they sat on a bank in Xochimilco and soaked their feet in the ancient waterways of the Aztecs" (259). The trip to the capital records the real presence of different forms of transportation, but it allows the girls to bypass the need for horses, carriages, or railcars—the physical demands of modernity—and move directly into the sensations of city life and the ancient power of the Aztecs. Urrea suggests here that restoring contact with Aztec culture may provide a means for healing the divide between Mexico's traditional and modern worlds—and for imagining new mixtures of physical, cultural, and spiritual experience.

Another episode that realizes the magical power of native places and indigenous beliefs is Teresa's temporary death. After a violent encounter with the ranch hand Millán, Teresa dies and then returns to life after four days in her coffin. Segundo finds her body in a grove, her head lying in the water. "Blue and white and red-yellow butterflies had settled on her. . . . A single hummingbird hovered near her left hand, then flew up and out of sight through the trees, gone in a flash of burning green and metal

blue" (318). After the narrator recounts vain efforts by an American doctor to bring her back to consciousness and the housekeeper's discovery
that "She's gone all soft," a short chapter describes Teresa's experience of
death. "How quiet it is," she thinks (324–25). She sees a deer; a coyote; "the
Mother"; trees with colorful leaves that fly like butterflies; the "humble
home" of Itom Achai, the Yaqui God; and God himself, who speaks to her
in Cahita, "brushes back her hair and hands her a rose" (326). This journey
occurs while friends and family pay their respects to her apparently dead
body; on the fourth day, Teresa opens her eyes and sits up.

Before Teresa's temporary death, the novel's "magic" was achieved
through explicit contrasts in historical perspective, class position, and
types of knowledge as the narrator showed his readers that any historical
reimagining requires a compilation of a great variety of voices and points
of view. After Teresa returns to life, however, the novel challenges the divisions between mind and body, rationality and indigenous belief, European
modernization and native Mexican tradition, an imposed national order
and sites of local resistance—and thus becomes a magical borderlands
novel. Before Teresa's death, *The Hummingbird's Daughter* imagines a perfectly possible heterogeneity. Afterward, its energies divide, requiring new
imaginative efforts to integrate the borderland's temporalities and cultural
diversity. North American readers may identify increasingly with the
rational Tomás, who struggles to protect Teresa, helps her to escape from
prison, and urges her to seek satisfaction in private, domestic life. One
part of Teresa does long for "a small cool house under trees. Where no one
would look at me. I would grow mint and corn and some tomatoes," as she
specifies her dream to her father. "I would grow cilantro and find a little
humble man and have a baby and I . . . I would be forgotten" (396–97). At
the same time, Urrea urges his readers to accept, too, the power of Mexico's
indigenous traditions and its marvels, as Teresa does. Tomás believes we
make our own destinies; Teresa believes otherwise. "God makes our destinies," she proclaims, and history seems to prove her right.

Teresa's resurrection initiates the period of chaos at the ranch, followed
by division and dispersal. At first people "came in small groups to see the
living dead girl" (339) who now smelled of roses—then the news spreads
and the crowd converges. "They walked from the shores of the sea. They
rode the new rail lines from Arizona to Guaymas, then rented wagons and
came east. They filtered down from the high peaks and the darkened canyons of the sierra" (351). After a few months, "Reporters found the ranch
infested with 10,000 campers" (352). More reporters come, then Cruz

Chávez, the chief of the Tigres from Tomóchic (or "Tigers of the Sierra"), and then Father Gastélum—all eager to test Teresa's power. Finally, the "real world," as Tomás calls it, arrives in the form of the army, invading the ranch a second time. When Tomás and Teresa flee to the north, they are apprehended again and taken to prison in Guaymas. With Teresa gone, the People atomize—they "went to the four directions."

> The Yaquis went north and the Mayos went south. The few Tarahumara ran back toward their sierras, and the Apaches galloped to Arizona. The Pimas moved west of Tucson, and the Seris walked toward the sea.
>
> Mestizos hurried toward Sinaloa, their dream of salvation shattered. The Arizonans and New Mexicans and Texans hove their wagons onto the dusty roads and made less haste—the Mexican army would not dare attack gringo caravans. But all along the way, people stopped them and asked, *Is it true?* And *Have they taken the Saint?* And they spread the word—they said, *Yes, she is gone.* They said, *Yes, she is dead.* They said the army was set to massacre them all. (446)

Teresa's life had renewed their beliefs and her death, they thought, foretold their own.

And yet, because the form of the novel transcends the limits of both rationality and traditional experience, seemingly decisive acts of abandonment or death are never final. Any single observer or cultural group glimpses only part of the story. Characters may leave one native place, never to return—but they also leave in search of another, still unknown, homeland. A narrative that stays on one side of the border cannot be complete, and Urrea's choice to end his narrative of Teresa's life at Mexico's northern border signifies his desire to keep her future and the meaning of her story open. The conclusion to *The Hummingbird's Daughter* resonates with possibilities that Teresa Urrea's real life did not always fulfill. In the novel, Teresa glimpses her own potential future while bound for the United States, and she is not sure how to interpret it. She encounters Huila in an empty car, back from the dead. Still inhabiting separate realms, like the spirit Virgil and the pilgrim in Dante's *Paradiso*, teacher and pupil climb toward the stars, which seem to be in constant motion, expanding in "ten million brilliant silver globes" (486). Huila commands her to look, and Teresa sees herself in each one: "In this globe, she was riding the train. In the next globe, she was a child. In the third globe, she was dressed in fine clothes, walking down a city street. She held children. She was pregnant. She was laughing. She was weeping" (486). Huila explains,

"Every moment of your life, every instant, looks like this. Do you see? You are always in a universe of choices. Any moment of your life can go in any direction you choose" (487).

From its beginning in Sinaloa in central Mexico through its migration north to Cabora and beyond, the novel has focused on a verifiably real universe, the region Irwin calls "the other borderlands." As it approaches the border itself, the "universe" becomes imaginary, a matter of choice. The topographical maps that arrived from Mexico City to guide Tomás's family and the people who choose to go with them to Cabora to escape punishment from Porfirio Díaz "had substantial swaths of the occult north seemingly erased. Frightening white spaces, some of them marked with the dreadful phrase 'Unknown Territory'" (111). By the end of *The Hummingbird's Daughter*, the territory north of the border looms as the continent's black place: "Nothing lay ahead of [Teresa and Tomás] but night. Night, and great, dark North America" (495). While the first figuration of the United States as "occult," "unknown," and "white" might indicate a deliberate effort on the part of official cartographers in Mexico to discourage emigration, the novel's final representation of the north indicates a continental divide broader than nationality and associates its darkness with both a natural cycle (of day or life) and sublimity (the greatness of scale that inspires the most intense, if still unspecified, feeling). With this figuration, Urrea effectively erases the economic and political dominance of the United States and inscribes his own imaginary borderland.

The novel's conclusion at the border also erases the historical record of Teresa's life in Nogales, Arizona, and El Paso, Texas, following her deportation in 1892. By ending the novel with Teresa and Tomás on a train about to cross the border, the novel reclaims Teresa Urrea as a triumphant Mexican, *mestiza* heroine. Urrea could have followed her struggles in the United States, where she married quickly and badly and then divorced, went to California in 1900 to demonstrate her healing powers and then joined a "Curing Crusade" that toured major cities and entertained Anglo audiences, and in 1904 finally broke her contract and returned with her two daughters to Clifton, Arizona. She died young of tuberculosis, in 1906, a local curiosity in the United States and almost forgotten in Mexico.[6] Instead, Urrea builds the narrative toward a dramatic demonstration of all of Teresa's proven and imagined powers, suggesting that she could forever be capable of healing innocent children, inspiring peace and devotion in even the most violent warriors, and looking squarely into a dark future with laughter and confidence.

   The novel's narrative technique and trajectory suggest that in the borderlands of the greater Southwest, "history," "reality," and "magic" are matters of location, perception, and belief. Magical borderlands fiction like *The Hummingbird's Daughter* dissolves the distinction between these domains to produce neither a meditation on material ruin nor a reconstruction of history but the embodied sensation of freedom. Such freedom, the novel suggests, lies in the ability to integrate the experience of the body, the memory of native landscapes, and the knowledge of many worldviews and scales of history—while remaining always in motion. If, as William Kittredge has proposed, a homeland is "a position from which to enjoy and withstand the gorgeous, evasive and invasive world," (43) the region's magical fictions offer its diverse and atomized readers a choice of positions and a poetics of survival in a world whose borders continue to disappear into dreams and reappear as ruins, ready again for real and imaginary reconstruction.

Notes

Introduction

1. Weston and Weston, *California and the West* 40.

2. Referring to Weston's photographs of Wilson on the Oceano sand dunes, Jonathan Spaulding writes, "If California has a muse, maybe this is it: a strong-limbed beauty flinging herself into the future, aware of her power, eager for all that life and love can bring" ("Bright Power, Dark Peace" 29).

3. Due to a technical error, the first negatives of the entire body were double-exposed. However, even if "[t]he picture that was a more complete biography of the man's last journey was lost," Wilson still found an eloquent narrative embedded in this unrealized image. She wrote, "The image on the ground glass was haunting in its double message: the desert had conquered the man with its scorching spaces and pitiless heat, but the man had succeeded in crossing that inhuman wasteland to die on a shady creek bank, with comforting objects around him" (Wilson, "The Weston Eye" 119–20).

4. Spaulding interprets the image as fully transcending the accident of discovery and the conditions of production. He writes, "Weston's treatment removes the victim from his immediate historical context and, instead, presents a more universal image of death. . . . The serene pose and glowing light on the face of the man, caught especially in the hollows of his eyes, echo Renaissance imagery of divine rapture, giving the scene not so much a feeling of suffering as of transcendence and peace" ("Bright Power" 43).

5. See Appadurai, *Modernity at Large*, and Nabhan, *The Desert Smells Like Rain* and *Arab/American*, among other studies. In *Xerophilia*, his study of Southwestern literature's affective relation to desert places, Tom Lynch foregrounds bioregions over political or cultural designations, arguing that with this approach "the 'Southwest' becomes reconceptualized as the meeting ground of a variety of interpenetrating arid lands bioregions in that portion of the United States that was once Mexico" (24). Although my analysis of Southwestern landscapes in this book is not organized around bioregional areas, like those proposed by Nabhan and Lynch, I share their commitment to investigating how literature articulates subtle relations between self and

place, "simultaneously determining and revealing the degree to which we feel estranged or at home" in the land (Lynch, *Xerophilia* 22).

6. See Kollin, ed., *Postwestern Cultures* xi.

Chapter 1. The Road

1. Migrants do not merely move; they leave one home and try to establish another. In the process, they gather together or "cluster," as if anticipating the difficulty of re-creating a new social group. Social historian Clarence Mondale describes this process as "staying in touch with one's own" (Mondale, "Place-on-the-Move" 55–57).

2. Dorothea Lange's well-known photograph "Toward Los Angeles, California, 1937" provides stark proof of the relation between class and mobility. At a time when posters for travel companies, like the well-known Deco-style poster for the Normandie cruise line, encouraged associations between style and speed, Lange reminded her viewers that such luxuries were bought at the price of steady employment for most workers. See Ann Dempsey, "Deco," in *Art in the Modern Era*; also James Guimond, *American Photography and the American Dream*.

3. Other examples are James M. Cain's *The Postman Always Rings Twice*(1934), *Double Indemnity* (1936), and *Mildred Pierce* (1941), all made almost immediately into film *noir*, and Chester Himes's *If He Hollers Let Him Go* (1945).

4. While acknowledging the need to define postmodernism in terms of the modernism specific to each discipline, Andy Grundberg in "The Crisis of the Real" defines postmodern architecture and dance in similar terms: "it attempts to revitalize the art form through inclusion rather than exclusion" (165). He concludes with the observation, "There is no place in the postmodern world for a belief in the authenticity of experience, in the sanctity of the individual artist's vision, in genius or originality. What postmodernist art finally tells us is that things have been used up, that we are at the end of the line, that we are all prisoners of what we see" (178).

5. As Scott Casper explains in his introduction to *Moving Stories*, a recent collection of essays on the topic, "Newer stories tell of . . . the forced migrations of Native Americans as Euro-Americans encroached upon their lands; the sorrows of leaving family, community, and culture; the ways in which discrimination and inequality, not just opportunity, followed migrants to their new homes" (xiii).

6. Application for Guggenheim Foundation Fellowship; original in archives of Guggenheim Foundation, copy in archives of Huntington Library, San Marino, California.

7. In a letter to his friend Willard Van Dyke, Weston wrote, "No, I have not done 'faces and postures,' except one dead man (wish I could have found more) and many dead animals; but I have done ruins and wreckage by the square mile and square inch, and some satires" (Weston to Van Dyke, April 18, 1938, in Calmes, *The Letters between Edward Weston and Willard Van Dyke* 35). In the same letter, Weston wrote that he regretted how American culture was being "severed from its roots in the soil—cluttered with nonessentials, blinded by abortive desires."

8. Weston to Van Dyke, March 28, 1938, in *The Letters* 34.

9. One entry contrasts the extreme quiet and cleanliness of the desert with the noise and dirt of the city: "We have read no newspapers, heard no radios, and little other noise but the wind. Now it's back to people, radios, jabber, and noise of cars, horns, trains, whistles. In Death Valley the dust and dry air kept us clean. Now we go back to city sweat and soot. Dirt, noise, and everything unimportant. But at least not for long,—we'll soon be off again" (Journal, April 17, 1937).

10. Wilson wrote in her Journal on April 12, 1937, "Up at fourthirty with a good gang of stars left. When the sun comes up against our canyon rockworks here, Edward trudges off with Cole into it, and I begin to wonder while clearing up camp stuff, how I ever thought I could finish a novel on this anything but leisurely tour."

11. Although it includes a photograph of Judge Walker's studio, where they were married, *California and the West* makes no mention of the marriage, concluding instead with a description of Edward making a negative from "the perfect setting of vineyards" (122), a subject that eluded him at the start of the trip.

12. Wilson would lament in *California and the West* over "the disadvantage of traveling with a photographer, that you become accustomed to looking at things from a photographic viewpoint." Whereas once she "would have rejoiced at the rich upholstery of underbrush, the unsettled land, the untracked mountains, the untamed river," after months on the road she came to find a "day-long negativeless drive . . . monotonous" (98).

13. To give another example, on their "Northern Circuit" trip in the fall of 1937, they pick up "a tall man in patchy brown clothes, a smattering of beard on his face" who claims to have walked twenty-three miles the previous day and needs a ride "to one of his mines, he has two of them." The man keeps talking, spinning one tale after another and becoming increasingly hard to follow "due to a slight liquor haze." The man finally explains, "its not good living by yourself all the time and never seeing people, thats why I need to get to talk to people sometime." When they drop him at his destination, they

discuss his situation and how much of his story to believe. Wilson concludes, "Our final verdict was that he was cook for a mine outfit" (Journal, September 29, 1937).

14. The characterization is Starr's; he writes in *The Dream Endures*, "To Weston's way of thinking, his camera had an obligation to transcend the mere documentation of geography, history, or sociology in the effort to depict Life itself, pure and simple" (223).

15. In *Through Another Lens*, Wilson refers to a letter Weston dated February 1943 that "had been drafted by me, as was still the case with most of his serious correspondence" (324). She also confesses that she "suffered a shock" to discover that Weston's extensive correspondence with Henry Allen Moe, the Guggenheim Foundation's secretary general, during their first Guggenheim year did not mention her contribution to the project at all: "My utter invisibility during these formative years—even when he talked about acquiring the Highlands property and building the house, was stunning to discover. I felt like one of the Russian non-persons airbrushed out of photographs taken with Stalin" (203–4).

16. Wilson reported, "The general theory we work out is that he either rode the rails or hitch hiked out here from Tenessee—the can stamped KY would be a Kentucky army post drinking can—that already broke and hungry he started off in this country having no idea of what a desert might be like—and the heat did the rest. The problem of Mr. Edwards calling him a 'sick man' on the same day that we found him, is easily solved by saying Edwards got the date wrong on his note, but against that the milk looked as fresh as milk can look, and several other signs made it sure that he had just died" (Journal, May 17, 1937).

17. "In true journalese they had 'propped' the dead man up against a 'stunted tree' from which a faded bandanna had 'fluttered.' And, of course, he was 'miles from water'" (*California and the West* 50).

18. Limerick concludes her essay, "The ruins of the Nevada Test Site, along with the ruins at the Hanford Nuclear Reservation, are the most serious and instructive western ruins of all, but the lessons they teach are kin to the lessons of Rhyolite. The West, these places tell us, . . . is . . . the region where we can most profitably study the interplay of ambition and outcome, the collision between simple expectation and complex reality, and the fallout from optimistic efforts to master both nature and human nature" (34).

19. Lowitt and Beasley, Introduction to *One Third of a Nation: Lorena Hickok Reports on the Great Depression* xxiv.

20. Hickok to Hopkins, Nov. 3, 1935, Box 11, Lorena Hickok Papers, Franklin D. Roosevelt Library, Hyde Park, NY, qtd. in Lowitt and Beasley xxiv.

21. *The Grapes of Wrath* "was perhaps the first important American novel to be written with its next stage, a film script, and its third stage, a film, vividly in the author's mind," according to Edmund Wilson. In the words of Kevin Starr, "Steinbeck's documentary evocations of the coming of the Dust Bowl, the tractoring out of sharecroppers, the migrations of the tin lizzies, the plowing of an orange crop in California, all of it laced with snatches of religious and folk music, quotations from the people, documentary close-ups and wide-angle vision, constitute a mixed-media technique flourishing at the center of Depression art." Starr's description confirms that collective documentary portraits of the Depression are defined by their mixture of visions and voices—and by their willful integration of those voices into a single narrative of dispossession and collective aspiration. See Starr, *Endangered Dreams* 257, 256.

22. Malone and Etulain, *The American West* 91. The cycle of drought lasted from 1931 to 1937, causing over 300,000 people to leave the Southwest to try to earn a living in California.

23. Kelley, "Travels with Steinbeck," *People* (April 24, 1989) 73, qtd. in Howarth 77. For the complete account of the projects that led up to Steinbeck's experience in Visalia, see Howarth 76–86.

24. Letter to Stryker, April 20, 1940, qtd. in Joan Myers, *Pie Town Woman* 104.

25. Maren Stange's study of FSA photography shows that Lee recorded transformations in rural life as well as white workers and their families either attending union meetings or coping with strikes; for example, one of Lee's images shows Mexican workers at Union Hall in San Antonio, Texas, awaiting their daily assignment. Stange, "'The Record Itself'" 1–5.

26. Consult the Library of Congress Prints and Photographs online catalog for Lee's Pie Town images, including those of the Caudill family.

27. Walker Evans, "Photography," in Louis Kronenberger, ed., *Quality: Its Image in the Arts* (NY: Atheneum, 1969) 180, qtd. in Galassi 137.

28. See Lee's photograph LC-USF33-012739-M5, "Mrs. Whinery working in her kitchen," in the Library of Congress Prints and Photographs digital archive.

29. Starr, *Material Dreams* 393. Starr shows the completion of ambitious public works (like the Hoover Dam and the Los Angeles aqueduct system) to be critical to the city's new status as national leader in agricultural, aircraft, and movie production. But the situation of Los Angeles within a national and increasingly global economy put pressure on now-settled immigrants to redefine the city both from within and through their relations with other regions.

30. West's ironic comparison of Homer with "Picasso's great sterile athletes, who brood helplessly on pink sand, staring at veined marble waves" fails to infuse this banal life with the heroism of art. On the contrary: as Bernard points out, this description casts doubt on even the greatest modernist ambitions. "His sterility and passivity could equally be transformed to the Picasso and read as a comment on the sterility and social impotence of the master work" ("'When You Wish Upon a Star'" 341).

31. Richard Simon argues that *The Day of the Locust. . .* is a Hollywood movie in novel form." He especially identifies Capra's *Mr. Deeds Goes to Town*(1936) as a major source for the novel's plot line and character types, explaining that "West's novel meticulously and systematically revises Capra's movie, elaborating and adding to it elements borrowed from a number of other movies of the period, among them *A Star is Born* (1937), *San Francisco*(1936), *In Old Chicago* (1937), *The Buccaneer* (1938), perhaps *Gone with the Wind*(1939)," as well as from several foreign films and the standard character types of B movies. See Simon 513–14.

32. In "Sturges and *The Grapes of Wrath*: *Sullivan's Travels* as Documentary Comedy," Kevin Hearle gathers evidence about Steinbeck's and Darryl Zanuck's extensive research into farm labor, including the publication of *Their Blood is Strong* and articles in the *New York Post*, *Collier's*, and *Life*, to support his argument that Sturges intentionally attacked the premise of *The Grapes of Wrath* as book and film in *Sullivan's Travels*.

Chapter 2. The Village

1. For a full discussion of the scholarship concerning the issue of Spanish American identity in New Mexico, see Nieto-Phillips's Introduction and Montgomery, *The Spanish Redemption*.

2. See Malone and Etulain, *The American West*, chapter 3.

3. Hickok to Hopkins, Socorro, New Mexico, April 27, 1934, in Lowitt and Beasley 234.

4. Hickok concluded that because the state's Spanish-American residents had a fairly low standard of living (and given their "Latin temperament," had little ambition), "they aren't a particularly serious relief problem, except that we'll probably have them on our hands forever unless we try to rehabilitate them in some way. It's largely a matter of education. They need to be taught what to raise, how to raise it, how to take care of their stock" (Hickok to Hopkins, Phoenix, Arizona, May 4, 1934, in Lowitt and Beasley 239; Hickok to Hopkins, April 27, 1934, in Lowitt and Beasley 235).

5. See the Library of Congress Prints and Photographs Online Catalog for examples of the photographs Lee made of Chamisal in July 1940.

6. For reproductions of these photographs, see Wroth, ed., *Russell Lee's FSA Photographs of Chamisal and Peñasco, NM*.

7. Nina Otero-Warren and J. F. Zimmerman, proposal sent to FWP director Henry G. Alsberg, December 10, 1935. Qtd. in Marta Weigle, ed., *Women of New Mexico: Depression Era Images* xi.

8. Alsberg, *FWP Manual for Folklore Stories* (1938), in the WPA New Mexico Collection, Fray Angélico Chávez History Library, Santa Fe, NM 6, 8.

9. Alsberg to Aileen O'Bryan Nusbaum, 1939, in Weigle, *Women of New Mexico* ix.

10. Christine Bold lucidly analyzes the guides' common form and ideology. By constructing a collective subject position, delineating cultural outsiders and insiders, naturalizing social differences, and introducing readers to their shared modernity, she argues, the guides developed a national consciousness from local materials. See Bold, *The WPA Guides:* 3–18.

11. Waters, letter to Mabel Dodge Luhan, February 1941. Qtd. in Holley 44.

12. For example, Charles Biggs quotes the recollection of an older man from Chamisal, a village in the Taos valley, that farms supplied local families during the Depression and that people in his community shared each other's labor and bounty; as long as a family had land, they didn't need money. See "Remembering the Past: Chamisal and Peñasco in 1940," in *Russell Lee's FSA Photographs* 5.

13. For an explanation of the acequia system, see deBuys, *Enchantment and Exploitation*; Rodríguez, "Honor, Aridity, and Place;" and Lynch, "Toward a Symbiosis."

14. For a discussion of Waters as "a forerunner of the attitudes embodied in Chicano literature," and especially for an investigation of the connection between Maria in *People of the Valley* and Ultima in Rudolfo Anaya's *Bless Me, Ultima*, see Barrera.

15. Even as the Murphys seemed to adopt the customs of the village, "they remained gringos and Irish" and "held to a certain cold objectivity which enabled them to see themselves apart from the land and the people" (126). As a result, they succeeded in devising a scheme that encouraged the villagers to pay off their debts to the store with land and, eventually, in forming a company that controls land and water rights for the entire valley.

16. See Ian Duncan, "The Provincial or Regional Novel," in *A Companion to the Victorian Novel*, ed. Patrick Brantlinger and William Thesing. Qtd. in Moretti, *Graphs, Maps, Trees* 52.

17. According to his wife, Waters especially identified with the idea of "'Being Within' used by the great Shawnee warrior-statesman Tecumseh to represent that spiritual essence universally and eternally embodied in all things: human, animals, birds, trees, rocks, mountains" (Barbara Waters, "The Final Task," in Deloria, *Frank Waters: Man and Mystic* 65).

18. Rebolledo, for instance, summarizes "narrative strategies of resistance" engaged by these writers, including attention to Spanish names and ethnic heritage, an implicit critique of the present through attachment to a past when Hispanos occupied a cultural center, experimental mixing of genres in the tradition of the *recuerdo* to test a feminine autobiographical voice, and playful translations between cultures. *Women Singing in the Snow*, chapter 1, 31–32.

19. She had been discussing "Spanish" recipes with a neighbor who asked whether she had seen an article in the magazine written by one "Mrs. D." "I had not seen it," Jaramillo explains, "so she gave me the magazine to take home to read it. It was a three-page article, nicely written and illustrated, but very deficient as to knowledge of our Spanish cooking. In giving the recipe for making *tortillas* it read, 'Mix bread flour with water, add salt.'" Then she comments sarcastically, "How nice and light these must be without yeast or shortening! And still these smart Americans make money with their writing, and we who know the correct way sit back and listen" (Jaramillo, *Romance* 173).

20. Reyes Martinez, FWP Reports, Sept. 4, Sept. 28, and May 8, 1937, WPA New Mexico Collection, Fray Angélico Chávez History Library, Santa Fe, NM.

21. Martinez, FWP Reports, Dec. 11, 1936, and Feb. 27, 1937, WPA New Mexico Collection, Fray Angélico Chávez History Library, Santa Fe, NM.

22. Martinez, "Foods of the Southwest," reprinted in Jaramillo, *The Genuine New Mexico Tasty Recipes* 28–30.

23. Muriel Haskell, FWP Reports, Feb. 7–27, 1936, WPA New Mexico Collection, Fray Angélico Chávez History Library, 2–3, 9. Rebolledo and Marquez cite the debate between editors and directors in Washington and Alice Corbin, then the director of the New Mexico Project, regarding Martinez's work. One editor commended his enthusiasm, but described his "flowery" and "over-written" reports as containing only a "splinter of folklore." Although Corbin characterized the work as charming and argued for "its extreme simplicity—and lucidity," the editor did not alter her assessment: "The general impression, after reading the papers submitted, is one of an adolescent who has been encouraged beyond his native ability," she concluded (qtd. in the Introduction to Rebolledo and Marquez, *Women's Tales* xxix-xxx).

24. See Padilla's discussion in *My History, Not Yours* 206. Sánchez also identifies the problem of the region's isolation in *Forgotten People: A Study of New Mexicans* (1940), a study that simultaneously celebrates the "cultural synthesis" of Nuevomexicanos and critiques "the damaging effects of cultural isolation" that will prevent their assimilation.

25. For a discussion of regional food festivals, see Busby, *The Greenwood Encyclopedia of American Regional Cultures: The Southwest.*

26. Martín-Rodriguez describes *The House on Mango Street* as "a text in which old oppressive metaphors and symbols of the domestic subordination of many Chicanas are reformulated into liberatory spaces of feminine literary communication" (73).

Chapter 3. The Bridge

An earlier version of this chapter was published in *Postwestern Cultures: Literature, Theory, Space* (U of Nebraska Press, 2007).

1. For a thorough explanation of Edgar Lee Hewett's efforts to preserve the Pajarito Plateau, see Rothman, chapter 4.

2. Burns describes these work arrangements in chapter 20 of *In the Shadow of Los Alamos.*

3. Lucy Lippard proposes, "Feminist landscape and the bomb do seem deeply connected, not just on a theoretical level, but also on an emotional one." Questions of power inform our "looking at almost every 'natural' landscape, and power is always a feminist issue" (*The Pink Glass Swan* 320).

4. Lefebvre developed his theories through the study of Venice, Tuscany, New York City, and Spanish-American towns, just as J. B. Jackson formed the basis for his comparative study of landscapes through travels in Europe and across the United States.

5. *Critical Mass* exhibition catalog (November 1993) 1.

Chapter 4. The Desert

Part of this chapter originally appeared in *Southwestern American Literature* 33:3 (Fall 2008).

1. Patricia Limerick expands on this point in the last chapter of *Desert Passages*, noting that the reversal of the desert's symbolic meaning came only with the rise of leisure and a substantial "margin of safety." Under these conditions, she explains, "Deserts that had not submitted to development were, to

the appreciators, the most authentic of places, where existence was stripped to its essentials, without presence and without artifice" (168).

2. In C. S. Peirce's semiotic definition, icons represent their objects mainly by similarity. For a full consideration of various theories of how icons signify, see *Iconology* by W.J.T. Mitchell, especially chapter 3, which analyzes the tension between an image's natural and conventional elements in Ernst Gombrich's seminal *Art and Illusion*(1956). For a specific discussion of Peirce, see page 56.

3. "The shining white image of O'Keeffe, as Stieglitz transformed her into the iconic natural body celebrated in his modernism, has been rendered time and again as the climax of modernism in New York in the 1920s," writes Kathleen Pyne in *Modernism and the Feminine Voice* xxvii. Pyne argues that in his photographs of the 1920s, Stieglitz drew on the "paradoxical constructions" of "the spiritual bride and the knowing virgin—a woman who simultaneously inhabits antithetical states of being" (221).

4. Chabot to O'Keeffe, March 13, 1948. Qtd. in Poling-Kempes, *Ghost Ranch* 152.

5. Elizabeth McClausland had already noted in a review of O'Keeffe's 14th Annual Exhibition at An American Place for *The Springfield Republican* that in her New Mexico paintings O'Keeffe had started to achieve "a greater directness and simplicity of statement, a more robust expression of the thing seen and loved and set down in paint" following years of sustaining her own myth. See McClausland, "Georgia O'Keeffe Shows Her Latest Paintings."

6. The *Catalogue Raisonnée, Volume Two* for O'Keeffe's painting lists twelve paintings or pastels of the Black Place: "The Black Place–No. 1, 1942"; "Black Hills with Cedar, 1942"; "The Black Place, 1943"; "Black Place I, 1944"; "Black Place II, 1944"; "Black Place III, 1944"; "Black Place No. IV, 1944"; "The Black Place III (pastel) 1945"; "Black Place I, 1945"; "Black Place, Grey and Pink," 1949"; "Black Place Green, 1949"; and the record for the unavailable "Black Place II, 1945."

7. Teuton continues to explain, "In the Pueblo worldview, becoming human is an achievement. It is a process that requires forming a notion of how we should live to allow the world to remain balanced and alive" (135–36).

8. Another important work produced by a Guild member is Peter Goin's *Nuclear Landscapes* (1991), which documents partially destroyed artifacts and lands from Frenchman Flat in Nevada to the Bikini Atoll islands. In this work, Goin focuses on the "relics, ruins, and structures emblematic of the nuclear age," such as the buildings and vehicles that nuclear blasts turned into warped debris, aiming to "elevate the objects within the photographs to iconic significance" (xxii). For a more extensive discussion of *Nuclear Landscapes*,

see my essay on "The Nuclear Southwest" in *The Blackwell Companion to Western American Literature and Culture*.

9. See Kuletz, Preface to *Tainted Desert*.

Chapter 5. The Border

1. See Anzaldúa, *Borderlands/La Frontera*; García Canclini, *Hybrid Cultures*; Castillo, "Borderlining," and Castillo and Córdoba, eds., *Border Women*.

2. García Canclini conducted research among residents of Tijuana, asking them to identify their own representative places and to evaluate the significance of other places he and his colleagues photographed. Key sites included Revolution Avenue and street corners with burros painted like zebras, places that seemed to show how "bilingual, bicultural, and binational oscillations" create ambivalent, postmodern "monuments" (*Hybrid Cultures* 235).

3. Rudy Adler, Victoria Criado, and Brett Huneycutt organized this project in the summer of 2005. Together they wanted to investigate the effects of tightened border security, and they developed "a way to document the border through the eyes of women and men on the line." They recruited migrants and Minutemen volunteers to photograph their experience, distributing cameras at shelters and observation sites with instructions about how to use them and how to send them back. After receiving seventy-three cameras and almost two thousand pictures, they edited the images and printed them with excerpts from interviews they conducted. The resulting book, *Border Film Project: Photos by Migrants and Minutemen on the U.S.–Mexico Border*, was published in 2007.

4. See Saldívar, *Border Matters* 66. The defining events for twentieth-century borderland literature were the Mexican Revolution of 1910 and the Bracero Program of 1941–1964. See also Tom Miller's Introduction to *Writing on the Edge: A Borderlands Reader*.

5. See Robinson, *Having It Both Ways*, and Kollin's development of this argument about the "anti-western" in "Genre and the Geographies of Violence" 559–60.

6. For example, see Rafael Pérez-Torres, *Movements in Chicano Poetry* 12. For a fine analysis of Ríos's poem "Day of the Refugios" in this context, see also Deters, "Fireworks on the Borderlands."

7. Aldama summarizes Islas's position and technique in the biography *Dancing with Ghosts*: "Islas carved out a new storytelling voice as he hybridized the many genres and styles found in literature on both sides of the U.S./ Mexico border and beyond. He used this voice to chart the many symbolic and real borderlands (cultural, linguistic, racial, and sexual) that threatened

to destroy but also to create new forms of life: Chicano/as struggling to inhabit a threatening and living-giving borderland world" (48).

8. Both Mama Chona and Miguel Chico accept this poem as Netzahualcóyotl's because their relative wrote that it was so. However, scholars agree that the Nahuatl king could not have written this work because its imagery and metaphoric language are so distinctly foreign. Indigenous chroniclers and historians recorded Netzahualcóyotl's speech and poetry while he was King of Texcoco; even if the poems were published without dates, these documents, along with recent biographies and close textual analysis, provide sufficient indication of what Miguel Leon-Pórtilla calls a "logical sequence" (79) of poems by this "most celebrated sage lord of Tezcoco" (88). Leon-Pórtilla claims that "All the earth is a grave" is a composition that "cannot be accepted as his work" and points to such incongruous phrases and images as "the roundness of earth which is a sepulcher" and "the royal purple vault" as proof (72).

9. For a discussion of the historical contexts for reading Aztec poetry, see Damrosch, "The Aesthetics of Conquest."

10. Citing the scholarship of Angel María Garibay, Brodman explains that a major category of pre-Columbian lyric poetry is the "canto de flores," song of the flowers, which typically expresses "the idea of poetry, 'flower and song,' as a means of achieving immortality" (*The Mexican Cult of Death in Myth and Literature* 10–11).

11. The poem suggests that the idea for *The Rain God* originated in the rush of feeling Islas experienced at the top of the magnificent temple. Islas attests, "[T]hese gods were real to me. They are not dead; and in the desert, the grave of Cuauhtémoc will flower and bear fruits" (*The Uncollected Work* 105–6; see also "Aztec Angel" in the same volume, 110–11).

Chapter 6. Magical Regions

1. According to Aldama's history of "magical realism," when Roh first introduced the term in 1925, he used it to describe visual modes of communication. See Aldama's Introduction to *Postethnic Narrative Criticism.*

2. See Faris, *Ordinary Enchantments* 21, 34. Faris proposes several primary features of magical realism: "an 'irreducible element' of magic," descriptions that "detail a strong presence of the phenomenal world," the ability to produce "unsettling doubts" in a reader who tries "to reconcile two contradictory understandings of events," and an ability to disrupt "received ideas about time, space, and identity" (7).

3. See Moretti, *Modern Epic*; *Magical Realism: Theory, History, Community*, edited by Zamora and Faris; and Menton, *Magic Realism Rediscovered, 1918–1981*.

4. For a discussion of the origins and imagery of Huitzilopochtli, see Boone, *Incarnations of the Aztec Supernatural*.

5. Shannin Schroeder discusses the technique of authorial reticence in chapter 1 of *Rediscovering Magical Realism in the Americas*, arguing that magical realist novels neutralize the opposition between the real and the supernatural through narrative innovation.

6. For a thorough account of Teresa's life in the United States, see Irwin 241–49.

Bibliography

Manuscript Sources

Georgia O'Keeffe Library. Georgia O'Keeffe Foundation, Abiquiu, NM
Georgia O'Keeffe Museum and Research Center, Santa Fe, NM
Wilson, Charis. Journal of Guggenheim Year, 1937–1938. Huntington
    Library, San Marino, CA
WPA Collection. New Mexico State Records Center and Archives, Santa
    Fe, NM
WPA New Mexico Collection. Fray Angélico Chávez History Library, Santa
    Fe, NM

Photography Sources

Beinecke Rare Book and Manuscript Library, Yale University, New Haven, CT
The Center for Creative Photography, University of Arizona, Tucson, AZ
Huntington Library, San Marino, CA
Library of Congress Prints and Photographs Division, Washington, DC

Published Sources

Adler, Rudy, Victoria Criado, and Brett Huneycutt. *Border Film Project:
    Photos by Migrants & Minutemen on the U.S.–Mexico Border*. New York:
    Abrams, 2007.
Agee, James, and Walker Evans. *Let Us Now Praise Famous Men*. 1941. Hough-
    ton Mifflin, 1988.
Aldama, Frederick Luis. *Dancing with Ghosts*. Berkeley: U of California P,
    2005.
———. *Postethnic Narrative Criticism: Magicorealism in Oscar "Zeta" Acosta,
    Ana Castillo, Julie Dash, Hanif Kuresishi, and Salman Rushdie*. Austin:
    U of Texas P, 2003.
Anderson, Eric Gary. *American Indian Literature and the Southwest*. Austin:
    U of Texas P, 1999.

Anzaldúa, Gloria. *Borderlands/La Frontera: The New Mestiza.* Third Edition. San Francisco: Aunt Lute Books, 2007.

Appadurai, Arjun. *Modernity at Large: Cultural Dimensions of Globalization.* Minneapolis: U of Minnesota P, 1996.

Arnold, Ellen. "An Ear for a Story, an Eye for the Pattern: Rereading *Ceremony.*" *Modern Fiction Studies* 45.1 (1999): 69–92.

Baer, Ulrich. *Spectral Evidence: The Photography of Trauma.* Cambridge: MIT Press, 2002.

Barrera, José J. "Frank Waters: Precursor of Chicano Literature." *Studies in Frank Waters XVI* (1994): 51–67.

Batchen, Lou Sage. *Las Placitas: Historical Facts and Legends.* Placitas, NM: Tumbleweed, 1972.

Bernard, Rita. *The Great Depression and the Culture of Abundance.* New York: Cambridge UP, 1995.

———. "'When You Wish Upon a Star': Fantasy, Experience, and Mass Culture in Nathanael West." *American Literature* 66.2 (1994): 325–351.

Bernstein, Jeremy. *Oppenheimer: Portrait of an Enigma.* Chicago: Ivan R. Dee, 2004.

Bird, Kai, and Martin J. Sherwin. *American Prometheus: The Triumph and Tragedy of J. Robert Oppenheimer.* New York: Knopf, 2005.

Bold, Christine. *The WPA Guides: Mapping America.* Jackson: UP of Mississippi, 1999.

Boone, Elizabeth Hill. *Incarnations of the Aztec Supernatural: The Image of Huitzilopochtli.* Philadelphia: American Philosophical Society, 1989.

Boyer, Paul S. *By the Bomb's Early Light: American Thought and Culture at the Dawn of the Atomic Age.* New York: Pantheon, 1985.

Brodman, Barbara. *The Mexican Cult of Death in Myth and Literature.* Gainesville: U of Florida Monographs/Humanities No. 44, 1976.

Browder, Laura. *Rousing the Nation: Radical Culture in Depression America.* Amherst: U of Massachusetts P, 1998.

Brown, Lorin W., with Charles L. Briggs and Marta Weigle. *Hispano Folklife of New Mexico: The Lorin W. Brown Federal Writers' Project Manuscripts.* Albuquerque: U of New Mexico P, 1978.

Bunnell, Peter, and David Featherstone, eds. *EW: 100 Centennial Essays in Honor of Edward Weston.* Carmel, CA: Friends of Photography, 1986.

Burciaga, José Antonio. "A Conversation with Arturo Islas." *Stanford Humanities Review* 2.3 (1992): 158–66.

Burns, Patrick. Introduction to *In the Shadow of Los Alamos: Selected Writings of Edith Warner.* Ed. Burns. Albuquerque: U of New Mexico P, 2001.

Busby, Mark, ed. *The Greenwood Encyclopedia of American Regional Cultures: The Southwest.* Westport: Greenwood, 2004.

Bustard, Bruce. *A New Deal for the Arts.* Washington, DC: National Archives Trust Fund Board; Seattle: U of Washington P, 1997.

Cabeza de Baca, Fabiola. *We Fed Them Cactus.* Albuquerque: U of New Mexico P, 1954.

Calderón, Héctor. *Narratives of Greater Mexico: Essays on Chicano Literary History, Genre, & Borders.* Austin: U of Texas P, 2004.

Calmes, Leslie Squyres, ed. *The Letters between Edward Weston and Willard Van Dyke.* Tucson: Center for Creative Photography, 1992.

Campbell, Neil. "Critical Regionalism, Thirdspace, and John Brinckerhoff Jackson's Western Cultural Landscapes." *Postwestern Cultures.* Ed. Susan Kollin. Lincoln: U of Nebraska P, 2008. 59–81.

———. *The Cultures of the American New West.* Edinburgh: Edinburgh UP, 2000.

———. *The Rhizomatic West: Representing the American West in a Transnational, Global, Media Age.* Lincoln: U of Nebraska P, 2008.

Cantú, Roberto. "Arturo Islas." *Dictionary of Literary Biography* Vol. 122 (Chicano Writers). Ed. Francisco A. Lomelí and Carl R. Shirley. Detroit: Gale Research, 1992. 146–54.

Caruth, Cathy. *Unclaimed Experience: Trauma, Narrative, and History.* Baltimore: Johns Hopkins UP, 1996.

Casper, Scott E., and Lucinda M. Long, eds. *Moving Stories: Migration and the American West, 1850–2000.* Reno: Nevada Humanities Committee, 2001.

Castillo, Debra A., "Borderlining: An Introduction." *Tijuana: Stories on the Border.* By Federico Campbell. Berkeley: University of California Press, 1995. 1–26.

Castillo, Debra, and María Socorro Tabuenca Córdoba, eds. *Border Women: Writing from La Frontera.* Minneapolis: U of Minnesota P, 2002.

Chabot, Maria, and Georgia O'Keeffe. *Maria Chabot–Georgia O'Keeffe: Correspondence, 1941–1949.* Ed. Barbara Buhler Lynes and Ann Paden. Santa Fe: Georgia O'Keeffe Museum Research Center, 2003.

Chandler, Katherine R., and Melissa A. Goldthwaite, eds. *Surveying the Literary Landscapes of Terry Tempest Williams.* Salt Lake City: U of Utah P, 2003.

Chávez, Denise. "Denise Chávez: Chicana Woman Writer Crossing Borders– An Interview." By Elizabeth Brown-Guillory. *South Central Review* 16.1 (Spring 1999): 30–43.

———. *Face of an Angel.* New York: Warner, 1984.

———. Interview with Annie O. Eysturoy. *This Is about Vision: Interviews with Southwestern Writers*. By William Balassi, John F. Crawford, and Eysturoy. Albuquerque: U of New Mexico P, 1990. 157–169.

———. *The Last of the Menu Girls*. Houston: Arte Público, 1986.

———. *A Taco Testimony: Meditations on Family, Food and Culture*. Tucson: Rio Nuevo, 2006.

Church, Peggy Pond. *The House at Otowi Bridge*. Albuquerque: U of New Mexico P, 1960.

Clark, T. J. *Farewell to an Idea: Episodes from a History of Modernism*. New Haven: Yale UP, 2001.

Colson, James B. "The Art of the Human Document: Russell Lee in New Mexico." *Far from Main Street: Three Photographers in Depression-Era New Mexico*. By Russell Lee, John Collier Jr., Jack Delano, and James B. Colson. Santa Fe: Museum of New Mexico, 1994. 2–9.

Conant, Jennet. *109 East Palace: Robert Oppenheimer and the Secret City of Los Alamos*. New York: Simon and Schuster, 2005.

Cooper Alarcón, Daniel. *The Aztec Palimpsest: Mexico in the Modern Imagination*. Tucson: U of Arizona P, 1997.

Damrosch, David. "The Aesthetics of Conquest: Aztec Poetry Before and After Cortés." *New World Encounters*. Ed. Stephen Greenblatt. Berkeley: U of California P, 1993. 138–58.

Daniel, Pete, Merry A. Foresta, Maren Stange, and Sally Stein, eds. *Official Images: New Deal Photography*. Washington, DC: Smithsonian Institution Press, 1987.

Davidov, Judith Fryer. "'The Color of My Skin, the Shape of My Eyes': Photographs of the Japanese-American Internment by Dorothea Lange, Ansel Adams, and Toyo Miyatake." *Yale Journal of Criticism* 9.2 (1996): 223–44.

———. "Narratives of Place: History and Memory and the Evidential Force of Photography in Work by Meridel Rubenstein and Joan Myers." *Phototextualities: Intersections of Photography and Narrative*. Ed. Alex Hughes and Andrea Noble. Albuquerque: U of New Mexico P, 2003. 41–62.

Davidson, James West, and Mark Hamilton Lytle. *After the Fact: The Art of Historical Detection, Vol II*. Fourth Edition. Boston: McGraw Hill, 2000.

Davis, Mike. *City of Quartz: Excavating the Future in Los Angeles*. New York: Verso, 1990.

———. *Dead Cities and Other Tales*. New York: New Press, 2002.

deBuys, William. *Enchantment and Exploitation: The Life and Hard Times of a New Mexican Mountain Range*. Albuquerque: U of New Mexico P, 1985.

Deloria, Vine, Jr. *Frank Waters: Man and Mystic*. Athens: Swallow Press/Ohio UP, 1993.

Delpar, Helen. *The Enormous Vogue of Things Mexican: Cultural Relations between the U. S. and Mexico, 1920–1935.* Tuscaloosa: U of Alabama P, 1992.

Dempsey, Ann. *Art in the Modern Era: A Guide to Styles, Schools, and Movements.* London: Thames & Hudson, 2002.

Denning, Michael. *The Cultural Front.* London: Verso, 1996.

———. "The Novelists' International." *The Novel Volume I: History, Geography, and Culture.* Ed. Franco Moretti. Princeton: Princeton UP, 2006. 703–725.

Deters, Joseph. "Fireworks on the Borderlands: A Blending of Cultures in the Poetry of Alberto Ríos." *Confluencia* 15.2 (2000): 28–35.

Deutsch, Sarah. *No Separate Refuge: Culture, Class, and Gender on an Anglo-Hispanic Frontier in the American Southwest, 1880–1940.* New York: Oxford UP, 1987.

Deverell, William. *Whitewashed Adobe: The Rise of Los Angeles and the Remaking of Its Mexican Past.* Berkeley: U of California P, 2005.

Diedrich, Lisa. "'A New Thought in Familiar Country': Williams's Witnessing Ethics." *Surveying the Literary Landscapes of Terry Tempest Williams.* Ed. Katherine R. Chandler and Melissa A. Goldthwaite. Salt Lake City: U of Utah P, 2003. 211–28.

Dodd, Elizabeth. "Beyond the Blithe Air: Williams's Postnuclear Transcendentalism." *Surveying the Literary Landscapes of Terry Tempest Williams.* Ed. Katherine R. Chandler and Melissa A. Goldthwaite. Salt Lake City: U of Utah P, 2003. 3–13.

Douglas, Mary. *Purity and Danger: An Analysis of the Concepts of Pollution and Taboo.* 1966. New York: Routledge, 2006.

Dunsmore, Roger. *Earth's Mind: Essays in Native Literature.* Albuquerque: U of New Mexico P, 1997.

Eaton, Allen H. *Beauty behind Barbed Wire: The Arts of the Japanese in Our War Relocation Camps.* New York: Harper, 1952.

Eldredge, Charles C. *Georgia O'Keeffe.* New York: Harry N. Abrams, 1991.

———. *Georgia O'Keeffe: American and Modern.* New Haven: Yale UP, 1993.

Eliade, Mircea. *The Sacred and the Profane: The Nature of Religion.* Trans. Willard R. Trask. New York: Harcourt, 1959.

Enyeart, James L. *Photographers, Writers, and the American Scene.* Santa Fe: Arena Editions, 2002.

Faris, Wendy B. *Ordinary Enchantments: Magical Realism and the Remystification of Narrative.* Nashville: Vanderbilt UP, 2004.

Fine, David. *Imagining Los Angeles: A City in Fiction.* Albuquerque: U of New Mexico P, 2000.

———, ed. *Los Angeles in Fiction.* Albuquerque: U of New Mexico P, 1995.

Finnegan, Cara A. *Picturing Poverty: Print Culture and FSA Photographs*. Washington, DC: Smithsonian Books, 2003.

Fleischauer, Carl, and Beverly Brannan. *Documenting America, 1935–1943*. Berkeley: U of California P, 1988.

Forrest, Suzanne. *The Preservation of the Village: New Mexico's Hispanics and the New Deal*. Albuquerque: U of New Mexico P, 1989.

Fox, Claire. *The Fence and the River: Culture and Politics at the U.S.–Mexico Border*. Minneapolis: U of Minnesota P, 1999.

Fox, William L. *Making Time: Essays on the Nature of Los Angeles*. Emeryville, CA: Shoemaker & Hoard, 2007.

Frank, Robert. *The Americans*. New York: Aperture, 1958.

Franklin, Wayne, and Michael Steiner, eds. *Mapping American Culture*. Iowa City: U of Iowa P, 1992.

Galassi, Peter, ed. *Walker Evans & Company*. New York: Museum of Modern Art and Harry N. Abrams, 2000.

Gallagher, Carol. *American Ground Zero: The Secret Nuclear War*. Cambridge: MIT P, 1993.

García Canclini, Nestor. *Hybrid Cultures: Strategies for Entering and Leaving Modernity*. Minneapolis: U of Minnesota P, 1995.

Giles, Paul. "The Deterritorialization of American Literature." *Shades of the Planet: American Literature as World Literature*. Ed. Wai Chee Dimock and Lawrence Buell. Princeton: Princeton UP, 2007. 39–61.

Goin, Peter. "Following the Line: The Mexico-American Border." *Spazio e società* July/September 1987: 22–37.

———. "Magical Realism." *Western Places, American Myths: How We Think about the West*. Ed. Gary J. Hausladen. Reno and Las Vegas: U of Nevada P, 2003. 253–55.

———. *Nuclear Landscapes*. Baltimore: Johns Hopkins UP, 1991.

———. *Tracing the Line*. Reno: U of Nevada P, 1987.

Gonzales-Berry, Erlinda. "Sensuality, Repression, and Death in *The Rain God*." *Bilingual Review: La Revista Bilingüe* 12.3 (1985): 258–61.

Graulich, Melody. "'Cameras and Photographs Were Not Permitted in the Camps': Photographic Documentation and Distortion in Japanese American Internment Narratives." *True West: Authenticity and the American West*. Ed. William R. Handley and Nathaniel Lewis. Lincoln: U of Nebraska P, 2007. 222–53.

Green, Jonathan. *American Photography: A Critical History 1945–Present*. New York: Harry Abrams, 1984.

Greenberg, Clement. "Four Photographers." *The Collected Essays and Criticism: Modernism with a Vengeance, 1957–1969*. Vol. 4, ed. John O'Brien. Chicago: U of Chicago P, 1993. 183–87.

Greenberg, Jonathan. "Nathanael West and the Mystery of Feeling." *Modern Fiction Studies* 52.3 (Fall 2006): 588–612.

Gregory, James N. *American Exodus: The Dust Bowl Migration and Okie Culture in California.* New York: Oxford UP, 1989.

Griffith, James S. *A Shared Space: Folklife in the Arizona-Sonora Borderlands.* Logan: Utah State UP, 1995.

Griswold del Castillo, Richard. *La Familia: Chicano Families in the Urban Southwest, 1848 to the Present.* Notre Dame: U of Notre Dame P, 1984.

Grundberg, Andy. "The Crisis of the Real: Photography and Postmodernism." *The Photography Reader.* Ed. Liz Wells. London: Routledge, 2003. 164–179.

Guimond, James. *American Photography and the American Dream.* Chapel Hill: U of North Carolina P, 1991.

Gusterson, Hugh. *People of the Bomb: Portraits of America's Nuclear Complex.* Minneapolis: U of Minnesota P, 2004.

Gutiérrez, David. *Walls and Mirrors: Mexican Americans, Mexican Immigrants, and the Politics of Ethnicity.* Berkeley: U of California P, 1995.

Hales, Peter Bacon. *Atomic Spaces: Living on the Manhattan Project.* Urbana: U of Illinois P, 1997.

Harvey, David. *The Condition of Postmodernity.* Oxford: Oxford UP, 1990.

Hearle, Kevin. "Sturges and *The Grapes of Wrath*: *Sullivan's Travels* as Documentary Comedy." *Steinbeck Newsletter* 7.2 (1994): 5–7.

Herrera-Sobek, María, and Helena Viramontes, eds. *Chicana Creativity and Criticism: New Frontiers in American Literature.* Albuquerque: U of New Mexico P, 1996.

Hirsch, Jerrold. *Portrait of America: A Cultural History of the Federal Writers' Project.* Chapel Hill: U of North Carolina P, 2003.

Hoffman, Abraham. *Unwanted Mexican Americans in the Great Depression: Repatriation Pressures, 1929–39.* Tucson: U of Arizona P, 1974.

Holley, Joe. "A New Mexican Writer's Long Life: Revisiting Frank Waters." *Southwestern American Literature* 29.1 (Fall 2003): 39–53.

Houston, Jeanne Wakatsuki, and James D. Houston. *Farewell to Manzanar.* Boston: Houghton Mifflin, 1973.

Howarth, William. "The Mother of Literature: Journalism and *The Grapes of Wrath*." *New Essays on The Grapes of Wrath.* Ed. David Wyatt. Cambridge: Cambridge UP, 1990. 71–99.

Hunner, Jon. *Inventing Los Alamos: The Growth of an Atomic Community.* Norman: U of Oklahoma P, 2004.

Hurley, F. Jack. *A Portrait of a Decade: Roy Stryker and the Development of Documentary Photography in the Thirties.* Baton Rouge: Louisiana State UP, 1972.

Inada, Lawson Fusao. *Only What We Could Carry: The Japanese American Internment Experience.* Berkeley: Heydey, 2000.

Ingenschay, Dieter, and Joan Ramon Resina, eds. *After-Images of the City.* Ithaca: Cornell UP, 2003.

Irwin, Robert McKee. *Bandits, Captives, Heroines, and Saints: Cultural Icons of Mexico's Northwest Borderlands.* Minneapolis: U of Minnesota P, 2007.

Islas, Arturo. *Arturo Islas: The Uncollected Work.* Ed. Frederick Luis Aldama. Houston: Arte Publico, 2003.

——. Interview with Ricardo Aguilar Melantzón. "Tórica with Arturo Islas." El Paso: UT at El Paso News (1987): 2–4.

——. *Migrant Souls.* New York: Avon Books, 1990.

——. *The Rain God.* New York: HarperCollins, 1984.

Jackson, John Brinckerhoff. *Discovering the Vernacular Landscape.* New Haven: Yale UP, 1984.

——. *Landscape in Sight: Looking at America.* Ed. Helen Lefkowitz. New Haven: Yale UP, 2000.

——. *The Necessity for Ruins and Other Topics.* Amherst: U of Massachusetts P, 1980.

——. *A Sense of Place, A Sense of Time.* New Haven: Yale UP, 1994.

James, Geoffrey. *Geoffrey James: Past/Present/Future.* Toronto: U of Toronto Art Centre, 2003.

——. *Running Fence.* North Vancouver, BC: Presentation House Gallery, 1999.

Jaramillo, Cleofas M. *The Genuine New Mexico Tasty Recipes.* 1939. Layton, UT: Gibbs Smith, 1981.

——. *Romance of a Little Village Girl.* 1955. Albuquerque: U of New Mexico P, 2000.

——. *Shadows of the Past/Sombras del Pasado.* 1941. Santa Fe: Ancient City, 1980.

Jenks, Deneen. "The Breathless Patience of Alberto Ríos." *Hayden's Ferry Review* 11 (1992): 115–123.

Jensen, Joan M. "'I've Worked, I'm Not Afraid of Work: Farm Women in New Mexico 1920–1940." *New Mexico Women: Intercultural Perspectives.* Ed. Joan M. Jensen and Darlis Miller. Albuquerque: U of New Mexico P, 1986. 227–55.

——. *Promises to the Land: Essays on Rural Women.* Albuquerque: U of New Mexico P, 1991.

Jewell, Edward Alden. "One Man Shows." *New York Times* January 28, 1945: 2.8.

Johnson, Denis. "Border of Sight." *Traces of Eden: Travels in the Desert Southwest.* Mark Klett and Denis Johnson. Boston: David R. Godine, 1986. n.p.

Justice, Daniel. *Our Fire Survives the Storm: A Cherokee Literary History.* Minneapolis: U of Minnesota P, 2006.

Kennedy, David M. *Freedom from Fear: The American People in Depression and War, 1929–1945.* New York: Oxford UP, 1999.

Kittredge, William. *Southwest Homelands.* Washington, DC: National Geographic, 2002.

Kollin, Susan. "Genre and the Geographies of Violence: Cormac McCarthy and the Contemporary Western." *Contemporary Literature* 42.3 (Fall 2001): 557–88.

———, ed. *Postwestern Cultures.* Lincoln: U of Nebraska P, 2008.

Kosek, Jake. *Understories: The Political Life of Forests in Northern New Mexico.* Durham: Duke UP, 2006.

Kowalewski, Michael, ed. *Reading the West: New Essays on the Literature of the American West.* Cambridge: Cambridge UP, 1996.

Kuletz, Valerie. *The Tainted Desert: Environmental Ruin in the American West.* New York: Routledge, 1998.

Lane, Anthony. "Ants in His Pants." *New Yorker.* September 14, 1998.

Lange, Dorothea, and Paul Taylor. *An American Exodus: A Record of Human Erosion.* New York: Reynal & Hitchcock, 1939.

Lee, Russell. *Russell Lee's FSA Photographs of Chamisal and Peñasco, New Mexico.* Ed. William Wroth. Santa Fe: Ancient City Press, 1985.

Lefebvre, Henri. *The Production of Space.* Trans. Donald Nicholson-Smith. Cambridge: Blackwell, 1991.

Leon-Pórtilla, Miguel. *Fifteen Poets of the Aztec World.* Norman: U of Oklahoma P, 1992.

Lewis, Nathaniel. *Unsettling the Literary West.* Lincoln: U of Nebraska P, 2003.

Libby, Brooke. "Nature Writing as *Refuge*: Autobiography in the Natural World." *Reading Under the Sign of Nature: New Essays in Ecocriticism.* Ed. John Tallmadge and Henry Harrington. Salt Lake City: U of Utah P, 2000. 251–64.

Limerick, Patricia Nelson. *Desert Passages: Encounters with the American Deserts.* Albuquerque: University of New Mexico P, 1985.

———. *Something in the Soil: Legacies and Reckonings in the New West.* New York: Norton, 2000.

Limerick, Patricia Nelson, and Mark Klett. "Haunted by Rhyolite: Learning from the Landscape of Failure." *American Art* 6.4 (Fall 1992): 18–39.

Limón, José E. *American Encounters: Greater Mexico, the United States, and the Erotics of Culture.* Boston: Beacon Press, 1998.

Lippard, Lucy R. *The Pink Glass Swan: Selected Feminist Essays on Art.* New York: New Press, 1995.

Lippit, Akira. *Atomic Light (Shadow Optics)*. Minneapolis: U of Minnesota P, 2005.

Lowitt, Richard. *The New Deal and the West*. Bloomington: Indiana UP, 1984.

Lowitt, Richard, and Maurine Beasley, eds. *One Third of a Nation: Lorena Hickok Reports on the Great Depression*. Urbana: U of Illinois P, 1981.

Lynch, Tom. "Toward a Symbiosis of Ecology and Justice: Water and Land Conflicts in Frank Waters, John Nichols, and Jimmy Santiago Baca." *Western American Literature* 37.4: 405–28.

———. *Xerophilia: Ecocritical Explorations in Southwestern Literature*. Lubbock: Texas Tech UP, 2008.

Lynes, Barbara Buhler. *Georgia O'Keeffe: Catalogue Raisonné*. 2 vols. New Haven: Yale UP, 1999.

———. "Georgia O'Keeffe: Identity and Place." *Georgia O'Keeffe: Circling around Abstraction*. West Palm Beach: Norton Museum of Art; New York: Hudson Hills Press, 2007. 38–51.

———. Introduction. *O'Keeffe's O'Keeffes: The Artist's Collection*. New York: Thames and Hudson, 2001.

Lynes, Barbara Buhler, Lesley Poling-Kempes, and Frederick W. Turner. *Georgia O'Keeffe and New Mexico: A Sense of Place*. Princeton: Princeton UP; Santa Fe: Georgia O'Keeffe Museum, 2004.

Lyon, Thomas J. *Frank Waters*. New York: Twayne, 1973.

———, ed. *A Frank Waters Reader: A Southwestern Life in Writing*. Athens: Swallow Books/Ohio UP, 2000.

Malone, Michael P., and Richard W. Etulain. *The American West: A Twentieth-Century History*. Lincoln: U of Nebraska P, 1989.

Mangione, Jerry. *The Dream and the Deal: The Federal Writers' Project 1935–1943*. Boston: Little, Brown, 1972.

Martín, Desirée A. "Possessing La Santa De Cabora: The Union of Sacred, Human, and Transnational Identities." *Crisscrossing Borders in Literature of the American West*. Ed. Reginald Dyck and Cheli Reutter. New York: Palgrave Macmillan, 2009. 179–195.

Martín-Rodríguez, Manuel. *Life in Search of Readers*. Albuquerque: U of New Mexico P, 2003.

Matsumoto, Valerie. "Japanese-American Women during World War II." *The American West: The Reader*. Ed. Walter Nugent and Martin Ridge. Bloomington: Indiana UP, 1999. 255–273.

McCarthy, Cormac. *The Crossing*. New York: A. A. Knopf, 1994.

McClausland, Elizabeth. "Georgia O'Keeffe Shows Her Latest Paintings." *Springfield Republican*. January 2, 1938.

McElvaine, Robert. *The Great Depression and the New Deal: A History in Documents.* New York: Oxford UP, 2000.

McWilliams, Carey. *North from Mexico: The Spanish-Speaking People of the United States.* 1948. New York: Greenwood, 1990.

———. *Southern California Country: An Island on the Land.* New York: Duell, Sloane and Pearce, 1946.

Meining, D. W. *The Southwest: Three Peoples in Geographical Change, 1600–1970.* New York: Oxford UP, 1971.

Meloy, Ellen. *The Anthropology of Turquoise: Reflections on Desert, Sea, Stone, and Sky.* 2002. New York: Vintage, 2003.

———. *The Last Cheater's Waltz: Beauty and Violence in the Desert Southwest.* Tucson: U of Arizona P, 1999.

Mendoza, Louis. *Historías: The Literary Making of Chicana and Chicano History.* College Station: Texas A&M UP, 2001.

Menton, Seymour. *Magic Realism Rediscovered, 1918–1981.* Philadelphia: Art Alliance Press, 1983.

Merrill, Christopher. Introduction. *From the Faraway Nearby: Georgia O'Keeffe as Icon.* Ed. Merrill and Ellen Bradbury. Reading, MA: Addison Wesley, 1992. 1–17.

Miller, Tom, ed. *Writing on the Edge: A Borderlands Reader.* Tucson: U of Arizona P, 2003.

Miller, Tyrus. "Documentary/Modernism: Convergence and Complementarity in the 1930s." *Modernism/Modernity* 9.2 (2002): 225–241.

———. *Late Modernism: Politics, Fiction, and the Arts between the Wars.* Berkeley: U of California P, 1999.

Misrach, Richard. *Bravo 20: The Bombing of the American West.* Baltimore: Johns Hopkins UP, 1990.

———. *Desert Cantos.* Albuquerque: U of New Mexico P, 1987.

———. *Violent Legacies: Three Cantos.* New York: Aperture, 1992.

Mitchell, W. J. T. *Iconology: Image, Text, Ideology.* Chicago: U of Chicago P, 1986.

Mondale, Clarence. "Place-on-the-Move: Space and Place for the Migrant." *Mapping American Culture.* Ed. Wayne Franklin and Michael Steiner. Iowa City: U of Iowa P, 1992. 53–88.

Monroy, Douglas. *Rebirth: Mexican Los Angeles from the Great Migration to the Great Depression.* Berkeley: U of California P, 1999.

Montgomery, Charles H. *The Spanish Redemption: Heritage, Power, and Loss on New Mexico's Upper Rio Grande.* Berkeley: U of California P, 2002.

Moretti, Franco. *Graphs, Maps, Trees: Abstract Models for a Literary History.* New York: Verso, 2005.

———. *Modern Epic: The World System from Goethe to García Márquez*. New York: Verso, 1996.

———, ed. *The Novel Volume I: History, Geography, and Culture*. Princeton: Princeton UP, 2006.

Myers, Joan. *Pie Town Woman: The Hard Life and Good Times of a New Mexico Homesteader*. Albuquerque: U of New Mexico P, 2001.

Myers, Joan, and Gary Okihiro. *Whispered Silences: Japanese Americans and World War II*. Seattle: U of Washington P, 1996.

Nabhan, Gary Paul. *Arab/American: Landscape, Culture, and Cuisine in Two Great Deserts*. Tucson: U of Arizona P, 2008.

———. *Cultures of Habitat: On Nature, Culture, and Story*. Washington, DC: Counterpoint, 1997.

———. *The Desert Smells Like Rain: A Naturalist in O'odham Country*. Tucson: U of Arizona P, 2003.

Nash, Gerald. *The Federal Landscape: An Economic History of the Twentieth-Century West*. Tucson: U of Arizona P, 1999.

———. "New Mexico Since 1940: An Overview." *Contemporary New Mexico, 1940–1990*. Ed. Richard W. Etulain. Albuquerque: U of New Mexico P, 1994. 1–24.

Nieto-Phillips, John M. *The Language of Blood: The Making of Spanish-American Identity in New Mexico, 1880s-1930s*. Albuquerque: U of New Mexico P, 2004.

O'Keeffe, Georgia. *Georgia O'Keeffe*. New York: Viking, 1976.

———. *Georgia O'Keeffe: Art and Letters*. Ed. Jack Cowart, Sarah Greenough, and Juan Hamilton. Boston: New York Graphic Society Books, 1987.

O'Neal, Hank, ed. *A Vision Shared: A Classic Portrait of America and Its People, 1935–1943*. New York: St. Martin's, 1976.

Oppenheimer, Robert J. *Atom and Void: Essays on Science and Community*. Princeton: Princeton UP, 1989.

———. *Robert Oppenheimer: Letters and Recollections*. Ed. Alice Kimball Smith and Charles Weiner. Stanford: Stanford UP, 1980.

Ortiz, Simon J. *Woven Stone*. Tucson: U of Arizona P, 1992.

Otero-Warren, Nina. *Old Spain in Our Southwest*. New York: Harcourt Brace, 1936.

Padilla, Genaro. *My History, Not Yours: The Formation of Mexican American Autobiography*. Madison: U of Wisconsin P, 1993.

Paredes, Raymund A. "The Evolution of Chicano Literature." *Three American Literatures*. Ed. Houston A. Baker Jr. New York: Modern Language Association, 1982. 37–79.

Pells, Richard H. *Radical Visions and American Dreams: Culture and Social Thought in the Depression Years.* New York: Harper and Row, 1973.

Perales, Marian. "Teresa Urrea: *Curandera* and Folk Saint." *Latina Legacies: Identity, Biography, and Community.* Ed. Vicki L. Ruiz and Virginia Sánchez Korrol. New York: Oxford UP, 2005. 97–119.

Pérez-Torres, Rafael. *Movements in Chicano Poetry: Against Myth, Against Margins.* New York: Cambridge UP, 1995.

Poling-Kempes, Lesley. *Ghost Ranch.* Tucson: U of Arizona P, 2005.

———. *Valley of Shining Stone: The Story of Abiquiu.* Tucson: U of Arizona P, 1997.

Poole, Peter E., ed. *The Altered Landscape.* Reno: U of Nevada P, 1999.

Pyne, Kathleen. *Modernism and the Feminine Voice: O'Keeffe and the Women of the Stieglitz Circle.* Berkeley: U of California P, 2007.

Quayson, Ato. "Fecundities of the Unexpected: Magical Realism, Narrative, and History." *The Novel Volume I: History Geography, and Culture.* Ed. Franco Moretti. Princeton: Princeton UP, 2006. 726–756.

Quinn, Karen E., and Theodore E. Stebbins, eds. *Weston's Westons: California and the West.* Boston: Museum of Fine Arts and Bulfinch Press, Little, Brown, 1994.

Rebolledo, Tey Diana. "Tradition and Mythology: Signatures of Landscape in Chicana Literature." *The Desert Is No Lady: Southwestern Landscapes in Women's Writing and Art.* Ed. Vera Norwood and Janice Monk. Tucson: U of Arizona P, 1997. 96–124.

———. *Women Singing in the Snow: A Cultural Analysis of Chicana Literature.* Tucson: U of Arizona P, 1995.

Rebolledo, Tey Diana, and Maria Teresa Marquez. *Women's Tales from the New Mexico WPA: La Diabla a Pie.* Houston: Arte Publico Press, 2000.

Rhodes, Richard. *The Making of the Atomic Bomb.* New York: Simon and Schuster, 1986.

Ríos, Alberto Alvaro. *Capirotada: A Nogales Memoir.* Albuquerque: U of New Mexico P, 1999.

———. *The Curtain of Trees.* Albuquerque: U of New Mexico P, 1999.

———. Interview by William Barillas. "Words Like the Wind: An Interview with Alberto Ríos." *Americas Review* 24.3–4 (1996): 116–29.

Roberson, Susan L., ed. *Women, America, and Movement: Narratives of Relocation.* Columbia: U of Missouri P, 1998.

Robinson, Forrest G. *Having It Both Ways: Self-Subversion in Western Popular Classics.* Albuquerque: U of New Mexico P, 1993.

Robinson, Roxana. *Georgia O'Keeffe: A Life.* New York: Harper & Row, 1989.

Rodríguez, Sylvia. "Honor, Aridity, and Place." *Expressing New Mexico: Nuevomexicano Creativity, Ritual, and Memory*. Ed. Phillip B. Gonzales. Tucson: U of Arizona P, 2007.

Rogers, Gary W. "The Mora Valley and Frank Waters's *People of the Valley*." *South Dakota Review* 31.1 (Spring 1993): 132–41.

Ronald, Ann. *Ghost West: Reflections Past and Present*. Norman: U of Oklahoma P, 2005.

Rothman, Hal. *On Rims and Ridges: The Los Alamos Area since 1880*. Lincoln: U of Nebraska P, 1992.

Rubenstein, Meridel. *Belonging: Los Alamos to Vietnam*. Los Angeles: St. Ann's, 2004.

———. *Critical Mass*. Museum of Fine Arts, Santa Fe, 1993.

Ruiz, Vicki, and Virginia Sánchez Korrol. *Latina Legacies: Identity, Biography, and Community*. New York: Oxford UP, 2005.

Rushdie, Salman. *Imaginary Homelands: Essays and Criticism 1981–1991*. London: Granta Books/Viking, 1991.

Salas, Elizabeth. "Adelina Otero Warren: Rural Aristocrat and Modern Feminist." *Latina Legacies: Identity, Biography, and Community*. Ed. Vicki L. Ruiz and Virginia Sánchez Korrol. New York: Oxford UP, 2005. 135–47.

Saldívar, José David. *Border Matters: Remapping American Culture Studies*. Berkeley: U of California P, 1997.

———. "The Hybridity of Culture in Arturo Islas's *The Rain God*." *Cohesion, Dissent, and Contemporary Cultural Boundaries*. Ed. Carol Colatrella and Joseph Alkana. Albany: State U of New York P, 1994.

Saldívar, Ramón. *The Borderlands of Culture: Américo Paredes and the Transnational Imaginary*. Durham: Duke UP, 2006.

Scarry, Elaine. *The Body in Pain: The Making and Unmaking of the World*. New York: Oxford UP, 1985.

Schroeder, Shannin. *Rediscovering Magical Realism in the Americas*. Westport: Praeger, 2004.

Serber, Charlotte, and Jane S. Wilson, eds. *Standing By and Making Do: Women of Wartime Los Alamos*. Los Alamos: Los Alamos Historical Society, 1988.

Shindo. Charles J. *Dust Bowl Migrants in the American Imagination*. Lawrence: UP of Kansas, 1997.

Silko, Leslie Marmon. *Ceremony*. 1977. New York: Penguin, 2006.

———. "Interior and Exterior Landscapes." *Speaking for the Generations*. Ed. Simon J. Ortiz. Tucson: U of Arizona P, 1998. 2–24.

Simon, Richard. "Between Capra and Adorno: West's *Day of the Locust* and the Movies of the 1930s." *Modern Language Quarterly* 54.4 (December 1993): 513–534.

Slotkin, Richard. *Gunfighter Nation: The Myth of the Frontier in the Twentieth Century*. New York: HarperPerennial, 1993.

Slusher, Katherine. "Alex Harris: Islands in Time." *Islands in Time*. 219–223.

Smyth, Russell. *Retracing Russell Lee's Steps: A New Documentary*. Austin: Communication Specialists and Southwest Texas State U, 1992.

Solnit, Rebecca. *A Field Guide to Getting Lost*. New York: Viking, 2005.

———. *Savage Dreams: A Journey into the Landscape Wars of the American West*. Berkeley: U of California P, 2000.

Spaulding, Jonathan. "Bright Power, Dark Peace: Edward Weston's California." *Edward Weston: A Legacy*. Ed. Jennifer A. Watts. London: Merrell; San Marino: Henry E. Huntington Library and Art Gallery, 2003. 29–53.

Spurgeon, Sara. *Exploding the Western: Myths of Empire on the Postmodern Frontier*. College Station: Texas A&M UP, 2005.

Stange, Maren. "'The Record Itself': Farm Security Administration Photography and the Transformation of Rural Life." *Official Images: New Deal Photography*. Pete Daniel, Merry A. Foresta, Maren Stange, and Sally Stein. Washington, DC: Smithsonian Institution P, 1987.

———. *Symbols of Ideal Life: Social Documentary Photography in America, 1890–1950*. Cambridge: U of Cambridge P, 1992.

Starr, Kevin. *The Dream Endures: California Enters the 1940s*. New York: Oxford UP, 2002.

———. *Endangered Dreams: The Great Depression in California*. New York: Oxford UP, 1996.

———. *Inventing the Dream: California through the Progressive Era*. New York: Oxford UP, 1985.

———. *Material Dreams: Southern California through the 1920s*. New York: Oxford UP, 1990.

Stebbins, Theodore E., Jr. "The Guggenheim Years: 1937–1939." *Edward Weston: Forms of Passion*. Ed. Gilles Mora. New York: Harry N. Abrams, Inc., 1995. 228–37.

Steinbeck, John. *The Grapes of Wrath*. 1939. New York: Penguin, 1997.

Stott, William. *Documentary Expression and Thirties America*. New York: Oxford UP, 1973.

Stryker, Roy, and Nancy Wood, eds. *In This Proud Land: America 1935–1943 as Seen in the FSA Photographs*. Greenwich: New York Graphic Society, 1973.

Sturdevant, Katherine Scott, ed. *Sundays in Tutt Library with Frank Waters*. Introduction by Joseph T. Gordon. Colorado Springs: Hulbert Center for Southwestern Studies, Colorado College, 1988.

Sturges, Preston, dir. *Sullivan's Travels*. 1941.

Susman, Warren. *Culture as History: The Transformation of American Society in the Twentieth Century*. New York: Pantheon, 1973.

Swain, Regina, and María Navaro. "Utopia." *Border Women: Writing from la Frontera*. Ed. Debra A. Castillo and María Socorro Tabuenca Córdoba. Minneapolis: U of Minnesota Press, 2002. 189–226.

Szarkowski, John. *American Landscapes: Photographs from the Collection of the Museum of Modern Art*. New York: Museum of Modern Art and New York Graphic Society, 1981.

——. "Edward Weston's Later Work," *MOMA* 2, Winter 1974–75. Repr. in Beaumont Newhall and Amy Conger, eds., *Edward Weston Omnibus: A Critical Anthology*. Salt Lake City: Gibbs M. Smith, Inc./Peregine Books, 1984. 158–59.

——. *The Photographer's Eye*. New York: The Museum of Modern Art and the New York Graphic Society, 1966.

Tateishi, John. *And Justice for All: An Oral History of the Japanese American Detention Camps*. New York: Random House, 1984.

Tatum, Stephen. "Cormac McCarthy." *Updating the Literary West*. Fort Worth: Texas Christian UP, 1997.

——. "Spectral Beauty and Forensic Aesthetics in the West." *Western American Literature*. 41.2 (Summer 2006): 123–45.

——. "Topographies of Transition in Western American Literature." *Western American Literature*. 32.4 (Winter 1998): 310–52.

Taylor, Paul S. *Mexican Labor in the United States: Imperial Valley*. Vol I. New York, 1970.

Teuton, Sean Kicummah. *Red Land, Red Power: Grounding Knowledge in the American Indian Novel*. Durham: Duke UP, 2008.

Uchida, Yoshiko. *Desert Exile: The Uprooting of a Japanese American Family*. Seattle: U of Washington P, 1982.

Udall, Sharyn Rohlfsen. *Carr, O'Keeffe, Kahlo: Places of Their Own*. New Haven: Yale UP, 2000.

Urrea, Luis Alberto. *Across the Wire: Life and Hard Times on the Mexican Border*. New York: Anchor Books, 1993.

——. *The Hummingbird's Daughter*. New York: Little, Brown, 2005.

——. *Nobody's Son: Notes from an American Life*. Tucson: U of Arizona P, 1998.

Veitch, Jonathan. *American Superrealism: Nathanael West and the Politics of Representation in the 1930s*. Madison: U of Wisconsin P, 1997.

Warner, Edith. *In the Shadow of Los Alamos: Selected Writings of Edith Warner*. Ed. Patrick Burns. Albuquerque: U of New Mexico P, 2001.

Waters, Barbara, ed. *Pure Waters: Frank Waters and the Quest for the Cosmic*. Athens: Swallow Press/Ohio UP, 2002.

Waters, Frank. *A Frank Waters Reader.* Ed. Thomas J. Lyon. Athens: Swallow Press/Ohio UP, 2000.

———. *People of the Valley.* 1941. Athens: Swallow Press/Ohio UP, 1969.

———. *The Woman at Otowi Crossing.* Ed. Thomas J. Lyon. Athens: Swallow Press/Ohio UP, 1987.

Watts, Jennifer A., ed. *Edward Weston: A Legacy.* London: Merrell; San Marino: Henry E. Huntington Library and Art Gallery, 2003.

Weigle, Marta, ed. *Hispanic Villages of Northern New Mexico: A Reprint of Volume II of the 1935 Tewa Basin Study with Supplementary Materials.* Santa Fe: Lightning Tree, 1975.

———, ed. *New Mexicans in Cameo and Camera: New Deal Documentation of Twentieth-Century Lives.* Albuquerque: U of New Mexico P, 1985.

———, ed. *Women of New Mexico: Depression Era Images.* Santa Fe: Ancient City Press, 1993.

West, Nathanael. *The Day of the Locust.* New York: New Directions, 1939.

Weston, Charis Wilson, and Edward Weston. *California and the West.* New York: Duell, Sloan and Pierce, 1940.

Weston, Edward. *The Daybooks of Edward Weston.* New York: Aperture, 1973.

———. "Of the West: A Guggenheim Portrait." *U.S. Camera Annual 1940.* New York, 1939. 37.

Whisenhunt, Donald W. *The Depression in the Southwest.* Port Washington, NY: Kennikat Press, 1980.

White, Richard. *"It's Your Misfortune and None of My Own": A New History of the American West.* Norman: U of Oklahoma P, 1991.

Wild, Peter. *The Opal Desert: Explorations of Fantasy and Reality in the American Southwest.* Austin: U of Texas P, 1999.

Williams, Raymond. *The Country and the City.* New York: Oxford UP, 1973.

Williams, Terry Tempest. *Refuge: An Unnatural History of Family and Place.* New York: Pantheon, 1991.

Wilson, Charis. "The Weston Eye." *EW: 100 Centennial Essays in Honor of Edward Weston.* Ed. Peter Bunnell and David Featherstone. Carmel: The Friends of Photography, 1986. 117–123.

Wilson, Charis, and Wendy Madar. *Through Another Lens: My Years with Edward Weston.* New York: North Point, 1998.

Wilson, Chris. *The Myth of Santa Fe.* Albuquerque: U of New Mexico P, 1997.

Wilson, Edmund. *The American Earthquake: A Chronicle of the Roaring Twenties, the Great Depression, and the Dawn of the New Deal.* 1958. New York: Da Capo Press, 1996.

———. "Hollywood's Dance of Death." *Critical Essays on Nathanael West.* Ed. Ben Siegel. New York: G. K. Hall, 1994. 72–74.

Wood, Nancy. *Heartland New Mexico: Photographs from the Farm Security Administration, 1935–1943*. Albuquerque: U of New Mexico P, 1989.

Worster, Donald. *Dust Bowl: The Southern Plains in the 1930s*. New York: Oxford UP, 1979.

The WPA Guide to 1930s New Mexico. 1940. Tucson: U of Arizona P, 1989.

Wroth, William, ed. *Russell Lee's FSA Photographs of Chamisal and Peñasco, New Mexico*. Santa Fe: Ancient City Press, 1985.

Yu, Henry. "Los Angeles and American Studies in a Pacific World of Migrations." *American Quarterly* 56.3 (2004): 531–43.

Zamora, Lois Parkman, and Wendy B. Faris, eds. *Magical Realism: Theory, History, Community*. Durham: Duke UP, 1995.

Index

About the Author

Audrey Goodman received a BA in English from Princeton University and a PhD in English and Comparative Literature from Columbia University. She is an Associate Professor of English at Georgia State University in Atlanta, where she also serves as Director of Undergraduate Studies.

Her first book, *Translating Southwestern Landscapes* (U of Arizona Press 2002), examines the Anglo art that defined the American Southwest at the turn of the twentieth century, arguing that encounters with Native American communities and desert environments produced literature and photographs that mediated their audience's desire for newness with the artist's knowledge of local terrain and regional customs. It won the 2003 Thomas J. Lyon Award for the Best Critical Book on Western American Literature from the Western Literature Association. A recipient of a fellowship from the Georgia O'Keeffe Museum Research Center in Santa Fe (2002–2003) and the Huntington Library in Pasadena (2008), Goodman is also the author of essays on Charles Lummis and Willa Cather, the iconography of the desert, and the nuclear Southwest.